D0984824

MONEY-MAKING REAL ESTATE

MONEY-MAKING REAL ESTATE

YOUR PERSONAL GUIDE TO SUCCESSFUL INVESTING

Carolyn Janik

VIKING

Published by the Penguin Group
Viking Penguin Inc., 40 West 23rd Street,
New York, New York 10010, U.S.A.
Penguin Books Ltd, 27 Wrights Lane, London W8 5TZ, England
Penguin Books Australia Ltd, Ringwood,
Victoria, Australia
Penguin Books Canada Limited, 2801 John Street,
Markham, Ontario, Canada L3R 1B4
Penguin Books (N.Z.) Ltd, 182–190 Wairau Road,
Auckland 10, New Zealand

Penguin Books Ltd, Registered Offices: Harmondsworth, Middlesex, England

First published in 1988 by Viking Penguin Inc.
Published simultaneously in Canada

LIBRARY OF CONGRESS CATALOGING IN PUBLICATION DATA
Janik, Carolyn
Money-making real estate.
Includes index.
1. Real estate investment.   I. Title.
HD1382.5.J35   1988   332.63'24   87-23103
ISBN 0-670-81137-8

Printed in the United States of America by
Haddon Craftsmen, Scranton, Pennsylvania
Set in Century Expanded
Designed by Mary A. Wirth

For
Julie and Ray Leiter
who inspired this book
and for
Ruth Rejnis
who listened through it

Author's Note

The anecdotes and examples used in this book are all based on actual projects and experiences. The names and identifying particulars, however, have been changed to protect the privacy of the individuals involved.

The real estate advice presented here is the very best I have to offer, the product of my study, research, and twenty years' experience in the real estate marketplace. You should remember, however, that each real estate transaction is truly unique, and you should always use *local* professional assistance when and where it is needed. Remember also that change is not only possible but probable in the real estate marketplace even though the essential principles of good investment practice are virtually timeless. Even as this book goes to press, a technical corrections amendment to the Tax Reform Act of 1986 is being considered in Congress. If it passes, it is almost certain to affect some real estate tax laws. No book therefore can stand in for advice regarding your specific and particular investment problem from a tax adviser, attorney, professional engineer, real estate agent, or other necessary adviser.

After considering the material in this book and the advice of your professional counselors, bear in mind that each investment decision is, in the end, *your* decision. Develop and use your own good judgment. I wish you success and good fortune.

—C.J.

Contents

MONEY-MAKING REAL ESTATE

· C H A P T E R   1 ·

Why Real Estate?

So you want to make money. Not just a good salary that will keep you comfortable from paycheck to paycheck but real money, the kind that will pay your way to a vacation in Australia, buy you a twenty-seven-foot yacht, secure your child's education, and allow you to stop worrying that Social Security will evaporate just as you become eligible. And you want to make this extra money without giving up the security of your job and without moonlighting yourself into a sixteen-hour workday.

Well, you're in the right place: *America, the land of opportunity.* Here you can invest your savings, put your money to work for you, as your grandmother used to say. You can invest in the stock market, the commodities market, precious metals, foreign currencies, art, oil, the Broadway theater, or any number of more or less risky ventures that could bring your dollars back a hundredfold.

Hold it! you cry. That's not quite what you had in mind. You want to make money but you don't want to get in over your head; you don't want to spend hours every day calculating new strategies and weighing hundreds of buy/sell options; you don't want to start biting your fingernails in day-to-day or long-term anxiety. And you *do* want to be pretty darn sure, right when you jump in, that your money-making venture will indeed *make money.* You want low risk and high reward. Now that's a plum, even in America. But, believe it or not, it's right there all around you, yours for the picking. Where? How do you get it?

If you'll pardon the platitude, you might start by listening a little more carefully to that grandmother who said "put your money to work for you," and to your grandfather, too, and maybe even to your parents. For generations, "old folks" told their children, "Buy land! God isn't making any more of it!" Many of those children nodded, smiled, and went about their business. But those who listened—those who bought land and the buildings upon it—grew richer.

Real estate has been the golden calf of American investment. No other investment medium has been so favored by our tax laws; nothing else has contributed so universally to the making of each and every American millionaire. During the past two decades, the words *real estate* and *riches* became almost synonymous. It seemed that every smart person with a little spare money was dancing around this glowing, growing investment vehicle.

But you probably know all that. You've probably heard both the old folks and the TV seminar salesmen talking about their various deals. You've probably read a few of the books. You may even have listened as a wealthy friend with a bulging real estate portfolio and a very good accountant leaned toward you and confided sotto voce, "Yup, I paid zero taxes last year." And now, you've probably discounted it all since tax reform has killed real estate investment.

Whoa! If that's what you've been thinking, you may just be making the most serious mistake of your investing career. Tax reform has indeed killed real estate as a tax shelter, but it has barely grazed real estate as an investment vehicle.

Despite the longer depreciation schedule, the elimination of the capital gains advantage, and the passive investment rules, real estate *can* be a major money-making investment if:

- You forget the motivation of tax shelter and invest in money-making real estate for the purpose of making money.
- You forget the idea that someone else will make you rich without risk or work on your part and take control of your own investing, *yourself*, using knowledge and eventually expertise that you acquire, yourself.
- You forget the no-money-down schemes and realize that real estate is an *investment*, an investment into which you must put both time and money in order to harvest good returns.
- You reevaluate the idea that a highly leveraged real estate investment is the best investment. To leverage in the real estate marketplace means to buy property with a minimum down payment and maximum financing. When the rate of property appreciation is fast,

WHY REAL ESTATE? • 3

leveraging can bring fabulous returns on a small cash investment. But high interest rates, a sluggish re-sale market, the need for positive cash flow, and/or the new tax laws can erase the benefits of leveraging.

- You forget the idea that you'll get rich *quick* and realize that you build wealth in the real estate marketplace gradually.
- You choose to invest in the real estate vehicles that are best suited to the time, money, and skill that you have available to you at a given point in your career.
- You choose to invest only in geographic areas that you know well.

Yes, tax reform has changed the motivations and the investment patterns and procedures of the past two decades, but it has changed none of the basic values and principles that have made real estate America's best investment. Primary among those was, and is, relatively low risk.

"How can you say that?" you ask. "Prices have dipped sharply in several parts of the country and in several different kinds of real estate investment as a result of tax reform."

True. But for the most part the dips were the result of panic selling, or of selling because leverage was creating negative cash flow that was no longer deductible, or of selling because the owner bought as a tax shelter and was unwilling to put in the time required to turn his shelter into a profitable investment. All of which have created bargains in the marketplace for the savvy investor.

Price adjustments are not a new thing created by tax reform. They've been around as long as real estate, in fact, as long as anyone has bought and sold anything. They occur as a result of overbuilding or underbuilding, population changes, industrial development, business failure, economic changes, maintenance and management procedures, life-style changes, local politics, and more. You can make such price adjustments work *for you* if you remember that real estate value is essentially a function of location, and the value of any given location is a function of *everything* that is happening around a given piece of property.

And remember *always* that real estate is a *low*-risk investment, not a *no*-risk investment. The obvious key to successful real estate investment is the choosing of properties that will appreciate in value during the time that the investor wishes to hold them. The *appeal* of real estate investment, however, is that this key is relatively easy to find and easy to use. More readily than in any other investment field, the nonprofessional real estate investor can make the right choices consistently and profitably. Let's take a quick look at why.

SECURITY

Real estate is just what its name implies: real property. You can point to it, stand on it, touch it, and say "This is mine." How different from the stock certificate which represents an intangible share in a corporation run by people you don't know in a place you never visit. Or from the particularly rare and valuable oriental rug which somehow gets "lost" by the dealer who was supposed to be cleaning it for you. Or from the signed-original Tiffany lamp that a visiting toddler knocks over and breaks.

Real estate is yours for as long as you want to keep it. Land, in theory at least, is indestructible, and buildings, if not indestructible, are certainly insurable. Land and buildings therefore are the ultimate secure investment: they will be there whenever you wish to see them; they are virtually impossible to steal; and their value almost always increases with time.

Some financial advisers will caution you, however, that because of its size, the legal strings attached to its ownership, and its large dollar worth per unit, real estate is an illiquid investment, that is, one that's difficult to turn back into cash. And to some extent this word of caution rings true. But every investment is illiquid at some price and liquid at another. Try to sell a hundred shares of AT&T at ninety dollars a share and you have an illiquid investment. Put a building on the market for twice its market value and you have an illiquid investment. But list that same building just under market value and your liquidity is usually determined only by the time it takes to close title. Meanwhile, the illiquid, stable, and substantial nature of the real estate investment vehicle makes it a favorite security among lenders. Nothing compares with real estate in the ability to stand as collateral for a quick, large, and/or long-term loan.

"Well, real estate may be secure, but it's *not* the perfect investment," you mutter quietly. You're probably thinking of areas where property values have gone down. And I agree with you: nothing is certain, depreciation *is* a possibility in the real estate marketplace. It is one, however, against which the smart investor can protect himself or herself. Why? How? Because real estate is a nonvolatile investment vehicle.

Changes in property value usually occur more gradually than the changes in other investment markets. A savvy real estate investor will learn to read the signs that will protect his or her investment and bail out long before a significant loss becomes a possibility. Yes, there is an occasional surprise in this marketplace, but never the wide, quick swings in value that drive some Americans to seek out copies of the *Wall Street Journal* while on vacation in Paris.

DEMAND

Society is built on real estate. Every person needs shelter and every business needs a workplace. And (even better news!) the demand for real property, especially residential property, is *going to increase.* Consider these facts:

• The number of single person households in the United States is growing at a rate faster than anyone anticipated twenty years ago. More single person households = the need for more dwellings.
• People are living longer. Add that to a birthrate which still continues to chug along and we have a growing population. Growing population = the need for more dwellings.
• There has not been enough housing built (especially rental housing) since 1980 to meet the growing needs of the population. Greater need than supply = higher prices, especially rents.
• Ours is both a wealthy society and a society that prizes leisure time. The demand for leisure-time shelter and services is growing. More demand = higher prices.

INVESTMENT APPEAL

We are a country of landlords and aspiring landlords. Is there a great fortune in the United States that does not include real estate ownership? And how about just plain ordinary fortunes? Is there a wealthy person anywhere who doesn't own real estate? Changes in our tax laws may affect what we buy, how long we hold it, and how we structure the debt, but they are unlikely to change our inclination to *own property*.

It's the American Dream, after all. Literally millions of Americans own small bits of this huge country. Those who are investors are using their bits to provide for extra cash now and/or a wealthy retirement later. For most of them, real estate investment is an "after hours" avocation. They work at it *because* their work is rewarded. In short, the attitude is positive and the rewards are significant.

TAX BENEFITS

You're probably thinking: Hold it! Didn't she just say *forget tax shelter*? I did. Tax shelter is dead, but not tax benefits. *Buildings are still depreciable.* The depreciation period, however, is now longer than the fifteen years established by the Accelerated Cost Recovery System (ACRS) in 1981.

That legislation was intended to stimulate the economy, but it was so tax-shelter oriented that it also stimulated the explosive growth of real estate limited partnerships in the early 1980s. These partnerships were designed and created specifically to provide tax shelter for the rich. When word finally got out that wealthy investors were reaping six, seven, ten, and more times their invested capital in yearly tax deductions, even the sleepiest legislator on Capitol Hill woke up to cry, "Something is wrong with our tax laws!" Because real estate had been so favored by those tax laws, real estate took the hardest of the blows dealt by the Tax Reform Act of 1986.

Depreciation as a tax benefit was not destroyed, however, it was changed. Residential buildings are now depreciated over 27½ years, commercial buildings over 31½ years. Which means that a smaller percentage of the purchase price can be deducted as a paper loss on the tax return each year, but some paper loss still exists. In fact, a building that is actually providing you with welcome pocket money each month can still show no taxable income.

To further prevent the wealthy from using real estate as a tax shelter, Congress established three classes of income: *ordinary income* (what you earn at a job), *portfolio income* (what you earn from stocks, bonds, and interest-bearing investments), and *passive income* (what you earn from businesses in which you do not actively participate). All rental real estate income was classified as *passive income* and taxpayers were not allowed to deduct losses from real estate holdings against their other categories of income.

Except, and this exception is a big one, those taxpayers whose adjusted gross income is less than $100,000 and who actively participate in the management of their real estate holdings may deduct real estate losses up to $25,000 against their ordinary income. For those taxpayers earning between $100,000 and $150,000 a year, the $25,000 deduction diminishes by one dollar for every two dollars earned over $100,000, thus phasing out to zero deduction at $150,000.

This provision allows the small investor to use real estate deductions to offset income and come away with a few extra dollars of spendable income per year. It cannot be used by those owning limited partnership shares as their only investment vehicle, however, since there is no owner participation in the management of real estate in a limited partnership. Thus the government has curtailed the excessive use of paper real estate losses to offset income from other sources, while maintaining a real estate tax advantage for the small investor.

So perhaps Uncle Sam isn't such a bad guy after all? Probably. And there's more. Local property taxes are still fully deductible, even if they are generated by vacant land which produces no income. And mortgage interest, maintenance costs, and management fees are all deductible against the income from a property before a taxable earnings figure is determined. The government therefore taxes you only on the real earnings of the property, minus the depreciation. Still not a bad deal. And of course you pay nothing on equity growth and appreciation until you sell the property.

GETTING STARTED

Real estate may no longer be the favored nephew of Uncle Sam, but it doesn't need to be! It is a sound investment medium that can compete favorably with anything else this country has to offer. So why not jump in? Why doesn't everyone get out there and start buying and selling on the road to riches?

Slow down. This road to riches is not a high-speed interstate. For every investor who rushes into real estate, there are at least five others—the smarter ones—who hang back wondering if they really want to travel that road, if they have enough know-how, and if they want the hassle of it all. Real estate may be one of the finest investment vehicles available to Americans, but it is neither risk free nor problem free. And it's not right for everyone.

To survive in the real estate marketplace, you must recognize its demands as well as its opportunities. You must know your own strengths and weaknesses. And you must choose the investment properties that are right for you.

Do I mean choosing the *right* small apartment building from among the seven available in your town at the time you're ready to invest? Not exactly, or at least, not at first.

The choice of an *investment vehicle*, that is, a type of real estate investment, should be the beginning investor's first step into the real estate marketplace. This is a little like walking down the midway at a carnival and deciding which booth to play. Are you better at throwing darts or flipping nickels into ashtrays?

No, I'm not being facetious. Imagine walking down the midway, booths and tents on either side, each housing a different investment vehicle. The signs might read CONDOS, LAND, SMALL APARTMENT BUILDINGS, COMMERCIAL/RESIDENTIAL PROPERTY, LIMITED PARTNERSHIPS, and so on. Inside each booth or tent, you wager your money on a game, a game with its own special rules. If you want to win and win often, you will pick the games that are best for you.

In the *real* real estate marketplace, "best for you" means the type of real estate best suited to your personality, skills, knowledge, lifestyle, and bank account. This choice is every bit as important as choosing a good *piece* of property because the degree to which the vehicle fits the investor will tremendously influence the odds for success.

Consider these vehicles for example: a multifamily house in disrepair; a private limited partnership that's buying a skyscraper apartment building with the idea of condominium conversion; a parcel of land ripe for subdivision; and a rental-pool condominium apartment in a jet-set resort area. In which of these investment vehicles are *you* likely to succeed? Which can best be managed in the time you have available for the investment? Which is best suited to your skills and knowledge? Which best fits your financial resources for up-front money and your ability to handle cash flow—both positive and negative? Which will bring you closest to your immediate or long-term investment goals?

Choosing an investment vehicle without considering its particular demands and characteristics can result in financial and even emotional disaster. Despite what you may hear, see, or read in the media, *there is no one real estate investment vehicle that is right for everyone.*

Buying, fixing up, and selling a run-down multifamily house, for example, demands rather different market evaluation knowledge, personal skills, and time and money commitments than starting up a syndicate for the building of a seven-million-dollar resort in Hawaii. The syndicator might fail miserably at the multifamily house project.

If you really want to use real estate investment to increase your present wealth, to assure yourself a comfortable and plentiful retirement, or perhaps even to allow yourself the luxury of quitting your job, you must be able to choose both the best investment vehicles for you and the best available properties. To choose among vehicles you must know yourself and your resources. The next two chapters will help you to do an evaluation and an inventory.

To choose the best available properties, you must thoroughly know the geographic area in which you're investing and you must get to know the rules and subtleties of the investment vehicle game in which you're playing. *That* is called expertise, and it takes time to develop.

This book will not make you an instant expert. It will help you to choose the vehicles appropriate to your life at any given point and it will help you to evaluate individual properties. It will point out some shortcuts and warn you of some pitfalls. *You* will make yourself an expert in your chosen field and location.

CHAPTER 2

Are You Right for Real Estate?

Today's real estate market is so vast and varied that almost everyone can find a corner in it somewhere, and a corner well chosen and tended can cushion a lifetime. But are *you* "almost everyone"? Are you right for real estate? You say you can't really picture yourself up there on television with those self-made millionaires who advertise the quick-rich seminars. In fact, you can't even picture yourself talking about zoning regulations at a cocktail party. Maybe there is no corner for you . . .

Take heart. You don't have to smoke cigars, wear onyx cuff links, use silver eye shadow, or buy perfume at $180 an ounce. Real people, everyday people, can succeed in the real estate investment game. I have worked with engineers, hairdressers, business executives, tenors, physicians, truck drivers, computer programmers, poets, and even an immigrant couple each of whom used an X to sign their closing papers. They *all* shared only one belief in common: that a little extra money helps in the pursuit of happiness.

Most of them, however, also possessed a common core of character traits. There *is* a real estate type. Let's look at the characteristics of the real estate personality.

POSITIVE ACTION AND REACTION

Real estate investment is for *active* people. No, you don't have to be a skier or a tennis buff. I mean *active* as opposed to *passive*. Those who make it as real estate investors don't wait around for things to happen to them. And when something beyond their control does happen, they don't sit at their kitchen tables crying "Woe is me!" or "What can you do?" They act.

The desire to step out and *do* something, to control one's own life as much as possible, is perhaps the most essential character trait of the successful investor. Good deals will rarely come to your door and knock. You must go out into the marketplace and look for them.

RISK TAKING

Historically, real estate has proven to be one of the safest investments in America. Yes, there have been recessions, periods of local price adjustments, and geographic pockets of diminished value, but the overall curve of investment return has been strongly upward. The vast majority of real estate investors *make money*. So why should a prospective investor be a risk taker?

Because buying real estate involves risk, risk of your money, your time, and sometimes your credit rating. Since real estate is relatively illiquid, it imposes a commitment upon the investor. You can't get out of your investment in 27 Happy Hollow Road in the same way that you can put 500 shares of IBM on the trading block and have your money out in a matter of hours. Virtually all real estate investments require some time to convert property to cash. Enacting a sale might take three weeks or three years.

And what if, while 27 Happy Hollow Road is up for sale, the local newspaper announces that the state has approved a new dump site on the land that abuts its back lot line? Will you lose money on your investment? It's entirely possible.

Or what if 27 Happy Hollow Road is an apartment house and four of its twelve tenants are behind on their rents, in fact real deadbeats? Now you must go to housing court for evictions. Months can pass before those units are again producing income. What if you can't cover mortgage payments, utility bills, local taxes, etc., with the rent from the remaining eight tenants? Are you willing and/or able to contribute out-of-pocket cash? Or will your credit rating be getting a little shaky? Will you recover? Probably, but the ice you're skating on has gotten thinner.

Even if you put but a very small amount of your own cash into buying a real estate investment, you still take on a responsibility for the property on the day that you close. Will you attend to maintenance, pay the bills, taxes, and mortgage payments, keep the property adequately insured, collect rents, settle tenant disputes, and in general be available? In taking on these responsibilities, you're risking the time and the money that they involve. Will that time and money be well rewarded? Usually, but there are no 100 percent sure bets.

DECISION MAKING

You stand before a florist's cart. Should you buy the red roses or the white roses? They're both so beautiful . . . the price is the same . . . you have enough cash for one bunch only . . . the white would look lovely in the dining room . . . but you heard that red last longer . . . Jennifer likes yellow best, but there are no yellow today . . . the red really have a sweeter scent . . . the white are so sophisticated and elegant. You walk around the flower cart. You walk away. You walk back. Red or white? Impulsively, you turn away and take the subway home. Without the roses.

A silly story? Perhaps. But exactly this kind of thinking and behavior are responsible for countless lost real estate deals every year.

Real estate investment properties must be carefully analyzed and evaluated one against another. Value, cash flow, potential appreciation, and taxes must all be considered. But finally a decision to purchase, a choice, must be made in order for you to *become* an investor.

It is at the decision point that some buyers become financially paralyzed. They walk around the properties. And away. And back again. And away again. And again, often until a decision is made for them by another buyer who snatches up one of the properties under consideration. In many instances the indecisive investor gets the leftovers or buys something less valuable on the rebound. Or the investment money simply gets left in the savings account.

To be a successful real estate investor, you must be able to decide among the opportunities available to you and then go forward on the basis of your decision. You must not stop and look back, rethinking and reconsidering what is already done. And you must not dwell on could-have-beens or might-have-beens or we-should-haves.

.   .   .

COMMITMENT

Some forms of real estate investment require only money. You put your share of cash in, someone else does the buying and managing, and still someone else does the accounting. You receive an annual report and you list your profits or losses on your tax return. The most popular money-only real estate investments of the '80s were called syndicates. They were actually limited partnerships.

Before tax reform, most investors thought of syndicates as investment without commitment, a sure thing: no work, nothing to lose, a great tax shelter. When they talked about their fabulous write-offs, they would forget to mention that their money was often *committed* without the opportunity for withdrawal for five to seven years! They would also forget to mention that they had little or no expectation of substantial profit when the syndicate was to be dissolved.

Today, most of the tax shelter of these limited partnerships is gone, but the commitment remains!

In hands-on real estate (the kind you buy yourself), you can sell out whenever you choose, but there is a different kind of commitment required. Most real estate investments make demands not only on your money but also on your time and your good conscience. It's a matter of responsibility.

As an investor, you must be willing to follow through on your dreams, your plans, and your promises. Before you decide to buy a four-family house, for example, you must be fairly certain that you won't be taking off next month to spend a year or two in Paris. Or, if you are, you must make arrangements for property management. Real estate investment requires commitment not only because good and responsible investors realize that property affects people, but also because unattended or poorly attended real estate will return far less profit.

LOGICAL AND RATIONAL EVALUATION

David Goldstick, a successful New York City lawyer and investor, made the best differentiation I have yet heard between the essential evaluations necessary to homebuying and to investment real estate. He said, "You have to love the place you're going to call home, at least a little, but there's no place for love in investment real estate."

One of the most common failings of beginning real estate investors is the evaluation of property based upon their own preferences. Many people who love sand and surf, for example, think a beachfront vacation home is a great investment. Having projected their love of the sea onto others, they assume that a given cottage will be in demand, that rents will be high, and that appreciation will be great. They dash into the purchase without considering location, economic conditions (present and projected), the comparative value of similar properties, and the projected return on the investment dollar. Sometimes they win.

More consistently successful investors, however, consider the purchase of property as they would consider any other business decision. They gather information, make comparisons, and finally give the nod to the option that best fulfills current needs and promises the best return on the time and money spent.

NUMBERS AND THE LETTER OF THE LAW

Have you ever thought about the tax and legal angles involved in converting a 29-unit, fully occupied apartment building into a condominium? Or how about the idea of building 400 low-to-moderate-income, single-family houses in a small suburban town, using factory-built modules, a sewer package plant, and zero-lot-line planning?

Contemporary real estate investors cannot fly by the seat of their pants any more than modern-day pilots can. The vehicles they handle are simply too complex.

It's true that some real estate investments require more consideration of the numbers, financial and otherwise, and more legal advice than others. All, however, are based upon two questions: *Can it be done?* and *Will it be profitable?* And those questions require numerical and legal answers. To be a successful real estate investor, therefore, you must respect numbers and legal constraints enough to research them to the best of your ability. And you must know enough to call in professional help when you need it.

ORGANIZATION AND MANAGEMENT SKILLS

If you dream of some day being chief executive officer of a syndicate that owns fifty buildings, you would do well to take a close look at your delegating skills. You won't be able to run your business alone, and your success will very much depend upon which tasks you assign to whom. With this delegation of course, goes supervision. Can you organize and manage people? Can you teach your managers to manage?

"Hold on!" you say. You only want to own a small apartment building or two. You're not looking to run a major corporation. Well, you're in the majority. Few of us really aspire to being entrepreneurs with our names emblazoned on the sides of buildings. We just want to be comfortable, or, well, maybe rich. To get rich in real estate you must be able to keep records, make and carry out plans, and yes, delegate, even if the delegating in your case means knowing when to call in a plumber after several attempts with Drāno and the plunger have failed.

FORESIGHT

There's an old adage in the real estate game that goes: if you want to get rich, buy when everyone else is selling and sell when everyone else is buying. It's good old-adage advice, but it doesn't always work.

Some of the biggest profits in real estate have been the result not of buying counter to the trend of the market but of buying in anticipation of the trend. Sometimes such foresight can be statistically based. A careful study of demographics and economic development, for example, may clearly indicate the need (in four or five years) of a shopping center where there is now a cow pasture.

Sometimes, however, foresight can be a matter of educated intuition. You walk through a neighborhood that might politely be referred to as "run down," yet you notice curtains in most of the windows; many stairways and stairwells that are free of litter and debris, and an occasional tricycle parked near a doorway. A new bus route in town goes to the main shopping area and then on the industrial park beyond the city limits and one of the new bus stops is two blocks from where you're standing. Is the six-family walk-up being sold on a HUD foreclosure with a minimum bid of $50,000 a good investment? I'd guess it might be.

IMAGINATION AND CREATIVITY

My brother came to the door of our parents' summer cottage while my husband and I were visiting one Sunday and said, "Hey! Come for a ride! I want to show you some land I just bought."

Always eager to look at land, we got into his car but were dismayed to find ourselves driving to his home.

"We can't see it in this car," he explained and piled us into a four-wheel-drive Jeep with oversized tires. I hung on to the roll bar as we rode a two-rut path through the woods. After the trees, mud, and thorn bushes, we took on a steep gravel bank, blowing a shower of pebbles behind us that seemed to threaten landslide at any moment. On the hill top, we got out of the Jeep.

The first thing I saw was not the lay of the land around us but a huge snake sunning itself on a rock not twenty feet away. I had difficulty listening attentively to my brother's talk of the small lake that would be created by new drainage patterns, the plans to level the gravel bank into gently rolling terrain, and a road and plat plan that would give a maximum number of families lake frontage. The place looked uninhabitable to me.

That was five years ago. Today you can drive your Mercedes along the route we traveled that Sunday without worrying about chipping its paint with flying pebbles or scratching its sides with blackberry thorns. The land is almost completely developed, the lots are all sold. My brother lives there, in a house with a magnificent indoor swimming pool and a hot tub.

Often success in real estate investment lies in being able to imagine what others cannot see or in being able to create something beautiful and appealing where there once was nothing anyone considered valuable.

Self-Confidence

Human renditions of Chicken Little walk about everywhere warning earnestly, "The sky is falling!" If you invest in real estate, you'll meet more than your fair share of them. The economy is about to go belly up . . . interest rates will be double by next year . . . you'd better get out of the land deal before they zone for apartments on the next parcel over . . . the market for condos is drying up . . . tax revision has killed the vacation home market forever . . . and on and on.

It's okay to listen to such talk. You might even want to do some investigating once in a while to see what truth there is in it. But essentially, the real estate investor must have confidence in his or her own judgment, enough confidence *not* to be swayed by the advice of friends and associates who have no financial stake in the investment at hand.

Self-confidence can also encourage perseverance, the willpower to continue on despite obstacles and set-backs. Some people call it stubbornness.

PATIENCE, TACT, AND SELF-CONTROL

Everyone knows that selling real estate takes time and that investor-sellers must be patient enough to wait for the right deal. Investors must also be patient and tactful enough to work with zoning boards that table variance requests month after month, with lenders tied up in their own paperwork, with subcontractors who don't show up on time or at all, with building inspectors with particular axes to grind, with housing courts anxious to listen to the doleful voices of tenants, and with sales and marketing people not always as motivated and efficient as one might hope.

Most of all, however, you must have enough self-control to avoid losing your temper. Book throwing, table pounding, shouting, walking out, and door slamming almost always lose both time and money, and often the deal itself. The successful investor learns to speak in a clear, well-modulated, and well-paced manner—to talk softly whether the stick being carried is a club or a broken branch.

SOCIAL CONTACTS

Hermits rarely make a killing in the real estate market. Investing in real estate is a social game. You must go into the marketplace, and you must be aware that you *are* in it whenever you're talking with people, meeting with people, even having lunch or playing golf with people, for it's there, among other people, that one hears most often about new investment opportunities.

The need for sociability does not end, however, with getting a hot lead and grabbing up the investment. As an investor, you must also be sociable enough to manage your investment. You must deal with people who owe you money and with people to whom you owe money. You must be willing to do an occasional favor and to call in favors owed when necessary.

In other words, dealing in real estate means dealing with people. You will find the job more pleasant and often more profitable if you can do it with a smile, a compliment, and an occasional good joke.

Negotiating Skill

Some three-year-olds quite successfully negotiate the postponement of their bedtimes almost every evening. Others try but only prompt an angry parental response and an *earlier* bedtime. All of which goes to say that there are indeed natural negotiators among us. If you're one of them, real estate investment is a calling you can hardly turn down.

If you aren't, or if you aren't sure, don't put away the book and go back to the stock market idea. Negotiating skill can be learned. I've devoted Chapter 15 to basic dos and don'ts and a few inside secrets I've learned along the way, but your real education in negotiating will be self-education. You will learn with each session and you'll come to know both your strengths and your weaknesses. And how to use them.

YOUR INVESTOR PERSONALITY PROFILE

Do you see yourself as a perfect investor? No? Don't worry. There is no such creature. No real person could score a 10 in every one of these categories, nor is there an investment vehicle that demands a 10 in all of them.

To start down the real estate road to riches you need only to see yourself as having good potential or as willing to recognize and deal with these character traits. Before you take the turn, however, you should carefully assess your strengths and weaknesses. There's a blank bar graph on page 19 to help you. Machine copy it and fill in the lines as accurately as possible; the higher the number, the more you have of a trait.

By doing this self-assessment you will be drawing your own investor personality profile. This bar graph will become an important tool in making your choices among investment vehicles. If you will be working with partners or a spouse in your real estate investing, do a profile for each member of your group. Then overlay the individual profiles to form a *composite* profile of your group strengths.

As I discuss each of the money-making investment vehicles in this book, I will include an investment demand profile based on this same bar graph. The demand profile will show my estimate of each vehicle's demands upon each of the character traits. Compare your personal and/or group profile to the demand profile for each investment vehicle

YOUR INVESTOR PERSONALITY PROFILE

	1	2	3	4	5	6	7	8	9	10
1. Positive Action and Reaction										
2. Willingness to Take Risks										
3. Decision-making Ability										
4. Commitment—the Will to Follow Through										
5. Logical and Rational Evaluation of Options										
6. Ability to Deal with Numbers and Finances										
7. Ability to Deal with Legal Constraints										
8. Organization and Management Skills										
9. Foresight										
10. Imagination and Creativity										
11. Self-confidence										
12. Patience and Tact										
13. Self-control										
14. Social Contact										
15. Negotiating Skill										

that you consider. Your strong points should be able to meet high demand points.

None of this, of course, is scientific. Your profile is *your* evaluation of yourself or your group and the demand profiles are *my* evaluations of the demands made by each of the investment vehicles and the investor personalities most likely to succeed at that investment. It is unlikely that any two profiles will ever match exactly, and it's absolutely unnecessary. We are seeking here to increase the probability of success. There are no certainties.

Think of your profile as a mirror into which you look before you go out into the marketplace. And remember that the image you see there may change somewhat with time and experience. Usually for the better!

I wish I could end here with "That's all there is to it," but I can't. You might well have a real estate personality ideally suited to your real estate investment vehicle of choice, but you'll still get virtually nowhere unless you can also effectively use the tools of the trade required by that investment vehicle. That's the next chapter.

CHAPTER 3

Tools of the Trade

Time, money, and knowledge are the tools of the real estate investing trade. They are the essential elements in every deal between a buyer and a seller, and they are more. Time, money, and knowledge are the coordinates that will determine your course in the real estate marketplace, and they are the specifications that will define the size and nature of your investment vehicles.

By way of example, consider these investors:

- A husband and wife, fifty-one and forty-eight, both working at office jobs. They have two kids in college, an excellent credit rating, plenty of time evenings and weekends, and good handyman skills, but they have virtually no spare money.
- A neurosurgeon, thirty-three and single. He has ample available cash and wants to invest in real estate that will appreciate in the next five years without showing significant taxable annual income. He has little knowledge of big-city real estate and almost no time that he can commit to the investment process.
- A woman college professor, thirty-seven, recently divorced, and living in a small one-bedroom apartment. She has flexible hours and $40,000 in cash (her half of the equity in the house the ex-couple just sold). Her income, however, is relatively small.

They all live in the same city. Among the available investment properties are the following:

- A block of eight co-op apartments, seven of which are occupied under rent control.
- A large, 50-year-old, one-family house in a neighborhood that is zoned for single-family dwellings but where more than half of the old houses have been converted to hold two or three apartment units.
- A two-bedroom ranch-style house that is run-down and dirty but structurally sound. It's located in an area where some houses have been remodeled and are well maintained while others seem about to fall apart.

Can you match the investor with the appropriate investment? You should come up with the following:

- The couple gets the little ranch-style house. They can buy it with an FHA-sponsored program called 203K that will provide mortgage money to cover up to 85 percent of the purchase price and the estimated cost of refurbishing. When the job is complete, they will sell for a profit. (Renting this property is probably not advisable since its rental income might not cover costs when maximum financing is used for purchase. This couple is unlikely to opt for negative cash flow.)
- The doctor gets the co-ops. His investment secures him a place to live and seven other appreciating apartments. If he (and his accountant) calculate carefully, he can invest just enough cash so that rental income equals costs, thus showing no taxable income from the investment. He doesn't need to be bothered with maintenance or supervision of his property investment, since the co-op's board of directors sees to that, but he will have to collect his rents.
- The divorced professor gets the large old house. She plans to divide it into three apartments, live in one, and rent the other two. She'll do some of the conversion and refurbishing work herself, relying on skills she learned as a home owner. Rents from the newly created apartments will augment her income while she is a resident landlord. (In fact, within a year or two, she should be living housing-cost free.) Meanwhile, her investment will appreciate both with the market *and* because it has become an income-producing property.

The theory here is obvious. A good real estate investment plan is most often a matter of matching the time, money, and knowledge available with the time, money, and knowledge required. Before we get into matchmaking, however, let's talk about the tools of the trade in a little more detail, taking them apart, as it were, to better understand how each affects your investment decisions.

TIME

There are two kinds of time in real estate: waiting time and working time. Both apply to some extent to every investment vehicle and every investment property, but with wide variables.

WAITING TIME

I'm using the term "waiting time" to mean the passing of time as a factor in financial return. Waiting time is the interim between the time you choose an investment property and the time it partially or completely fulfills your goals and you liquidate it.

In your observation of real estate dealings around you, be aware of how waiting time differs not only from one investment vehicle to another but also between similar properties within the same vehicle. Raw land as a vehicle generally has a long waiting time. Refurbished single-family homes are usually turned over quickly. But take two tracts of undeveloped land. One may take ten years before appreciation brings its market value to your selling and profit goals. The other might be turned over for a more modest profit in ten months. Or consider a run-down single-family house. You might refurbish the house and achieve your profit goal in three months, or you might choose to rent the house for five years and then sell.

These wide variations occur because the waiting time necessary for a satisfactory profit is determined by a combination of and balance between four factors:

• the nature of the investment vehicle;
• the local supply and demand for that vehicle;
• the desirability of the particular piece of property; and
• your specific investment goals.

Weigh these four factors as you consider the probable holding time of an investment property and then add in the *cost* of waiting. Professional investors call this cost the time value of money.

Let's say you are willing to wait five years to achieve a certain dollar return from your investment. You buy a property for $100,000, and you want to make $40,000 profit. You'll sell in five years for $140,000, right?

Almost never! Besides the obvious factors such as the cost of interest on your loan, the pluses and minuses associated with taxes, the cost of maintenance and insurance, the cash flow from the investment, and the sales commission and closing costs, you must figure in the time value of money. In all likelihood, $140,000 will not buy as much at the time you sell the property as it would have at the time you bought it. When you think you're ready to sell, therefore, ask yourself: *how has inflation affected the value of the dollar during the time I held this property?* If the property appreciated at or below the rate of inflation, you have not achieved your $40,000 profit goal. You may not even have stayed even! So add inflation to your $100,000 base price before setting your selling price.

You should also consider the return potential of the money that you invested in the property at the outset. Let's say you put $20,000 down to buy this $100,000 property. Consider how much that $20,000 would have earned for you in a moneymarket fund with no work, no worry, and complete liquidity. Factor in the taxes you would have had to pay on that interest income and add the figure you come up with to the $100,000 plus inflation figure before you add on your $40,000 hoped-for profit. Then leave some room for commissions and negotiating and ask yourself if the market in your area will support the price you need to achieve your profit goal. If not, you may have to wait a little longer, adjust your profit goal, or add some features to the property that will make it more desirable.

If you need help working out these figures with tax laws and expenses factored in, you might consult a financial adviser who will walk you through the process. You might also treat yourself to a good business calculator, the kind most real estate agents carry around in their pockets.

If you faithfully do this kind of time-value consideration for every property that cries out "Buy me!" you'll never be swayed by talk of big-bucks profit with time as a factor. When you hear, "Pay cash for this land and you'll double your money in ten years!" you'll know that the offer is *not* a good deal. You can do better by putting your cash into government-backed mortgages.

SOME FACTORS IN CALCULATING YOUR PROFITS

BUYING

Original purchase price _____

Closing costs (include lender points, attorney _____
    fees, mortgage application fees, survey fees,
    etc.)

Original cost of purchase _____

SELLING

Annual profit/loss reported on tax returns _____

The time value of money (the difference in the _____
    purchasing power of the dollar between the
    time you purchased your property and your
    proposed selling time)

Alternative possible rate of return on the capital _____
    investment

Probable selling costs and commissions _____

Probable market value of the property _____

Profit goal _____

WORKING TIME

Working time is the amount of *your* time that you must devote to a real estate investment. It is time *doing* something—looking for the investment property, keeping the books, doing repair work, planning a subdivision, or trying to settle a dispute between your tenants over where to keep bicycles.

Working time is an important factor in investment appeal and, like waiting time, it varies among vehicles and from one property to another. Lots of working time but very little waiting time, for example, can be very appealing, especially if you have a block of time to devote to your investment. A long wait but virtually no working time can also be very appealing. But beware of an investment that demands a long waiting time and a lot of working time, for you may not really make money in it at all.

Before you take on an investment that has high working time demands, ask yourself, *What is my time worth?* Could you make more spending the same number of hours moonlighting at a part-time job? If so, look for another investment. But don't forget to figure in tax advantages when you're doing these calculations.

Also, before you jump into any real estate investment, consider your stage of life and your life-style. Do you have and are you willing to give up the working time necessary to make a particular investment property profitable?

MONEY

Despite what real estate's snake-oil salesmen may tell you, it is very difficult to invest in real estate if you are flat broke and in debt. The seller who is willing to take nothing down and hold the mortgage for a buyer who has no cash reserves and is not paying his bills is usually motivated by one or both of the following conditions: (1) he needs or very badly wants to get rid of that piece of property, or (2) he's making a killing on the price. You, as the buyer, would do well to find out which and why before taking on the responsibility of ownership. Even with nothing down.

There are some government programs and even some loan programs at established lending institutions that allow you to purchase a property without a down payment. But you had better have something to offer in place of the money, like a superb investment (a "sure thing") that the lender can't afford to refuse, or a shared appreciation deal, or a joint venture, or, at the very least, a successful personal history with similar investments, a very good credit rating, and/or handyman, legal, or construction skills that have been tested and proven. And you still must pay the closing costs.

Oh, you read about deals where the buyer actually walks away from the closing table with someone else's crumpled green stuff in his or her pocket? There have been some of those. But if you are planning to fiddle with numbers on a contract to make a deal look different than it really is, you had better watch out! Uncle Sam does not like prices on paper that are thousands of dollars higher than the real amount of cash exchanged in order to let a buyer pocket cash at the closing, claim higher depreciation losses while owning the investment, and report a smaller profit when the property is sold. And your friendly neighborhood banker may not be so friendly anymore if he were to discover that his loan was at 130 percent of the real cash exchanged rather than 80 percent of the price named on the contract.

If you are serious about investing, however, you *can* begin with a very small nest egg and succeed handsomely, even as you faithfully walk the straight and narrow. Some investment vehicles do require big bucks up front, but they're usually not for beginners anyway. Your choice of vehicle and property will almost always depend upon how its money demands fit with your money resources. Before you go out to spend a penny, however, you should understand how the elements of investment money-demand break down.

Start-up Cash

A real estate investor needs start-up cash in much the same way that a farmer needs seed money: it's hard to reap a harvest without it. Your seed money may be your down payment, but not always. With 100 percent financing, for example, you need only enough cash for closing costs and refurbishing. Or you might own a building that you want to convert into a condominium. Then your start-up cash will be money spent on legal fees. Or you might want to buy and develop land. Here your start-up fees will go on and on and on—surveys, plat plans, road bonds, construction materials, wages, and more, all before you collect a penny in return.

It's important that you evaluate the different demands for start-up cash made by different investments and then compare those investments against each other in terms of projected return and probable waiting-time and working-time demands. You may find that an investment which requires a large amount of start-up cash will turn over very quickly and at a very good return. It's probably worth borrowing for. It might even be worthwhile to get a group together to raise the start-up cash even though you'll have to split the profits. Or you may find that an investment with very little start-up cash required demands both waiting time and working time beyond the limitations you have set. Your goal, of course, is to find an investment that combines good potential return with start-up costs and time demands that you can handle.

•　　　•　　　•

CASH FLOW

Some investments, apartment buildings for example, start generating cash almost as soon as the buyers and sellers push their chairs away from the closing table. Others, like the land development just mentioned, demand a heavy negative cash flow almost until the investment is liquidated. Still others, most limited partnerships, for example, and many rental pool condominiums, neither demand nor generate significant cash during the period of ownership. Their advantages were once in the paper losses that created tax shelter. Today their advantages are in the possibility of appreciation or, with restructuring, in the possibility of some small positive cash flow while awaiting maximum appreciation. Again, the goal of the smart investor is to match cash flow (negative or positive) with his or her financial resources.

Positive cash flow is the amount of cash you have left in your bank account after paying all the expenses associated with the investment. Negative cash flow is the amount of cash you must put in to keep an investment afloat. If at your particular stage of life you have little spare cash and rather significant and constant cash drain, you should seek an investment likely to generate positive cash flow. If you can afford a negative cash flow, you might well choose an investment with rather steady cash drain but a potentially large return upon sale. The negative cash flow would eliminate the possibility of paying federal income taxes on the investment while you held it and would be deductible from the profit when the property was finally sold. Or the annual loss could be deducted against the profits from other rental properties that you actively manage.

TAXES

There are two kinds of taxes that affect real estate: local assessments and federal income tax laws. The principles of local taxation have seen little change (with the exception of California's Proposition 13) over many years. Essentially, towns and sometimes counties raise money by taxing property. Each piece of property is assessed for value and then taxed according to the established mill rate for a given tax year. (A mill is one-tenth of one cent. It is the measure used in this country to state the property tax rate.)

It doesn't take a Harvard degree to realize that the cost of holding a piece of property in a town with a low tax rate and low assessments on property will be less than the cost of holding a piece of property in a town with a high tax rate and high assessments. The smart investor, however, will also be very much aware of politics and economics in the local area of his/her investments, for local tax structure (assessment and rate) can and does change. A significant change could upset the delicate balance of profitability in an investment and could even affect resale value by diminishing desirability.

It is in terms of federal income tax law that real estate has become a new ball game. Because losses (both paper and real) generated by a real estate investment are no longer fully deductible against ordinary income, real estate debt structure and cash flow must be calculated more carefully when determining the *value* of an investment property. As I have said, real estate still has tax advantages, but it is no longer a place to hide money from the IRS. As we talk about the various investment vehicles in this book, I will try to put tax law effects into perspective as a buy/sell criterion for each vehicle. Because these laws are subject to shifting political winds, however, I strongly advise you to review the cash flow of an investment with a qualified tax adviser or accountant *before* you buy and *before* you structure property debt.

THE BOTTOM LINE

How much will I make? That *is* the question, right? Yes. And no. A better question might be: *Does this potential bottom line adequately compensate me for the time—both working and waiting—that I've devoted to the investment and the financial risk I've taken?* In other words, is it really worth it?

I'm sure you've heard people bragging, "I've just made fifty grand!" Often you can put a pin in their balloons by asking, "What did it cost you?" or "How long did it take?"

KNOWLEDGE

Without knowledge in the real estate marketplace, you might just as well put your money on a roulette wheel or spend your time studying *The Racing Form*. There are two types of knowledge that can influence your financial rewards in the investment game: real estate savvy and special skills. Let's look at the savvy part first.

SAVVY: INVESTMENT VEHICLES

So far I've been doing a lot of talking about matching your personality, life-style, strengths, goals, and resources to the investment vehicles that best suit them. To do this, as I've said, you must understand both what you *bring* to an investment and what it *demands*. In other words, you must be savvy to your own nature and to the nature of the investment vehicle.

While only you can call up the first kind of savvy, the remaining chapters of this book are focused upon real estate investment savvy. Each chapter, except the last, will initiate you into a basic understanding of the demands, risks, and opportunities inherent in one particular type of vehicle and will help you to judge the appropriateness of that vehicle to your particular needs and goals.

SAVVY: INVESTMENT PROPERTIES

Once you've chosen a vehicle, you must choose to buy a particular piece of property. Here savvy is a question of:

- knowing what makes a given property valuable;
- being aware of certain clues to its *future* worth;
- being able to anticipate potential problems and either avoid them or solve them; and
- knowing when to sell.

This kind of property savvy is hard to come by and most investors learn it only after making a few mistakes. Learn it you must, however, for buying, owning, and selling property piece-by-piece is the action that makes money. Without this action, all your study is but theory.

For just a moment, think of your life in the real estate marketplace as a day at the races. If you were to spend the afternoon studying track records, the horses, the jockeys, the post positions, and every Super Picks card on sale, you might well pick horses that finished in the money in almost every race. But if you never placed a bet, you would take home nothing in winnings. In the same way, you might perfectly match an investment vehicle to your resources and goals but the match would mean nothing unless you put your money on a particular piece of property that eventually increased your wealth.

The problem, of course, is how to pick the right horse or the right property. To help you in the real estate marketplace, I have decided to put the good old American dollar sign to use. Whenever an important money-making indicator is mentioned in discussing the various investment vehicles in this book, I will place a $ in the margin. Use these indicators with your other knowledge to help you judge which *particular piece of property* will make you a winner.

SAVVY: LOCATION

Location is the word that sets real estate apart from every other investment opportunity and makes each piece of property unique. Location savvy has two requirements:

• knowledge of the particular site, that is the lot, neighborhood, condominium community, etc.; and
• knowledge of the geographic area.

Not always, but almost always, your best real estate investment opportunities will be in geographic areas, often in the very neighborhoods, that you know well, areas where you know people and where you can anticipate economic changes and consumer demand. Familiarity is often a key to success in the real estate marketplace.

SPECIAL SKILLS

Do you know how to:

• hang wallpaper;
• file a variance request;
• choose a good tenant;
• drive a backhoe;
• fight your way through red tape;
• do plumbing, electrical work, or roofing;
• read a mortgage agreement;
• get a parcel of land surveyed?

Some real estate investments are easier and more profitable for those who have these and other special skills. Your skills may indeed be a factor in determining where you enter the marketplace. Use them. But don't be afraid to face the need to learn new ones. Skills learned in handling one investment vehicle may lead you to another, even more profitable venture.

USING THE TOOLS OF THE TRADE

There's one I haven't mentioned yet: luck. Yes, that elusive lady is very much present in the real estate marketplace. And she's as fickle as ever. So welcome her when she pays you a visit, but don't count on her. Time, money, and knowledge may not be as provocative, but they certainly are more reliable. Evaluate them in your life before each investment opportunity and you will markedly increase your chances for financial success and personal satisfaction.

"Evaluate" is, of course, the key word in that bit of advice and you'd be entirely justified in asking, "How, *exactly*, does one rank and judge time, money, and knowledge in terms of each and every real estate investment opportunity?" These real estate tools of the trade are changeable, sometimes intangible, and not always measurable. No check-the-proper-box survey could possibly provide any significant degree of accurate or applicable information. Evaluation therefore is work, and work that you're going to have to do *yourself*. But the difficulty of the task should not discourage you from attempting this very important taking stock.

There are actually three steps in attempting to evaluate real estate's tools of the trade against a contemplated purchase. The first is to take personal stock. To help you do this I've drawn up a personal evaluation form on page 33. Make a few photo copies and fill in the blanks to delineate for you, *on paper*, your limitations and your resources in the marketplace.

The second step is to apply the tools-of-the-trade criteria to the specific investment you're considering. On page 34, I've done a mock property evaluation. Your information, of course, will be different, but the approach should be very similar.

The third step is entirely dependent upon steps one and two. Having completed both a personal and a property tools-of-the-trade evaluation, you should compare them. The essential question of the comparison should be: *do your personal resources and goals match the demands and potential rewards of the investment you're considering?* If you cannot answer *yes* to that question, you should reconsider your purchase and your motivations very carefully.

TOOLS-OF-THE-TRADE PERSONAL EVALUATION

TIME

WAITING: _____   [How long are you will-
         _____   ing to hold this invest-
                                     ment?]

WORKING: _____   [How many hours,
                                     days, or weekends are
         _____   you willing to work at
                                     your investment?]

MONEY

START-UP: _____   [How much do you
                                      have for start-up costs?
          _____   Can you get additional
                                      cash on a short-term
          _____   basis?]

CASH FLOW: _____   [Do you need a posi-
                                       tive figure? How much?
           _____   Or, how much of a
                                       negative cash flow can
           _____   you carry?]

TAXES: _____   [What type of benefits
                                   are you seeking?]
       _____

EXPECTED RETURN: _____   [How much do you
                                             realistically hope to
                 _____   make?]

KNOWLEDGE

INVESTMENT SAVVY: _____   [What special informa-
                                              tion or familiarity do
                  _____   you bring to this invest-
                                              ment? Consider all
                  _____   members of your in-
                                              vestment group when
                  _____   making this evaluation.]

SPECIAL SKILLS: _____   [List all training, talents,
                                            and experience perti-
                _____   nent to real estate in-
                                            vestment or
                _____   development.]

TOOLS-OF-THE-TRADE PROPERTY EVALUATION

Property: 21 acres in Highland Township   Price $210,000

TIME

WAITING: probably no more than five years. Maximum profit will be shortly after the Interstate is complete.

WORKING: low demand; little to do unless we decide to go for preliminary subdivision approval.

MONEY

START-UP: $60,000 down; seller will carry balance in interest-only mortgage at 9 percent for a maximum of eight years.

CASH FLOW: negative; $13,500 per year in interest
<u>   2,300</u> per year in taxes
$15,800 per year negative cash flow

TAXES: property taxes deductible. Interest not deductible annually but it can be carried forward and deducted from the profit on sale.

EXPECTED RETURN: should be very high. Housing demand is increasing and moving toward the area of the property. The land might also be suitable for industrial or office building development if we can get the zoning changed. On raw land, figure $700,000. On 17 one-acre lots sold to a builder as a package, figure $1,200,000. Industrial or office building use would be higher.

KNOWLEDGE

INVESTMENT SAVVY: economic projections good;
zoning laws acceptable now;
drainage patterns excellent;
potential for water = wells good in surrounding areas;
sewerage treatment = septic; good drainage;
road layout = probably one curved cul-de-sac.

SPECIAL SKILLS: it would be nice if we knew a surveyor!

And now let's turn to the investment vehicles themselves. Each of the next eleven chapters discusses a particular type of real estate and each begins with an investor profile or profiles that sketch very briefly an "ideal" buyer for that type of investment. Look for yourself in these sketches, but don't limit your reading to the profiles that fit your self-image. Sometimes reading a "well, maybe" chapter or reading a chapter purely out of curiosity even though the investor profile is 180 degrees out of line with both your personality and your position of the moment will give you new ideas for today's investments and for tomorrow's plans. Life-styles change. The kind of property that's your best bet at one point in your life may be unsuitable for another. Ten years from now you could be following a road you never dreamed of taking.

· CHAPTER 4 ·

Multifamily Houses

Dick and Janet Ferber have $19,000 in cash savings. They are both working now, but they want a baby and a house. If Janet stops working, they can't afford the mortgage payments on a house. If she keeps working, they won't be able to raise their child as they want to. Investment vehicle of choice: a multifamily house.

· · ·

A detached single-family house on a nice quiet street . . . that's the housing dream of over 80 percent of the home-buying public. To get one, many aspiring home owners rent the cheapest possible apartment and put every spare penny into savings accounts. Meanwhile prices rise in the real estate marketplace, always a jump ahead of them. It seems they will *never* qualify for the mortgage they need.

Fixation on a dream house blurs the marketplace facts of life for these unsuccessful home buyers. They forget that the detached single-family house is an *expensive* form of shelter. Oh, it's true enough that mortgage interest, tax deductions, appreciation, and equity growth are a means to savings, but it's also true that a house means maintenance costs, both anticipated and unanticipated, the lawn calls out for fertilizer, the water heater springs a leak, the roof needs new shingles. The single-family-home owner must carry all the expenses associated with maintaining the property *and* the monthly mortgage payments, *alone.*

"It's worth it!" you say. "Home owners have privacy and autonomy. It's the best way to live!"

If it fits your life-style and *if* you can afford it. But there's an easier way to get there than saving your pennies, a way that will also launch you into beginner status as a real estate investor. The smart young home buyer on a limited budget chooses the multifamily house and gets someone else to help meet those monthly payments and maintenance costs.

CHECKPOINTS FOR THE INVESTOR

Numbers and Finances

In a good, owner-occupied, two-family house, the tenants should pay approximately 50 percent of the monthly mortgage, tax, and insurance payment at the outset. That percentage should be even higher in three- to six-unit houses, and it should rise the longer the property is held. This income is an important factor in choosing a successful first purchase for it is an indication of future resale value.

To test for resale value, consider yourself an investor who is *not* planning to occupy a unit. Such an investor will want the investment to come as close to a positive cash flow as possible. He will rent both units with the expectation that the sum of the rents will come close to paying the expenses of the building (including carrying the mort gage). The closer they come, the better the investment usually looks, since rents tend to go up over the years at a faster rate than carrying costs. A balanced or just slightly negative cash flow at the time of purchase will, therefore, almost certainly become positive, and positive cash flow plus appreciation and equity growth are the goals of most multifamily house investors.

And now consider the situation again with yourself as an owner-occupant investor. In the first year you own a two-family house, you pay half the monthly payment due the bank and virtually all of the miscellaneous maintenance costs. (It's a good idea to keep a few thousand dollars in a money market fund that first year for unexpected expenses!) After five years of ownership, however, you're living in the house essentially cost free, and appreciation has transformed your $5,000 down payment into $25,000 in equity.

The amount of rental income that a property generates at the time of purchase is also an important factor in enabling you to buy the

INVESTOR DEMAND PROFILE

	1	2	3	4	5	6	7	8	9	10
1. Positive Action and Reaction	▓	▓	▓	▓	▓	▓	▓	▓		
2. Willingness to Take Risks	▓	▓	▓	▓						
3. Decision-making Ability	▓	▓	▓	▓	▓	▓				
4. Commitment—the Will to Follow Through	▓	▓	▓	▓	▓	▓	▓	▓		
5. Logical and Rational Evaluation of Options	▓	▓	▓	▓	▓					
6. Ability to Deal with Numbers and Finances	▓	▓	▓	▓	▓	▓	▓			
7. Ability to Deal with Legal Constraints	▓	▓	▓	▓	▓	▓				
8. Organization and Management Skills	▓	▓	▓	▓	▓	▓	▓	▓		
9. Foresight	▓	▓	▓	▓	▓	▓	▓			
10. Imagination and Creativity	▓									
11. Self-confidence	▓	▓	▓	▓	▓	▓				
12. Patience and Tact	▓	▓	▓	▓	▓	▓	▓	▓		
13. Self-control	▓	▓	▓	▓	▓	▓	▓	▓		
14. Social Contact	▓	▓	▓	▓	▓	▓	▓			
15. Negotiating Skill	▓	▓	▓	▓						

property. A lender qualifying prospective home buyers for a multi-family purchase will add the monthly rent payments to their other income. Good rental income therefore can literally make home ownership possible.

POSITIVE ACTION

It takes positive action aplenty to put aside for a time your dream of a single-family home with a pretty yard and a garage of your own and choose instead to start out with an investment property. You must decide to take on the responsibilities of a landlord and to put up with the annoyances of sharing outdoor space, stairways, porches, and dividing walls (or floors or ceilings) with other people. Those who take the step, however, are usually rewarded with healthier bank accounts and ultimately nicer single-family houses than those who save their pennies and start out with a cottage or a condo.

RISK TAKING AND FORESIGHT

The risks in buying a multifamily house for owner occupancy are small and focused primarily on location, maintenance costs, and the local economy. You *can* lose money on your investment, however, if even one of these key factors turns sour. To avoid real depreciation in value and increase your odds for profit, be sure of the following:

- The house you buy is located among similar or better houses.
- The neighborhood is stable or improving and adjacent to stable or improving neighborhoods.
- The house is structurally sound and the major systems (heat, plumbing, and electricity) are in good working order.
- There is a steady or increasing demand for rental housing in the area. Beware of areas that are hot spots, however, since they often attract entrepreneurs who build apartment houses in excess of need, bringing about a high vacancy rate and thus forcing *down* rents and building value. (In the recent past, such downward pressure in investment value occurred in several major cities in Texas and Florida.)

If you take these key factors into consideration and if we as a country can avoid another mortgage crunch similar to that of the early eighties, you can pretty much count on selling your multifamily house for a substantial profit within five to seven years or less. You may have to live a little longer with your house listed for sale than you would like, however, since multifamily properties usually sell less quickly than single-family properties.

$ If you plan, eventually, to use the equity in your multifamily to help purchase another home for yourself and/or other investment property, it's usually a good idea to have a contract of sale (that is a ready, willing, and able buyer for the place you are selling) *before* you sign any contracts to buy any other real estate. This is a safety net that can save you thousands of dollars in double interest payments while you carry two properties. And since the property you're selling is an investment property, you can often arrange to continue on as a tenant until you are ready to move into your next purchase.

There is virtually no risk of rent control or tenant-group problems in your purchase of a multifamily house. Rent control does not usually affect two- to six-family buildings, especially if they are owner-occupied. There is also little risk that you will find yourself living with tenants whom you think are undesirable, unless you chose them yourself. Our government allows you, the owner-occupant, the final word regarding with whom you will share your house. Do not discriminate, however, solely on the basis of race, religion, sex, age, marital status, or national origin. Any other reasonable objection is acceptable.

COMMITMENT

You may have read in the newspapers about buildings inspectors finding code violations in apartment houses near you. The landlords faced fines of thousands of dollars. What if that happened to you?

You need not worry. The odds are you'll never see a buildings inspector in your house unless he happens to be an invited guest. These good people rarely visit owner-occupied multifamily houses. The commitment to being a "good landlord" therefore rests with your sense of responsibility (nudged perhaps by your desire for profit when you sell).

LEGAL CONSTRAINTS

There are some other legal entanglements you must handle, however. Primarily, the lease. You should have one. Most jurisdictions across the country will recognize an oral lease (a handshake agreement) as binding for short periods of time, but it's very hard to prove exactly what you shook hands on if a dispute arises.

You can get a form lease from your local stationery or office supply store. Read it through and cross out anything that does not apply. You may also add any desired restrictions or agreements—no smoking in the house, for example—before you offer it to your tenants to sign.

If you take a security deposit, be sure that you check your state policy on the payment of interest. Some states require it, some do not. You can find out by calling your state attorney general's office.

MANAGEMENT SKILLS

Keeping track of your tenants' rent payments, paying the bills associated with your property, and keeping accurate records (for the IRS) of improvements and expenses associated with the rented space of your property are about the only record keeping and money management you'll be required to do. Some owners will also organize their time for leaf raking, lawn mowing, stair sweeping, refusal removal, etc., but most will just do these tasks as needed and not think very much about time allocation.

More highly refined management skills may be called upon, however, to enforce rules. You did tell your tenants that cars were not to be parked on the patio area! Yet there it is, your tenants' son's friend's red hearse.

CREATIVITY

Imagination is fine for making wall hangings or beautiful flower beds but when directed toward a multifamily house, it can actually be a detriment to maximum profit. Living rooms decorated in jungle motif or six-inch-wide floor-to-ceiling windows added to the bathrooms may turn off both tenants and prospective buyers. Clean, simple, and functional are the key words in redecorating or refurbishing a multifamily.

SELF-CONFIDENCE AND DECISION MAKING

I guarantee that there will be decisions beyond to buy or not to buy in this, your first investment experience. *Which tenant to choose, which improvements will add to resale value, when to sell,* to name just a few. And every time you make one, you will need enough self-confidence to stand by yourself. *What-if* and *we-shoulda* are always hanging about the real estate marketplace. Try to ignore them.

RATIONAL EVALUATION

Perhaps your most difficult and important decision will be *which multifamily shall I choose?* Here you must add up the numbers and consider the market indicators, but you must also leave room for some nonlogical, even irrational responses. If you are going to live in the house you buy, it is important that you love it a little, or at least like it. Owner-occupants who buy only by the numbers sometimes find themselves very unhappy. The emotions associated with *home* take over and very often precipitate a selling time long before optimum profit time.

PATIENCE, TACT, AND SELF-CONTROL

Anyone who must live in the same building with other people needs a fair share of these virtues, and the need intensifies when the other people live in *your* house and owe you money each month. Try to be:

- consistent—the same rules all the time.
- tolerant—other people have other values, not necessarily better or worse than yours.
- firm—"The party must stop at 1 A.M." *means* 1 A.M.
- nonviolent—do not use threats or physical force. There are other ways to deal with noncompliant tenants. If they realize that they can indeed be moved into the street, their behavior usually changes.

SOCIAL CONTACT

$ Getting to know people in the neighborhood is an important part of being a good landlord. An area with a high percentage of owner-occupied houses is usually better maintained and therefore more marketable for rental and resale than a neighborhood where everyone is a tenant. *Before* you buy, find out who owns the nearby houses and how many of those owners live in their buildings.

Talking with other landlords can also help you in handling tenant problems, getting tips on good repair people (plumbers, roofers, win-

COULD-YOUS FOR WOULD-BE LANDLORDS

Could you:

- Insist that your tenants get rid of the eight-week-old toy poodle puppy they smuggled in despite your *no pets* rule?

- Make room in the driveway for the four-wheel-drive, go-everywhere Bronco with spotlights and musical horns that the teenage son of your long-time tenants just brought home?

- Evict a tenant three months behind in his rent who has been out of work for six months?

- Ignore a stream of overnight male guests in the apartment of the female tenant who lives above you?

- Replace the washer on a leaky faucet?

- Pick up the candy wrappers, paper airplanes, skate boards, sand pails, and stray pieces of clothing left about by your tenants' children?

dow washers, etc.) and charging fair rents. Recommendations for new tenants and leads to new property coming up for sale in the area also often come over the back fence, not to mention an occasional buyer.

NEGOTIATING

You're worried. Price haggling just isn't your thing. You can't even ask a garage-sale proprietor for a two-dollar discount without feeling funny. How can you ever negotiate in real estate?

Don't worry. Negotiating for a multifamily house is easier than negotiating for a single-family house, or even a car. Why? Because there is less emotion involved. Remember, this is a business deal. The concept of *home* is less overriding. You can negotiate with the sellers in terms of market value (what are similar properties selling for?) and in terms of the ratio of income to the cost of the property and the expense of maintaining it. And of course you'll read the negotiating chapter at the end of this book.

TOOLS OF THE TRADE

WAITING TIME

Some investors buy a run-down multifamily and rather quickly do enough fix-up to warrant increasing the rents and therefore the value of the property. Such properties can often be sold at substantial profit as soon as the work is complete. During at least part of the renovation time, however, these buildings must be wholly or partially vacant and the cash flow is always negative. It's a situation where you need money to make money.

Fix-up and immediate resale therefore is out of the question for investor/occupants like Dick and Janet Ferber. They need part of the house for shelter and they need the income from the other part to meet the monthly payments. In fact, it will usually take a year or so for appreciation to wipe out buying expenditures on closing fees and mortgage points and a bit longer yet to cover the anticipated closing fees and commissions due upon selling.

If you are young and getting started like the Ferbers, figure three years minimum occupancy/holding time before your fix-up efforts and housing appreciation in general amount to enough added equity for profitable resale. Seven years is usually a maximum waiting time in multifamily houses, but in areas of slow growth and minimal housing appreciation, it's not unusual.

In areas where there is a rental housing shortage, however, the profitable turnover time could be much shorter since the housing crunch puts upward pressure on the value of all rental property. Such was the case outside Boston where Dick and Janet Ferber did buy a somewhat run-down two-unit multifamily. With the permission and cooperation of the tenants, they put in new ready-made kitchen cabinets, had the long-dirtied oak floors sanded and stained, and did some painting inside and out. After fourteen months, they were finished and impatient. For them, the waiting time was enough. They sold for a $40,000 profit after all expenditures and closing costs, both buying and selling, had been deducted. And they were so high on their success that they put aside their single-family house dreams for a little while longer and bought a four-unit multifamily house (again somewhat run-down) only three blocks from the site of their original purchase.

•   •   •

Working Time

The working time demanded by a multifamily investment house in which you are an owner-occupant is only slightly more than the time you would put into a single-family house. The driveway needs shoveling, the trim needs painting, a toilet gets clogged, a squirrel gets into the attic, a light bulb goes out in the back stairwell—it's just like home, only it's the home of two or more families.

There's also a small working time demand in keeping records of rent receipts and maintenance expenditures, perhaps an hour a month.

Start-up Cash

Start-up cash requirements are variable. Mortgages may be obtained with as little as 5 percent of the purchase price down, with FHA, VA, or private mortgage insurance backing. In fact, if the price is right and your income high enough, you might even be able to buy a multifamily with nothing down and a VA-guaranteed mortgage. You can get more specific information from the Veterans Administration and from any lender that writes VA and FHA loans. The noninsured mortgage down payment requirements for most owner-occupied multifamily houses are 20 to 25 percent of the purchase price or appraised value.

When a property is being sold by an investor, you can sometimes get a second mortgage note for part or all of the down payment money you need, and at a favorable interest rate. Ask for it. If you don't ask, you'll never know if the seller was willing or not.

A few sellers are even willing to take back a purchase money mortgage for the entire selling price. Be sure you can carry the payments if you're offered such a deal. Remember there is no lender or other uninterested party doing qualification calculations. You must test your own resources. If you are too easy on yourself (or perhaps just too optimistic) you could lose the property to foreclosure, leaving behind all your hard work and the equity growth that should have been yours.

A good credit rating will be important in your qualification for financing at a conventional lender, as will the condition of the building. Most lenders are hesitant to give maximum financing to buildings in need of immediate repairs unless you have plans and drawings for the fix-up, estimates of cost, and projections of the future building value after the fix-up is complete. *And then* the lender often wants you to borrow the cost of the building *plus* the cost of fixing it up. There are

also some government-sponsored loan programs to help in rehabilitation situations. (Ask your nearest FHA office to send you information
on the 203K program.) But rehab is really a different ballgame from
finding a good multifamily in which to live. Let me save it for the next
chapter.

CASH FLOW

An owner-occupied multifamily house often has a negative cash flow
for several years. Remember, however, that the negative cash flow is
primarily *your* half of the mortgage payment. Think of it as rent with
very positive returns. Even in fully rented multifamily houses (those
which are not occupied by the owner), investors do *not* get rich on
positive cash flow. The attraction of the investment vehicle for non-
occupying owners is primarily in potential appreciation.

TAXES

Filing a federal tax return is slightly more complicated for the multifamily homeowner than for the single-family homeowner, and you
might do well to seek professional help at least the first time through
the process. Basically, the portion of the house you occupy is treated
exactly as a single-family house. If it's a two-family, you may deduct
50 percent of the mortgage interest and local property taxes you paid
in a given year. If it's a three-family, you may deduct one-third, a
four-family one-fourth, etc.

What about the part that's rented? That is treated as passive real
estate investment. You tally your costs by depreciating one-half (or
whatever percentage applies to your rental units) of the purchase price
over 27½ years. To this you add the same percentage of the property
taxes and mortgage interest paid and the same percentage of maintenance costs that apply to the entire property (exterior house painting, for example, or driveway repairs) and the *full* cost of maintenance
that applies specifically to the rented units (a new kitchen floor, for
example, or the repair of leaking pipes in the wall of the shower).
These are your costs.

Then you have income, which is of course the total amount of rent
you collected during the year. When you have calculated both costs
and income, you compare the totals.

If *income* exceeds *costs*, you report the amount in excess as income on your tax return. However if *costs* exceed *income* (which they are likely to do because of the depreciation allowance, which is a paper loss or cost), you come under the provisions of the new tax law, which says that the yearly losses of passive real estate investment are *not* deductible against ordinary income and must be carried forward as losses to a profitable year or until sale.

"That's terrible!" you cry. "It's going to send multifamily housing values right down the drain!"

No, because most owners of multifamily houses are middle-income people and the government has left an incentive program of sorts to such investors. If you actively participate in the management of your property (choose tenants, collect rents, keep records, arrange for maintenance, etc.) and if your adjusted gross income is under $100,000 a year, you can deduct up to $25,000 in loss (the amount by which costs exceed income) against your ordinary income. (This $25,000 figure diminishes gradually for incomes exceeding $100,000 until it becomes zero at $150,000.)

When you sell your multifamily house, your profit is not a *capital gain* (this term no longer exists in this post-tax-reform age), it is ordinary income. But calculating the amount of profit isn't so easy. Cost of improvements lowers your profit, but the depreciation allowances you took over the years may well raise it again. I urge you to do these calculations with a tax accountant.

EXPECTED RETURN

When you are buying a piece of property, comparison is the best way to estimate the expected return upon a future sale. Find out how much similar property has appreciated over the past five years. The best place to do this is in the office of an experienced real estate agent. He or she can advise you both from personal observation and from a comparables file (records of past transactions) kept in the office.

Remember, however, that nothing stays the same in the real estate marketplace. If you choose well, and with a little luck, you could very well outperform all past records. Or vice versa.

KNOWLEDGE

Home maintenance skills (everything from plumbing to gardening) are an asset in keeping maintenance costs low. And a little knowledge of common construction practices and standards will help you eliminate some structurally questionable buildings from consideration. When it comes right down to deciding upon a purchase, however, it is usually wise to employ a professional home inspection firm to do a professional evaluation. The cost is small when you consider it as a safety check, a second opinion that is written, methodical, and objective.

I'm entering *interviewing and selecting tenants* here under knowledge for want of a better place, but really the process is an art, one that is learned by doing. To help you begin, however, I'll list a few pointers. Check for:

- good credit history
- good (steady) job
- good references
- no pets (or pets limited to your approval)
- not likely to be transient (Frequent turnover can cut deeply into your cash flow. Young, unattached singles and business executives on assignment are likely to be transient.)
- positive vibes (Don't discount your responses to the prospective tenants. Sometimes those feelings you can't quite put into words are very valid indicators.)

EIGHT QUESTIONS
TO ASK PROSPECTIVE TENANTS

1. Where are you living now?
2. How long have you lived there?
3. Why are you leaving?
4. What kind of work do you do?
5. How long have you been doing that?
6. What are you looking for in a place to live?
7. Of those features, what is most important to you?
8. If you were a landlord, would you choose a person like yourself for a tenant? Why?

Finally, up-to-date knowledge of what's going on in the town and the local area will help you to judge the probability of appreciation and the holding time to your profit-goal achievement.

HOW TO BUY ONE

Most multifamily houses are listed for sale by real estate agents, although you will occasionally see a for-sale-by-owner ad in the local papers. Before you buy, *go shopping*. You should see virtually everything that is for sale in your local area at the time you're ready to buy. Then make comparisons.

- Compare current asking prices to the selling prices of similar houses that have been sold during the past year. (The real estate agent can get this information for you in most parts of the country.)
- Compare the ratio of rental income to the asking price among all the houses which interest you.
- And compare the projected rental income with the projected cost of ownership at a given price. (The cost of ownership includes mortgage payments, taxes, insurance, and maintenance.)

Occasionally you may have some difficulty inspecting occupied apartments in houses that you are considering. Do not accept "Well, the upstairs apartment is just like the downstairs" from an agent or a seller. See for yourself! If you can't get into an occupied part of the house, make your offer-to-buy contingent upon your satisfactory inspection of the occupied units. With a signed contract of sale, the owner should have no problem getting access to an occupied unit.

Besides the profit indicators already mentioned, consider:

- Multifamily houses rent and sell better when they're not on a main traffic artery but still within a few blocks of public transportation.
- Off-street parking is a big plus. A garage for each unit is even bigger.
- The quality of the public schools affects the selling price of all residential real estate since it affects the desirability of the town itself as a place to live.
- Safe areas rent and sell best. Late on a Saturday night visit every property that you are seriously considering.

• Low municipal taxes contribute to the desirability of resale multi-family houses.

The largest numbers of available multifamily houses are to be found in and around virtually all American large and mid-sized cities. Single-family houses predominate in the suburbs, but even there you may find scattered clusters of older multifamily houses or old mansions that have been converted into multifamily houses. In rural areas, multi-family houses that were built as such are rare, but many farm houses have accessory apartments. Often these farmhouses are sold separately when a farm is converted to a tract development. A lucky investor sometimes happens upon one of these large houses and snatches up a bargain.

Most of the multifamily houses that you'll see will date from before World War II, since the big trend in housing for almost thirty years after the war was in single-family tracts. In the past decade, however, condominiums have become increasingly popular. As a result of this growing public acceptance (or perhaps reacceptance) of owned shared-space housing, there seems to be a renewed interest in multifamily building. In some new planned communities now under construction, developers are including clusters of multifamily buildings which are being marketed primarily to owner-occupants. Home buyers seem to see them as an alternative to condominium living, and a far more profitable alternative at that. If you can find such a development of new multifamily houses in your area, it's probably a good investment. The newness of the buildings alone will make the properties desirable for many years to come and will also keep down the maintenance costs.

If you intend to occupy the multifamily house that you choose, you must be certain that a unit will be vacant at the time of the closing. Get information about the leases for the current tenants. Do they survive after a change in ownership? When is a vacancy expected? You can stipulate in the contract that you will not close until a specified unit is vacant. You should also state in the contract that the vacant unit be left in *broom clean* condition. That may mean handprints on the walls, but at least you won't be faced with the chore of carting someone else's trash to the dump.

•   •   •

SOME SUCCESSFUL INVESTORS

RETIRED PEOPLE

After paying off his wife's medical bills and the funeral expenses, Joe Pustelnik found himself with only $10,000 remaining in his lifetime savings account. It didn't take much figuring for him to realize that his rent would eat up over half his pension and Social Security income each month now that his wife's checks no longer came in. He saw the $10,000 disappearing in but a few years, leaving him dependent upon senior citizens' public housing or his children's support.

His Polish pride found that prospect distasteful and his Polish ingenuity found a solution. He gathered his three children together and suggested a joint investment. He and each of them would contribute $5,000 toward the purchase of a four-family house. Joe would live in the smallest of the units, assume all rental management duties, and pay a token $100 a month rent for his "superintendent's apartment." That $100 and the rent from the other three units would cover the mortgage payments, taxes, and other carrying costs.

The plan worked beautifully. In five years, despite some repair and maintenance outlays, the property was actually showing a good-sized positive cash flow. Then, in the sixth year, Joe Pustelnik died suddenly. He still had $3,000 in that lifetime savings account, and he left his children that and something more.

The four-family house they had all purchased for $100,000 sold for $167,000. After closing costs and the mortgage were paid off, each of Joe's three children got back his or her $5,000 investment *plus* $17,993, a parting gift from a father who did not want to be a burden to them.

A multifamily house can provide low-cost housing for owners on a fixed retirement income while rents and property value keep pace with inflation. If a retiree is unable to do maintenance work and if landlord tenant rapport is good, a particular tenant's rent might be reduced somewhat in return for grass cutting, snow shoveling, and general fix-up work. Or if the retired owner is particularly active, he, she, or they may look upon maintenance and decorating as an outlet for spare time and energy.

•   •   •

SINGLE PARENTS

Elizabeth Cuccia's husband finally signed the divorce papers after four years of "unknown whereabouts" because he wanted *his* half of the profit from the sale of their modest house. The divorce decree specified child support payments, but Elizabeth had few hopes that checks would arrive in the mail. She had $37,000 in cash from the divorce settlement, three children (the youngest of whom suffered from cystic fibrosis and needed both supervision and care), and a dog. Her search for an apartment was heartrending. No one believed she could actually support her family and no one really wanted her problems around. After two stress-filled rentals, she put $32,000 down on a three-family house with a tiny fenced backyard and an old-fashioned garage that was too small for her Toyota but plenty big enough for bicycles, sleds, and lawn equipment.

She even went on to find the "perfect" tenant for the second-floor apartment, a retired couple who were willing to watch the children and help with the care of her youngest during her working hours in return for a small reduction in rent.

Housing is often a problem for single parents since many of the "best addresses" will not accept children or are just too costly for one income. Owning a multifamily house may be an ideal solution to this housing problem. With ownership comes security, autonomy, acceptance for the children, and a rental income that will supplement the single parent's take-home pay. With ownership also comes the right to have pets if you choose. And again, if a tenant is just right, the owner may be able to arrange for some after-school supervision for the children, or perhaps help with house maintenance jobs.

LONG-TERM INVESTORS

Yvonne and Al Black began investing in real estate in their late forties when Yvonne inherited $40,000. With the money, they bought two two-family houses, structuring the mortgages so that income from the rentals would almost cover all expenses and carrying costs.

Five years later, they were showing so much positive cash flow from each property that it hurt to mail in their tax returns in April. So they refinanced. Because they owned property in a very rapidly appreciating area, each of the houses was now worth almost double the original price. Yvonne and Al structured the new debt similar to their first venture into the marketplace (at the outset the rental income would fall just short of covering all expenses), and they came from the bank with enough cash to buy three more multifamily houses.

Real estate would be their retirement fun fund. They intended to hold these properties, even buy more if possible, until they reached retirement time. Then, with reduced income, they would pay less tax on the sale of each as it was sold to pay for the travels they had dreamed of for a lifetime.

Investors interested in self-supporting property that will insure their greater wealth in ten or more years often find multifamily houses an appealing option. Maintenance can become a problem, however, when several properties are owned simultaneously. Tenants are less careful in a fully rented house than in an owner-occupied house, and they are essentially unsupervised since the income from one multifamily can rarely support the fees of a managing agent and still show positive cash flow.

It's up to the owner, therefore, to run spot checks on his property and to attend to the myriad of small maintenance tasks that always crop up. Some of these are just mosquito bites ("My faucet is leaking!") requiring no more than an hour's work. But fifty mosquito bites in a short period of time can be very annoying.

Sometimes an arrangement can be made with a tenant in each of the multifamily houses to attend to the small complaints. And sometimes one particularly reliable tenant may take over the job of maintenance for all the properties owned by his landlord. This kind of responsibility requires much reduced rent or an hourly wage, however. And still the owner must check in and check up on record keeping and expenditures.

MOVING ON

Many investors specialize in multifamily houses. Once appreciation has increased their equity sufficiently, they either sell or refinance in order to get down-payment money to buy more property of a similar nature. The obvious advantage in this investment plan is experience. You develop a sense for the potential worth of properties in a local area and you develop property management skills.

The chief disadvantage, of course, is the increasing demand on management time as your investment portfolio expands. Maintenance costs also are somewhat higher in relation to income when you hold a number of multifamily houses than in some other comparable investments.

Those investors who find that managing a number of properties scattered about an area is too cumbersome, time-consuming, and/or expensive sometimes switch vehicles and purchase a small apartment building. Owning blocks of condominium or cooperative apartments is another alternative that demands less management time.

Investors who have considerable time, are particularly creative, or enjoy rehabilitation work and investors who discover that they do not like the role of landlord sometimes move from multifamily house ownership into buying and fixing up run-down houses for quick re-sale. Speculators who like high-risk/high-reward situations often move from small city multifamily houses into rental vacation properties.

Generally multifamily houses are a safe and profitable investment vehicle. They require but little specialized knowledge and are encumbered with minimal legal restraints. They are not, however, the fast track to millionaire's row.

· CHAPTER 5 ·

Handyman Specials

Tom and Clara Roselle both work at office jobs. They have two kids in college, an excellent credit rating, plenty of time evenings and weekends, and good handyman skills. But they have only a small amount of available cash. Investment vehicle of choice: the handyman special.

· · ·

To get a feel for the handyman-special marketplace you might try to imagine one of those rich-quick seminars so touted in the mid-'80s. Or perhaps you attended one. If you did, you'll remember the scene.

It might have been in a conference room or an auditorium in Anytown, USA. You remember the assistants stopping at the end of each row to pass out an "Investment Evaluation Sheet" to each person.

Then Percival Quickrich strides to the podium and greets his new students. He asks them to look at the first question on the sheet they have just been given. It reads:

The most profitable real estate going right now is

apartment buildings
land
syndicates (limited partnerships)
run-down single-family houses

"Okay everyone," shouts Quickrich, "mark your answer." He waits a few moments and then asks, "Is everyone finished?"

There's a general affirmative murmur.

"Great! Let's see what we get," continues the leader. "How many of you voted for apartments?"

There is a scattered show of hands.

"How many for land?"

Another scattering, somewhat fewer in number.

"How many for limited partnerships?"

Not a single hand is raised.

"How many for run-down single-family houses?"

Slightly more than 70 percent of those in the audience raise their hands.

"That's it folks! You got it!" shouts Quickrich. And punching his right arm into the air, he continues, "*Houses* are the way to wealth! Let's go for it! Go for it! Come on everyone, join in. Go for it! Go for it!"

The enthusiastic investor-audience joins him in a ringing cry of "Go for it!" Everyone in the room is on the road to riches.

For most of them it will be a dead end, a dream built upon unrealistic expectations and limited information. There *is* money to be made refurbishing run-down houses, but it is not easy, nor risk-free, nor without competition. It is also not for everyone.

The idea of making big bucks fast by buying handyman specials far below market value, fixing them up without using paid labor, and reselling at top market price is the pipe dream of the vast majority of American armchair investors. Those who leave their living rooms and actually *go* into the marketplace to make their fortunes soon discover that it is also one of the most demanding of all available investment vehicles. Let's look at the demand profile.

CHECKPOINTS FOR THE INVESTOR

POSITIVE ACTION AND SELF-CONFIDENCE

Real estate fever is contagious. When the market is hot, *everyone* wants in. Even the most run-down properties are snatched up by investors hoping to make a killing after doing a little painting and papering. If you want to get in on the best deals in a hot market, you must be willing to *act*. Competition for good investment property is keen and there is little time allowance for mulling it over or hemming

INVESTOR DEMAND PROFILE

	1	2	3	4	5	6	7	8	9	10
1. Positive Action and Reaction										
2. Willingness to Take Risks										
3. Decision-making Ability										
4. Commitment—the Will to Follow Through										
5. Logical and Rational Evaluation of Options										
6. Ability to Deal with Numbers and Finances										
7. Ability to Deal with Legal Constraints										
8. Organization and Management Skills										
9. Foresight										
10. Imagination and Creativity										
11. Self-confidence										
12. Patience and Tact										
13. Self-control										
14. Social Contact										
15. Negotiating Skill										

$ and hawing. Some investors even go so far as to knock on doors asking if anyone in the neighborhood is planning to sell.

In a slow market, when mortgage money is expensive or hard to get or when an area is economically depressed, many houses go begging and run-down properties sit long on the books. There are real price bargains to be had at such times, but buying takes a good deal of self-confidence. Are you choosing well? Will the market turn? Will the neighborhood appreciate? How about the geographical area in general? What are the positive indicators? Can you rent until the turn? These are only a few of the questions that will play bumper cars in your brain. Sometimes getting a good investment bargain means taking positive action when everyone else is holding back.

Social Contact

$ Most of the best deals in run-down single-family houses never get into the real estate office listing book. If you really want to deal in this kind of property, you must tell everyone who'll listen that you're looking to buy. Rumors of divorce, transfer, foreclosure, or estate sales should start your motor running. Most often you will hear that kind of news *from other people*. When it gets into the newspaper, competition for the property will increase tenfold, and most likely the price will go up.

Commitment

Once you've made the decision to refurbish a run-down house, you've got to commit yourself to the work. Every day the house is off the market or unrented costs you money (mortgage interest, taxes, utilities, etc.), so you can't afford much time off. The work may seem fun while you're riding on the excitement of the purchase and the anticipation of future gain during the first few weeks, but there will come a time when you want to throw the paintbrush through the window. Or perhaps it will rain for three days straight and you'll stop in to work in the cellar only to find four inches of water over the floor. At times like these you'll need to remember the importance of commitment, for, strangely enough, half finished houses sell *less well* than handyman specials. Buyers are suspicious souls and ask "What happened?" or "What's wrong?"

PATIENCE AND TACT

When you run out of wallpaper and the man in the paint store tells you it will be two weeks before he can get you another roll from the same dye lot, you may be able to grin and bear it and turn your efforts to laying new tile on the bathroom floor. But you may not be so tranquil when you wait at the property an entire day for a dishwasher that never gets delivered. And your blood pressure is sure to rise when you call the plumber and he says, "If I can't come tomorrow, I won't be able to come for three weeks."

Delays, mistakes, tie-ups, call them what you will, frustrations are inevitable in the business of handyman specials. Figure the time you think you need for refurbishing and add half again.

SELF-CONTROL

One of the dangers of the handyman special is emotional stress. This investment is a full-time job that is usually taken on by amateurs working part-time with unfamiliar tools and under time pressure. When things go wrong (and they will), it's all too easy to lose your temper and point the finger of blame at your spouse or partner. Laugh if you can or at least try to put the problems in perspective. Remember the money you'll make when the job is done. Cut out that magazine ad for a week in London and tape it to your refrigerator!

DECISION-MAKING ABILITY

The decision to buy is just the beginning in this investment vehicle. Redoing the run-down house calls for a decision a minute. Well, maybe not that often, but it may seem that way. Plans are made and then rethought. Obstacles are encountered. Often a decision must be made on the spot, without the opportunity to consult with partners. You must be willing to make such decisions and to take responsibility for them.

FORESIGHT AND IMAGINATION

These two character traits go hand in hand: foresight to judge the future saleability of the property; imagination to choose the improvements that will enhance saleability. Prophecy and creativity can be dangerous, however, unless grounded upon logical and rational evaluation of the property and careful attention to monetary and legal constraints. Otherwise you may overimprove or choose "improvements" that actually detract from market value.

RATIONAL EVALUATION

When buying a run-down house for refurbishing and resale, you must put aside your concepts of *home*. Many novice investors look at a house and say, "Ugh! I would *never* live in such a thing!" They often miss excellent investment opportunities because of personal bias.

Try to keep your personal tastes out of your investment decisions, for tastes and especially attitudes toward *home* are always colored by emotions. Investment property should be purchased with your head in complete control.

A LOOK AT LOTS

POSITIVE FACTORS	NEGATIVE FACTORS
Rectangular or regular in shape	Pie shaped or irregular
Near center of block or on a cul de sac	Corner lot or near commercial property
Level	Below road grade or with a steep upward driveway
Treed	No trees
Good landscaping	No landscaping
Good foundation planting	Foundation barren or overgrown
Lot size appropriate to house and surrounding neighborhood	Large lot that cannot be subdivided with much unusable land (higher taxes—more maintenance)

NUMBERS AND FINANCES

If you don't pay careful attention to numbers and finances when buying a run-down house, you may end up working for the same hourly wage as the teenager who bags your groceries. You *must* have accurate estimates for:

- Your monthly carrying costs—mortgage, taxes, insurance, utilities, etc.
- The cost of materials for the work that must be done.
- The time required to do the work.
- The cost of necessary subcontractors—plumbers, electricians, masons, heating contractors, roofers, etc.
- The realistic selling price for a comparable house in move-in condition. (Ask your real estate agent to show you the comparables file.)

LEGAL CONSTRAINTS

Before you add a garage or raise the roof for two more bedrooms, you must check zoning laws and building codes in the town where the property is located. You cannot extend an addition beyond the setback lines specified in the zoning laws without a variance approved by the planning board. And you must have a building permit to raise the roof or make any other addition to living space. If you start work without the proper approvals, town officials can go to court to order a halt, and your house may stand in the rain with its "improvement" side covered by plastic sheeting for several months. Planning boards are also less likely to act quickly or favorably when an investor has attempted to bypass their authority.

If you are renovating an older house, you should think twice before doing work that requires a building permit. Many older houses do not meet the standards of local building codes but are allowed to continue in use under grandfather clauses. When an investor begins renovation, however, housing officials can require that all working systems of the house be brought up to code standards. This requirement usually makes a renovation far more expensive than bargained for.

•   •   •

MANAGEMENT AND ORGANIZATION

You will not need to concern yourself with property management skills unless you decide to rent your refurbished property. You will, however, need some good organization skills to get the refurbishing accomplished. Tasks must be prioritized, supplies must be ordered and collected, subcontractors must be scheduled, bills must be paid, and records must be kept.

But all this work need not be done by *one* person. In fact, division of labor is often a key to successful handyman-special investing. Tom and Clara Roselle were experts at it from the start and, ironically, the *way* they divided the work became a rewarding contrast to their primary jobs and therefore as much a part of the satisfaction of investing as their cash rewards.

Tom's was a staff job. His days were filled with budgets, long-term plans, personnel problems, and endless meetings at which he had learned to choose and balance his words in order to make his points without offending "higher-ups" with different views. Clara was stuck in a bookkeeping job that allowed her little freedom. She was told what to do and when to do it.

Tom longed for *work*, physical, creative, hands-on work, jobs one could point to and say, "This is what I did today." Clara longed for responsibility and freedom, for the opportunity to run a project without someone peering over her shoulder to see that she was adhering to "company policy."

Their handyman-special investment was an incredible success. Together they found a two-bedroom house in a neighborhood that was something of a hodgepodge of style and quality but whose backyard abutted a new development of houses selling for $50,000 or more higher than their investment property.

After agreeing that this was their investment gem, they each assumed different work roles. Clara did all the planning and paperwork. She found the best mortgage-money deal, applied for it, got plans drawn for the expansion of the attic into dormered living space, followed through on building permits, kept records of estimates and actual expenditures, and scheduled and paid all subcontractors. If there was ever a question or a problem, Clara ran it down and resolved it.

Tom picked up his hammer and transformed a shack into a Cape Cod with some Victorian touches that might well have made the front cover of *Home* magazine.

Tom and Clara bought their run-down shack for $58,000, put $18,000 into the property (money which they got from the bank on a home-improvement loan), and sold four months later for $109,700. They took that trip to London, put $10,000 into their college tuition fund, and then bought the house *next door* to the one they just completed!

NEGOTIATING SKILL

How well you negotiate will have a very real effect on how much you make from your investment. Since refurbishing is often a relatively short-term investment, every dollar you negotiate off the asking price is quite literally a dollar in your pocket. Read chapter 15 carefully and then hone your skills with every negotiating session.

RISKS

If you ignore the investor-demands of this investment vehicle, it can be among the highest risk vehicles you'll ride. Among the fatal errors are the following:

- not accurately estimating market value—paying too much;
- not including acquisition and selling costs in profit estimates—mortgage points, survey fees, closing fees, real estate commissions, and transfer taxes;
- underestimating refurbishing costs;
- underestimating refurbishing time;
- missing an important structural flaw when inspecting the property;
- overestimating your abilities.

If you accurately evaluate the property and your abilities, however, the single-family house in need of refurbishing can be a most profitable investment and one of the least risk vehicles available. Why? There's an escape hatch in the purchase. Single-family houses are in high rental demand and a period of rental can usually carry you through a down time in the market (or a slightly overestimated value) to a time when the sale will be profitable indeed.

•   •   •

TOOLS OF THE TRADE

There's a logical question to be asked here and I can sense your asking it: *Why recommend an investment vehicle with such high investor demands to Tom and Clara Roselle, a middle-aged couple with a heavy drain on their income and little spare cash?* Because they have exactly the tools of the trade required for this investment.

The run-down single family house is an excellent entry-level investment vehicle for the home owner turning investor. The skills learned in the home-buying and home-ownership process are applicable to the investment, and knowledge of the local area is built in. Necessary cash for refurbishing can be obtained through government-insured loans or from private-sector lenders. From that point on, it's a matter of motivation and hard work.

WAITING TIME

The waiting time required for the *profitable* sale of a refurbished single-family house is dependent on four factors:

- the price paid for the property;
- the cost of refurbishing;
- the market value of surrounding houses;
- the available working hours for refurbishing.

$ Even with shiny new everything or added rooms, few houses will sell for more than 20 percent above the going price in the neighborhood. Before you buy, therefore, get accurate figures on recent sales in the area. If you plan to sell as soon as you complete the fix-up, use this equation as a guideline:

purchase price + refurbishing costs + acquisition and transfer costs + profit
= market value in the neighborhood

If the figures on the left side of the equation add up to more than 20 percent above the market value, the odds are against a quick sale.

If you plan to rent the house for a period of time, you need not adhere to this equation, especially if you buy in an area that's becoming more desirable. The rent will ease cash flow problems and appreciation will increase your profit over time. Two to five years is the average holding time for a rented single-family house.

WORKING TIME

The working time required for profitable sale is dependent on:

- the condition of the property;
- the number of people participating in the work;
- the skill of the workers.

It is in working time that the big split occurs between refurbishing, renovating, repairing, and rebuilding. These terms are often used almost interchangeably, but let's take a moment here for some differentiation.

REFURBISHING: Every investor dreams of finding the plum that's priced well below market yet needs only paint and elbow grease, and perhaps a little new floor covering—to make it appealing. The working time required by such properties is low and the potential profit is high. Realistically, however, such houses are few and far between. Most American home owners are very much aware of property value even though they may have allowed maintenance to slide.

RENOVATING: The dictionary says "renovate" means to make new. Renovation also implies an upgrading, a restoring to the gracefulness of original appearance. It is quite different from "rehabilitation," which means to make liveable again, without implying any commitment to style or grace. Good renovation is usually more expensive, more extensive, and more time-consuming than refurbishing.

REPAIRING: Something, usually many things, are broken or nonfunctioning. Repairing a house is costly because buyers expect a working furnace or a roof that does not leak. They're usually unwilling to pay extra for these necessities, whereas they may well pay extra for new wall-to-wall carpeting or a ceramic tile floor in the kitchen. If you invest in a house in need of repairs, you should buy it considerably below the neighborhood market value.

REBUILDING: There are houses for sale into which you might pour repair money and still have a structure that is barely holding together. "Rebuilding" usually means gutting or near-gutting of the house and starting over with the frame and foundation. Surprisingly, however, it is sometimes more profitable than repairing. When rebuilding is complete, you usually have a new-looking product to sell. If the neighborhood is good, your profits can be very great indeed. The risk in investing in a house in ramshackle condition is a risk of your skills as well as your money. You will almost certainly have to hire some subcontractors in order to pass state and local building code requirements. Beyond that, the questions are how much can you or members of your group do, *and do well*, and how quickly?

COST RETURN CONSIDERATIONS

LOW COST WITH HIGH RETURN

Landscape and clean yard
Paint
Wallpaper
New kitchen flooring
Sand and refinish hardwood floors

HIGH COST WITH HIGH RETURN

Kitchen remodeling
Bathroom remodeling
Addition of bathroom
Addition of bedroom(s)
Enclose breezeway for family room
Addition of garage
Addition of screened porch or deck in rear

HIGH COST WITH LITTLE OR NO RETURN

Bracing, buttressing, or rebuilding foundation
Roof replacement
New plumbing
New septic tank, dry well, or leech lines
Termite damage repair and elimination of termites
Chimney repairs
Repair wet basement, waterproof, and re-grade
Driveway repairs

START-UP CASH

If you have a good credit rating, little is needed. It is possible to obtain one mortgage to cover the cost of purchase *and* fix-up. Here's how it's done:

1. select the property and sign a contract contingent upon your being able to obtain the financing you need;
2. obtain professional estimates for the cost of work to be done;
3. go to an appraiser and obtain an appraisal of the value of the property as it will be after the work is complete;
4. take your plans, estimates, appraisal, and purchase contract to a lender.

You can obtain all-inclusive financing through a conventional mortgage lender or you can apply for a HUD-insured program called 203K. Under the HUD program there are limits on the amount that can be borrowed, but eligible expenditures include windows, stairs, walls, floors, roofing, wiring, plumbing, solar energy installations, room partitions, modernizing baths, kitchens, electric service, energy conservation, air conditioning systems, expanding living area, and adding apartments. For more specific information on current limitations contact the HUD office nearest you.

If you're seeing dollar signs after reading this but your checking account reads *empty*, bear in mind that you do need *some* start-up cash. You must pay the appraiser and the mortgage application fee, and you will need $1,000 or so for an earnest money check with the offer-to-buy. There may also be an escrow deposit of up to 10 percent of the purchase required until closing. It's possible to borrow this money (with a credit line on another house you might own, for example) but most conventional lenders like to see the money in *your* account in *their* bank before they agree to lend you what you need. If you do borrow this start-up cash, remember to add interest to your cost of purchase.

CASH FLOW

Single-family handyman specials are negative cash flow investments; the property generates no income until it is sold. Since it can consume a good deal of cash in the interim between purchase and sale, all-inclusive financing is advisable. No matter what type of financing you use, however, be sure that you have the needed cash allocated and ready. If you don't, you'll incur added cost and time delays in obtaining short-term loans. (Not to mention added anxiety.)

If you choose to rent after refurbishing, the odds are you'll still have a somewhat negative cash flow, for a year or two anyway, since the rent tag on a single-family house is usually about the same or less than comparable space in an apartment building. Meanwhile, your costs as a landlord (mortgage payments, taxes, maintenance) are almost invariably higher. So as you write your personal checks to help pay the mortgage, console yourself by thinking about the appreciating value of the property.

TAXES

Expenses incurred by refurbishing real estate for the purpose of resale are not deductible against the investor's ordinary income in the year they occur. They must be carried forward and deducted against the profit upon sale whether it is in the same year as the purchase or a year following the purchase. (Unless, of course, your *primary* occupation is fixing up and reselling houses and you're doing several at one time.)

If you fix up your handyman special and decide to rent it, however, you will have some tax advantages available to you. Once the property becomes rental real estate, it comes under the passive investment laws. People with adjusted gross income of $100,000 or less may deduct up to $25,000 a year in property-related losses against their ordinary income as long as they actively participate in the management of the property. Those with incomes between $100,000 and $150,000 have a gradually phased out deductability available. Losses above $25,000 a year must be carried forward to a profitable year, deducted against the profitable sale of the property, or deducted against other passive investment income.

Bear in mind also that capital gains are a thing of the past. All investment income now is treated as ordinary income. There is a small benefit in this change for the handyman-special investor in that you no longer must wait six months after purchase in order to sell your property at the best tax rate. You can sell as soon as you complete the work!

The new law has also eliminated the sticky question: *who is a dealer?*

Before tax reform, if you bought and sold too many properties in one year (and there was some question as to how many was too many), the IRS could consider you a dealer in real estate rather than an investor and thus tax all your profits as ordinary income. Investors who wanted capital gains treatment therefore had to limit the number of purchase/sale deals in a given year and often rented property while they juggled the number of sales, holding time, and new purchases. Today you may do as many buy/sell deals in one year as your time and money allow. This new freedom may result in fewer rental houses on the market and therefore somewhat higher rental income for those investors who do choose to rent their properties.

You should be aware that residential property depreciation schedules have a 27½-year term as of 1987. Depreciating property over 27½ years rather than over 15 years (as in 1981) or 19 years (as in 1986) diminishes the amount of paper losses deductible each year. A property therefore is more likely to show a taxable profit in a given year (or at least less of a loss). The tax bite upon sale, however, is likely to be slightly lower since you will have written off a smaller percentage of the building's original cost and will therefore be using a higher base price from which to calculate profit.

Deductions of mortgage interest, local property taxes, and maintenance and management costs are still allowed against the income from the property. If these costs exceed income from the property, and you do not qualify for the $25,000 loss deduction, the loss they generate can be carried forward to a profitable year or until sale, or it can be deducted against other passive investment profits. Rehabers who purchase houses built before 1935 can also take a tax credit of 10 percent of the cost of refurbishing.

EXPECTED RETURN

Most neophyte investors overestimate this figure. There is money to be made in handyman specials, but not enough to catapult you into a league with J. Paul Getty. Your best returns will be the result of savvy selection of location. The turnaround of a neighborhood can cause value to jump by tens of thousands of dollars in a matter of months, and that kind of appreciation requires absolutely *no work*!

• • •

SKILLS

I won't consume unnecessary space with a review of the handyman skills helpful in doing a fix-up, anyone who's ever lived in a house knows what they are. But I do want to mention a skill that's almost always overlooked: *shopping*.

Yes, shopping. Smart shopping techniques can save money, every penny of which, as the old adage goes, is a penny earned, except that in the real estate marketplace those pennies are really dollars.

Do you or a member of your investment group know where to get wallpaper, paint, plumbing supplies, lighting fixtures, floor covering, etc. at really low prices? Do you know where to find authentic restoration hardware, half-round moldings, a kit for a flagstone entranceway, or the spray nozzle for a dishwasher? You can start collecting shopping information long before you make your first investment, and you should keep an up-to-date file even after you've become a seasoned veteran. Such a file will save you time and money.

KNOWLEDGE

When you buy a handyman special that you intend to sell for a profit, you should know the housing features that appeal to the greatest number of potential home buyers and select property with as many of them as possible. In today's marketplace, look for:

- at least one bathroom or lavatory on each floor
- eat-in kitchens
- a front entrance foyer—most people object to front doors that open into the living room
- a gathering room (family room, great room, den) less formal than the living room but on the main floor of the house. (Basement rec rooms have small buyer appeal.)
- garage space

Avoid houses that have the following features:

- traffic patterns with walk-through rooms: the kitchen at the center of a house is an exception. Objection to walk-through dining rooms is moderate; objection to walk-through bedrooms is very high.
- dark kitchens

- long windowless hallways or particularly narrow hallways
- bathrooms without a window or skylight
- minimal closet space

In doing your fix-up, you should also be aware of currently fashionable features you might be able to add to a property to increase buyer appeal. (But remember: don't improve beyond what the neighborhood price can support.) High-fashion items heralding the approach of the '90s include these:

- skylights
- decks
- sunrooms
- whirlpool bathtubs
- front porches or covered entranceways
- Victorian touches in lighting, windows, style
- leaded glass
- two-story open foyers, living rooms, or family rooms

LOCATION

The value of a given location is a composite of many factors, probably chief among them is the character of the surrounding housing. When you house hunt for investment property, look for:

- areas close to higher-priced new construction
- areas where scattered houses have already been refurbished or renovated
- areas that are stable and well kept in which the investment property is the smallest and/or the only run-down house
- a house in a municipality with a highly regarded school system
- a small house in a town comprised primarily of high-priced houses.

Easy access to public transportation and interstate highways is usually a positive feature, but avoid houses that abut or overlook these facilities. And *listen* when you inspect a prospective investment property. Highway noise pollution is a factor in many residential areas and a definite detriment to sales.

•   •   •

SELLING YOUR PROPERTY

Unless you have a red hot seller's market in your area and a person in your investment group willing and able to take phone calls and drop everything to drive over and show the property, it's usually a good idea to use a real estate agency in selling. For maximum exposure,

---

IF YOU RENT

- Have a written lease.
- Hold a security deposit equal to at least one month's rent.
- Do an inspection of the property *with the tenant* before occupancy. Use a written checklist to note the condition and contents of each room. When the inspection is complete, both the landlord and the tenant should sign and date the checklist. Follow the same procedure (if possible) when the tenant moves out. Damages to be deducted from the security deposit should be noted at that time.

Checklist format:

ROOM	CONTENTS	CONDITION
Kitchen		
Living room		
Bedroom #1		
etc.		

- Do *not* rent with an option to buy. Options favor only the buyer. In an option contract, the future sale price is set on the date tenancy begins. If the house appreciates dramatically during the rental period, the tenant gets a bargain. If the house does not appreciate well, the tenant can walk away without obligation. *There is no advantage to the seller in an option as part of a rental lease.*
- Do *not* allow a tenant *right of first refusal.* The right of first refusal allows the tenant to match an acceptable offer from another buyer and take the house. This arrangement must be noted in a listing contract and many buyers will avoid considering a property with a *right of first refusal* rider. Real estate agents usually support this reluctance and steer buyers to "clean deals."

choose a residential broker with an office located close to the property.

Be sure to use a multiple listing service if one is available in your area. For a quick sale, determine your price with careful regard to market value in the neighborhood.

If you choose to rent the property for a few years before selling, be aware that it will probably need some degree of fixing up again before going on the market. There is considerable controversy as to whether it is better to list a rented property with the tenants in residence or to wait until they vacate. The proponents of the first option will tell you that houses show better with people living in them. Which is true if your tenants are willing to cooperate with the broker, are relatively neat, and haven't covered the walls with religious pictures or political posters. Proponents of the second option will mention tenants who undermine saleability by bad-mouthing the house, leaving clutter about, and being uncooperative with real estate agents who want to show the property. They will also tell you that no *home* buyer wants to deal with eviction problems. Which is also true.

SOME SUCCESSFUL INVESTORS

THE YOUNG

Despite Clara and Tom Roselle's obvious suitability for and success with this investment vehicle, you should not assume that handyman specials only appeal to middle-aged couples with empty nests. Nothing could be farther from the truth. Think about Craig Hall, for example. As an eighteen-year-old college freshman, he put all his savings ($4,000 in 1969) into the purchase of a run-down multifamily house near the campus. He turned that down payment into $49,000 in less than two years and began a process of buying and selling residential real estate that would skyrocket him to wealth in the multimillions of dollars before the age of twenty-seven. He went on to become CEO of over a dozen companies, an author, a lecturer, a banker, and an adviser to various government, private sector, and community welfare organizations.

Success with handyman specials is more a matter of motivation than age, or even experience. This investment vehicle can be the right choice for ambitious and persevering young people, single, married, or in groups.

The Live-in Variation

If you're adventurous and don't mind a little sawdust on your toast, you might undertake refurbishing, renovating, or remodeling a house that's both your primary residence and your first investment property. Madeleine Benda, a young woman on her way up as an investment tax adviser to a large master limited partnership, did just that. Knowing that Manhattan co-ops were priced out of sight and that rental apartments were not only hard to find but also without tax benefits, she crossed the river and bought a three-story townhouse in Hoboken.

The year was 1981, the price tag $43,000, and the place a god-awful mess. The cracks in the plaster walls and ceilings vied with the spiderwebs for intricacy of pattern. The brown-painted floors had scuffed gray trails along the traffic patterns. The bannister was broken, both the roof and the cast-iron waste pipes leaked, and the wiring was so poor that Madeleine couldn't make coffee and toast at the same time without blowing a fuse.

Madeleine hired contractors to do the immediately necessary repair work, just enough to make the place livable, and then began her work of transformation. She found tremendous satisfaction in working with color and texture, whether it was staining woodwork or hanging wallpaper. The difference was visible and work progressed toward a goal, a far cry from the abstract theories and numbers she juggled all day.

Colored shapes of light from the leaded glass windows in the front doorway played across the grain in the oak floors and the pattern of her oriental carpets when she sold the property in 1987. You say you want to know the selling price? It was $229,500.

Madeleine Benda had put $10,000 down when she bought the house. During the first four years of occupancy she spent $29,000 on refurbishing work. Her cash outlay of $39,000 therefore had a gross return of $190,500. Even after paying off the mortgage and calculating in buying and selling expenses, she had come away with over $148,000 additional cash in only 6½ years. Even considering the fact that the appreciation rate in her area was among the highest in the nation at the time she sold, the rate of return on a $39,000 cash investment was pretty good, don't you think?

The live-in variation of handyman specials works well for investor/owners who know they will need considerable time to complete refurbishing work but want to do most of that work themselves. The chief advantage is money: the cost of carrying the property during fix-up is also paying for a place to live. I must warn you, however, that this live-in investment does not usually work well for families with very young children. The dangers and hardships of children living in and with unfinished construction are obvious.

GROUP INVESTMENT

The five—two Bills, a Dave, a Kevin and a Keith—walked together along a road near the corporate complex every noon hour. From November through March they passed the lime green and fieldstone house with the peeling gray trim and the broken screen door hanging by one hinge. Its people had moved out just after Christmas. On a Wednesday in March, Kevin remarked that the muddied and faded FOR SALE sign looked almost as desolate as the house.

"You know, we ought to buy the place," mumbled one of the Bills, almost to himself.

"You gotta be kidding!" was the general response. "That dump!"

"No, really," he continued more positively. "We could probably get it cheap and if the five of us worked on it together, we could probably have it ready to sell in two or three months."

"I heard the company's bringing in fifteen hundred new people in the next year," chipped in the other Bill. "Let's take a look in the windows."

The five signed a contract to buy the property on Saturday. They had negotiated $47,000 off the asking price and they had negotiated the right of occupancy and the right to begin repair work immediately, *before title closed!*

There was of course some risk in starting the work before taking title, but the five guys intended to raise the purchase money by taking out equity lines (second mortgages) on the homes in which they each were living, so there was no mortgage contingency, and they had arranged for an insurance policy that would cover them and the property while they worked on it.

It took five weeks to close title. Two weeks after that the now cream colored and fieldstone house went back on the market with a price tag $35,000 higher than its original asking price. A contract of sale, negotiated down $3,000 from the asking price, was signed three weeks later. Title closed in six weeks.

The total time elapsed was sixteen weeks, and since most of the refurbishing was cosmetic, the expenditures were minimal. Total gross profit per investor: $15,800 in less than four months.

Groups of fewer than ten people can quite successfully pool their money and talents to buy and fix up handyman specials. A word of caution, however. Before you buy, it's important to agree upon the assigned tasks of each member of the group, the hours of working time, the amount of money to be spent on refurbishing, the extent of the refurbishing itself, and the probable selling price. Do this *on paper.*

THE RETIRED INVESTOR

Frank Coles was nudged out of his corporate job by a "management incentive program" designed to cut staff. As an incentive to his early retirement, the company offered to pay him an additional year's salary in one lump sum. At age fifty-three, Frank found himself with $67,000 in cash and no job.

He was feeling physically fine and he didn't really know what to do with himself for the next twelve years before reaching sixty-five, the age he had always considered for retirement. Almost to kill time, he bought a handyman special and launched a new career.

Generally, the fix-up on each property he purchased would take three to four months. When it was complete, Frank would list the house for sale and go on vacation. When he returned, he would begin looking for another property.

Frank never worked on more than one property at a time, he hired as few outside workmen as possible, and he never became obsessed with completion dates. After twenty-eight years of working within the corporate hierarchy, this man was organizing his own time, setting his own goals, and maintaining his own standards. Frank Coles felt like a sea gull gliding on the wind.

Some years he netted $50,000 from his handyman special business; other years it was closer to $35,000. But in either case, when added to the early retirement pension he was receiving from the corporation, it was more than enough.

The idea of the handyman special appeals to many retired people as a means of making a little spare money. Be a little wary if you fit this profile, however. Beyond the dreaming, designing, thinking, and buying stage, the *work* demands of a handyman special can be far more physically taxing than anticipated. Time can also become a demanding factor unless you have plenty of capital and don't mind paying property taxes and other expenses while the work progresses slowly.

Even the retired investor in excellent physical health may find that he or she needs to hire some assistants. Licensed or professional subcontractors are, of course, one option, although an expensive one. Those investors with knowledge and experience but limited endurance might also consider hiring men and women from a nearby college or technical school to work under their supervision or the supervision of the technical school teachers. These young people usually appreciate both the money they earn and the opportunity for experience.

MOVING ON

Buying, fixing up, and reselling run-down houses can be a training ground for a full-time, big-bucks real estate career. Besides the obvious real estate and building skills you will be learning as you ride this investment vehicle, you will also be establishing credit and credibility with local lenders and subcontractors. Perhaps you will even begin developing some contacts with attorneys, planning board members, and buildings inspectors.

With remodeling experience behind you, larger projects will seem less overwhelming. Road signs from this stage in your investment career point to building new houses from precut materials or modular construction units, tract development, custom home building, conversion of factory or warehouse space into condominium apartments or condominium commercial space, and the purchase of unprofitable apartment complexes with the intent of performing a turnaround to positive cash flow and profitable resale.

If full-time real estate employment is your goal, a few handyman specials are a good place to test your mettle. If you like the work and are good at it, choose one of these fast track roads.

· CHAPTER 6 ·

Land!

At age thirty-eight, Marian Forsythe inherited slightly more than $100,000. She, her husband, and their two daughters are living comfortably on their current income and foresee no financial difficulties ahead, even during the college years. Marian would like to use this inherited money to secure a comfortable retirement, but she wants to spend absolutely minimal time on managing her investment. Investment vehicle of choice: land.

· · ·

When I was a girl, my parents vacationed with us, their three children, in south Florida every February. Among their favorite pastimes was a drive north from Miami Beach along route A1A. Long before we reached Hollywood, there was nothing between the road and the ocean but sand and sawgrass.

"Let's buy some of this land," my mother would say every year.

And every year my father would laugh, a great, loving, very-much-amused laugh. "Ha! Ha! Ha! You want to *own* a piece of worthless sand that nothing will grow on!"

They never bought the piece of land that would have cost them little more than one of the fur coats my mother wore in January.

Today, multimillion-dollar hotels and condominiums stand on the "worthless sand" my father scoffed at. One acre, cheap by any standards when they first saw it, now sells for many times their annual income.

"But how can anyone tell what will happen in thirty years?" you ask.

No one can. Not for sure. That's why land investment is risky and long term, and why it takes a kind of sixth sense that can anticipate future trends and needs. It also takes a good deal of creativity and makes demands on a few other character traits, too. Let's look.

CHECKPOINTS FOR THE INVESTOR

NUMBERS AND FINANCES (AND TAXES)

If you're one of those people who regard numbers as friendly guides that will keep you out of financial trouble, you'll find yourself feeling very much alone in this investment vehicle. Numbers and finances fill in only a small part of the land investment picture. Even the experts, land developers and speculators, regard price-per-acre as but a factor for consideration.

This is not to say that you shouldn't give due regard to your research on nearby land values and recent appreciation history. Just remember also that you're dealing in an inexact science—very inexact and not really a science at all. Appreciation can be tremendous within five or ten years if your estimates and hunches are right, or negligible in your lifetime if you guess wrong or are just unlucky. Land is a marketplace where the old conservative advice holds water: *Do not invest in land any money that you may need in the foreseeable future.*

Raw land is among the most illiquid vehicles in the general field of real estate, which is itself regarded as illiquid. All of which means: *land is hard to sell.* In fact, it's hard to get your money out of a land investment even when it *has* appreciated considerably. Why? Because land is not only hard to sell but also hard to mortgage. Most conventional lenders will not write mortgages on undeveloped land. The best you can hope for is a daring private investor willing to give a mortgage at a high rate for a short term. (This "investor" is more often than not the seller!)

Why this difficulty in financing? Because the value of land is never very clear until a buyer appears on the scene with a bid. Without this ready, willing, and able buyer, appraisal is something of a guessing game. Each piece of property is unique and there are no real compa-

INVESTOR DEMAND PROFILE

	1	2	3	4	5	6	7	8	9	10
1. Positive Action and Reaction	▓	▓	▓	▓	▓	▓	▓			
2. Willingness to Take Risks	▓	▓	▓	▓	▓	▓	▓	▓	▓	▓
3. Decision-making Ability	▓	▓								
4. Commitment—the Will to Follow Through	▓	▓	▓	▓	▓	▓	▓			
5. Logical and Rational Evaluation of Options	▓	▓	▓	▓	▓	▓				
6. Ability to Deal with Numbers and Finances	▓	▓	▓	▓						
7. Ability to Deal with Legal Constraints	▓	▓	▓	▓	▓	▓	▓			
8. Organization and Management Skills	▓	▓	▓	▓	▓	▓	▓	▓		
9. Foresight	▓	▓	▓	▓	▓	▓	▓	▓		
10. Imagination and Creativity	▓	▓	▓	▓	▓	▓	▓	▓		
11. Self-confidence	▓	▓	▓	▓	▓	▓	▓	▓	▓	
12. Patience and Tact	▓	▓	▓	▓	▓	▓	▓	▓	▓	
13. Self-control	▓	▓	▓	▓	▓					
14. Social Contact	▓	▓	▓	▓	▓	▓	▓	▓		
15. Negotiating Skill	▓	▓	▓	▓	▓	▓	▓			

rables, no handy file of recently sold similar properties, to check your guess-at-value against. Worse yet, the value of land can change drastically with the ruling of a zoning board or with the opening or closing of a major employer in the area.

And what about tax benefits? Undeveloped land provides no shelter. The federal government sees the potential economic life of land as limitless and allows *no* depreciation on this investment. State and local property taxes are deductible annually on your federal income tax returns, but under the Tax Reform Act of 1986 you cannot deduct annually the interest you pay on a loan that uses the land as its collateral. Instead you must keep records on interest paid and deduct the total amount against the profit when you sell your land.

If your land produces some income (rental to a hunting club, for example), you may deduct interest paid on the land mortgage against this income. The interest will almost always exceed the income and the net result will be a little extra pocket money.

"Why bother with the figuring?" you ask. "It seems as though the 'ability to deal with numbers and finances' character trait should rate a one not a five in this investor demand profile."

Not true. Total disregard for numbers and finances can be disastrous. Before buying, you should check and double-check to be sure you can comfortably meet the carrying costs of your land investment: taxes, insurance, and the interest on any loans on the property. Then you should negotiate the best price you can get in order to keep those costs to a minimum.

NEGOTIATING SKILLS

Negotiating over land can go on for months. It's dependent upon how strongly a seller wants to sell, how strongly a buyer wants to buy, how far apart they are on price and financing terms, and how many contingencies are being negotiated for inclusion in the contract.

To move their land in the marketplace, many sellers take back purchase money mortgages for most or all of the price. Financing terms therefore are often as much a part of the negotiations as price concessions. And some negotiated terms, an assumable loan at a below-market interest rate for example, may even be major factors in profitable near-term resale.

Among the contingencies common in a contract to buy land are the following:

- Preliminary subdivision approval—will the town allow the tract to be divided into smaller parcels or lots?
- Percolation tests—does water drain into the land fast enough to satisfy local standards for the kind of development that has been proposed?
- Zoning changes—will the town allow different usage of the land than that which is currently imposed under its zoning laws?
- Approval of environmental control agencies—how will the proposed development affect the environment? Approval is now required from both federal and local agencies in most areas of the country.
- Removal of environmental restrictions—density restrictions might be removed, for example, if a sewer processing plant were to be built.
- Permission to hook into municipal sewer facilities—most municipalities have usage limitations on their sewer processing plants. A buyer will want proof that he can hook in.
- Others—some so strange you might think they came straight out of a science fiction magazine. Others as sensible as, Is there an access road that fire trucks can negotiate?

A contract might be held in abeyance for from six months to two years (or more) while each of its contingencies is tested and met.

Many experienced land buyers do not even go to contract when they spot a piece of land they might want. Instead, they negotiate a selling price and purchase a long-term option at that price. A year is a common option time. One or two available renewals for an additional year each at an additional fee are also common and a definite plus to the buyer. With such options in hand, these experts proceed with their tests or studies. They buy *only* if the land meets all contract contingencies and thus proves suitable to their development plans.

Using an option in the purchase of land establishes the price, ensures that no other buyer can put in a higher bid and take the property while it's being studied, and allows the holder of the option to walk away with only a small loss if he or she cannot implement the hoped-for use for the land. I highly recommend it.

If you buy land, one day you will probably become a seller of land. When that day comes, remember that the selling process can be very long and complicated. Negotiating skills are often severely tested in this marketplace, and patience and tact are just as often sorely tried.

Patience, Tact, and Self-control

Once negotiations for your land purchase are complete, you will still need a good supply of patience, for this vehicle moves slowly. If you plan to hold the land for appreciation only, as Marian Forsythe does, patience is built into your buying plan. If, on the other hand, you decide to apply for preliminary subdivision approval as a means to making your land more valuable and salable to a developer, you will need not only patience but every scrap of tact you can gather. Why? Because you'll be dealing with the local planning commission or zoning board. Your presentation of your proposal and your persuasive powers will become all important. A poorly chosen adjective, disregard for protocol, a little too much pressure on the wrong person, a demeanor that's a little too slick—such small things can turn a decisive vote against you.

What about self-control? Well, if your land is to stand idle, you won't need much. You can go to your property and kick, pound, yell, dig, even bulldoze. The land won't complain. But if you go before a planning commission, you'll need self-control that would make St. Peter proud. People who get angry, shout, call names, or become vindictive or sarcastic at meetings that might just go long into the night almost always lose. Sit still at the meeting. Let your lawyer do the talking, even leave the room if you must. Cool down with a walk on your land, or chop down a tree if you can use the firewood, but do *not* resume talking with the officials in power until you can do so in a quiet, rational voice.

Decision-making Ability

After the decision to buy a parcel of land is made, the need for this personality trait diminishes to a real estate low. There are few decisions required for land that is left to idle its way to appreciation. And even for land that is to be subdivided, many of the necessary decisions will be made by engineers, surveyors, and municipal officials, each of whom will take a good deal of time in arriving at a decision. So if land is your investment vehicle, you can feel free to consult, confer, ponder, and project to your heart's delight.

POSITIVE ACTION

You don't have to act quickly if you choose to invest in land, but you *do* have to get out of your easy chair. To buy land intelligently, you must walk it; and to walk it, you must find it.

Land investment begins with watching several local newspapers for ads and putting your name out to a number of real estate agents. Running down the leads you'll get from these sources will be a good education. You *may* even find something you're willing to consider.

If you are really serious about investing, however, you'll go on to the next step. It's at the tax collector's office. Ask to see local tax maps, and go over them sheet by sheet. You're looking for acreage with the name of the owner printed neatly in the center. When you see a likely piece, leave the tax map and go to the large street map of the town that usually hangs in the municipal building somewhere. Find the land on the town map and take a drive by it. Is it well located? Is the terrain suitable for development? Is it, in fact, property that you might want to own? If so, give the owner a call. Don't worry that the land is not listed for sale. Most undeveloped land is for sale at a price. Tell the owner that you're interested and arrange to walk through the property.

The initiative that it takes to make an appointment to inspect unlisted land and then to make an offer when no price tag is in place is often well rewarded. In fact, the best land deals are usually hunted down and negotiated privately, without the use of newspaper ads or real estate agents.

LOGICAL AND RATIONAL EVALUATION

It's important not to get caught up in fairy-tale dreams of owning a deep pine forest, or a mountain top, or the farm you vaguely remember from your childhood. Not all land is valuable, and value is not necessarily tied to the size of the tract or its beauty. Demand and feasibility for development are more realistic determinants of value.

The fifty-by-one hundred city lot may bring much more appreciation than two hundred acres on top of Mount High Hopes. The city lot may be perfect for a lawyer's office, or a convenience store, or, at the least, a multifamily house, whereas those two hundred hilltop acres will be worth little until the demand for housing in the area jacks the home-building profit margin high enough to support the cost of putting in a road and bringing in utilities. Or until the government decides it needs *your particular mountain top* for a satellite tracking station.

Among the factors considered positive signs of good return on a land investment are the following:

- Considerable frontage on an established road. Lots with current road frontage can often be subdivided from the tract and sold to support the cost of building the road into the interior of the property.
- Level or gently rolling land. Development is easier on such terrain. Building on the side of a cliff, for example, takes fill and even when complete is hard to sell.
- No running streams. Building bridges is expensive and discourages many developers.
- Good drainage. Most developers do not want the hassle of fighting basement water problems. If septic tanks are to handle the sewerage from development, drainage becomes even more important, and subdivision approval may hinge upon percolation tests and soil composition reports.
- The availability of drinking water, either from wells or a municipal supply.
- Proximity to currently functioning utility and phone lines. Developers must pay by the running foot to have these brought into the tract.
- Proximity to an interstate highway. The land should be convenient to but not abut the highway for residential development. For commercial development, land at or near interchanges is prime property, although it may take some time to find the right buyer.

RISK TAKING

Land is risky business because:

- There is usually no positive cash flow.
- It's illiquid—hard to sell if you're crashing.
- Its value is often related to future developments, and the future is unpredictable.
- Luck plays a rather large role in the script.
- Time is a factor, and time requirements are often long.
- Development is subject to approval by local governing bodies. And the mood of a town is not always rationally based.

Land as an investment vehicle is and should be the choice of the risk taker or the investor with money he or she can afford to lose. If you tend to be a worrier, and especially a worrier over factors you cannot influence, there are other investments better suited to your personality. Look into condominiums, multifamily houses, or small apartment buildings. These have sustaining income. They also have plenty to worry about *and* plenty that you can do things about!

LEGAL CONSTRAINTS, MANAGEMENT SKILLS, AND COMMITMENT

$ One of the best ways to make money on a land purchase is to do the paperwork for a builder. Most builders want to *build*, and they resent time required for "briefcase work." They also resent the time spent standing before a planning commission, and they fear the risk of being turned down.

Getting a zoning change, variance, or preliminary subdivision approval can take many months and can cost a good deal of money. You'll be required to have a professional survey done and you'll need a professionally drawn plat plan for the layout of the development. Most municipalities require that you employ a state-certified professional engineer for this work. Even plans for the minor subdivision of one lot into two lots can cost well over a thousand dollars.

You will also need information on drainage, water supply, and soil content. Your local U.S. Department of Agriculture County Extension Office can help you with these. Many municipalities, however, now require professional certification of environmental conditions and the potential effects of development. You may be forced to hire a geologist or other specialist to obtain such certification. This, of course, will cost still more money. And then, when you finally present your perfectly drawn and thoroughly certified plans to the planning commission in a public hearing, you may have to answer the protests of private environmental protection groups (Save the Deer, for example) or of earnest citizens who want Ruralsville to remain rural. Finally, you may even have to go to court if you think you've been unlawfully denied permission to develop an area.

If you go to court, the time span between idea and approval can easily be years. But once you get into such a hassle, there is usually little room for turnaround. You are committed, like it or not, for you have an illiquid investment that, once it encounters legal difficulties, is virtually unsalable until those problems are resolved. To resolve them, you will need to gather knowledgeable people around you to give advice, to oversee what has to be done and is being done, to schedule and negotiate each step, and to alter course if necessary. This is a battle that takes a cool head and an organized approach. Tact and strategy become paramount to success, and who you know becomes much more important than perhaps it should be.

If you're successful in going to court for a zoning change, your profits from the sale of your land can be tremendous. If you're unsuccessful, the legal fees involved in the effort can wipe out any potential for a profitable sale for many years to come.

SOCIAL CONTACT

If you buy land, let it sit idle for twenty years, and then sell it at whatever the market will bring, you need never meet anyone in the town or even the state where the land is located. If you aim for a quicker sale, however, or for increased profit, knowing a few influential local citizens or better yet sharing membership with them in local religious, social, or political groups, will become important.

Everyone knows that much of the work of the United States Congress is carried on in committees and over lunch, and, in just the same way, many of the agreements between a planning board and a landowner are arrived at after many private and informal talks. I don't mean to imply bribery or illegal influence peddling here. That does happen, but it happens far less frequently than most people think. I do want to point out, however, that ideas are often listened to with a more open mind in an informal, nonpublic setting, and without time pressure.

Knowing and socializing with local people can also be instrumental in gathering "hot leads" for the sale or purchase of land. A friend in the postal service tells you that the government is looking for a place to locate a post office in the Five Corners section of your town. You might just be able to buy up the most appropriate spot in the area! Or you hear that the Wellricks are getting divorced and want nothing more to do with the subdivision plans for their forty acres; you may be able to buy for cash at an excellent price! Word of desire to sell or buy often comes across the luncheon table or the fairway long before it hits the newspapers or the real estate listings.

FORESIGHT AND CREATIVITY

John Adelli, a real estate broker and a friend of mine, used his foresight to make his fortune. An interstate route that would connect Philadelphia and New York City was partially completed but being held up by a suit in the state court system, filed by environmentalists anxious to protect the wildlife in a park through which the road would run. Adelli believed that concessions would be made to the wildlife group but that the road would eventually be completed. When it was, he thought, virtually all the land along the route would become a potential suburb to one of the two great cities it connected.

Adelli bought three farms in three different towns along the proposed route of the interstate. Then he rented them back to farmers. The price tags were $180,000, $340,000, and $223,000, respectively. Was he a millionaire to shell out all that cash? Not at all. Because these were working farms with buildings on them he was able to get mortgages. His total cash outlay was $153,000, money he had recently realized from the sale of two small apartment buildings.

For nine years, Adelli held the farms with negative cash flow high enough to keep him in a rather too-small house and prevent him and his family from enjoying vacations any more grand than a week or two at the Jersey shore. His wife grumbled occasionally and his friends made jokes about "Farmer John."

Fortunately, however, the interstate was completed before John's eldest child was ready for college. By that time, John had also obtained preliminary subdivision approval for all three tracts of land. One he sold to a builder for a net profit of $900,000. He used this money to help him put roads through the subdivision of the second farm. The fourteen ¾-acre lots there are selling for $150,000 to $180,000 *each*. Adelli is keeping the third farm for "later."

Three cheers for foresight! What about creativity? Another friend, Alphons Schultz, provides a good example. He saw an advertisement in the classifieds for sixteen acres at $5,000 an acre. There must be something wrong, he thought, but he called anyway. There was. Two-thirds of the land was in a flood plain, essentially unbuildable. But that didn't stop Al.

He took an option on the property and went to work designing a cluster of condominiums on the high ground and recreation space to be owned and maintained by the condominium association on the low ground. The town saw the plan as a means of putting problem land to good use and also absolving itself from responsibility for the flood plain land since it would be owned by the condo association rather than dedicated to the town. They granted approval of Al's plan.

Al Schultz exercised his option, buying the tract at $80,000. He sold the following week to a developer for $294,000. Of course there were engineering costs, legal fees, closing costs, etc., etc., etc. And plenty of reward for his creativity.

SELF-CONFIDENCE

In order to act upon a vision, however, you must believe in yourself. You must believe enough to take on an investment which may well be long term, which has the likelihood of years of negative cash flow, which promises nothing, which may get tied up in committee, and which calls out to Lady Luck. Your dream may be laughed at and your plans vocally opposed. "It's impossible!" "You'll never make it!" "Worthless land!" "Money down the drain!" You'll hear all these words and more. If you're successful, however, you can laugh all the way to the bank.

THE TOOLS OF THE TRADE

WAITING TIME

Having already told you that waiting time on land is usually long, I thought I'd mention here some income-producing ideas that might help the waiting time pass a little more profitably (or less painfully). Consider:

* renting the land to nearby apartment dwellers for use as garden plots;
* renting the land to a hunt club for pheasant or deer hunting, or to a kennel club for dog shows or field trials;
* renting the land to the Boy Scouts or Girl Scouts (or other such organization) for hiking and overnight camping;
* establishing a tree farm for evergreens and selling cut-your-own Christmas trees two weekends a year. This use might bring about an agricultural assessment and thereby lower taxes;
* renting the land to a farmer for pasture;

- renting to local groups for art shows or flea markets;
- renting to a cross-country ski club or snowmobile club.

Before you take on any of these projects, however, check with your insurance agent to be sure you're covered for liability.

WORKING TIME

Working time in land investment runs to opposite poles. If you simply allow your land to appreciate with time, you will have virtually no working time after the purchase. But if you decide to go for a zoning change or a preliminary subdivision approval, you will spend many hours on your investment.

START-UP CASH

Here, too, land investment runs to opposite poles. You may need only a small amount of initial cash if a seller is willing to take back a purchase money mortgage. Or you may be able to negotiate an installment purchase contract, sometimes called a land contract. In this kind of transaction, a price is agreed upon and then divided into a given number of payments to be made upon named dates. The deed to the property does not pass from the seller to the buyer, however, until all or most of the payments have been made.

$ If you elect to use an installment purchase contract, be sure that it includes a clause that allows you to prepay without penalty. With this protection, you can proceed with plans to increase the value of the land by subdividing, rezoning, or even building upon the tract while being secure in the knowledge that you can sell when you're ready and pay off the holder of your land contract with the proceeds from the resale.

$ If a seller wishes to spread the income from the sale of land over time and will not allow prepayment, try to negotiate a *release clause* in the contract. Under this provision, you can subdivide and sell a lot or lots. The original seller (the holder of your installment purchase contract) releases that land to the new buyer and takes the money toward payment of a scheduled installment.

At the other end of the start-up cash spectrum is the all-cash deal. If your seller will not finance your purchase, all cash may be the only option open to you since few conventional lenders will write mortgages on undeveloped acreage. Land therefore makes a good investment for windfall cash such as an inheritance or the winnings of a lottery ticket.

CASH FLOW

It's almost always negative. Even if you use some of the income-producing ideas listed under Waiting Time above, you'll probably still need to put in some cash of your own each year. Be sure you can afford this cash drain before you invest in any piece of property, no matter how enticing. Remember, your land *can* be sold off at auction by the local government for nonpayment of taxes.

TAXES

Just to summarize what has already been mentioned:

- Income from the sale of land is taxed as ordinary income.
- There is no depreciation deduction allowed on undeveloped land.
- All expenses incurred in carrying investment land—insurance, mortgage interest payments, maintenance visits, survey fees, attorney fees, etc.—may be carried forward and deducted from the profit upon sale for federal income tax purposes. Local property taxes, however, are deductible annually.
- Income from the land rarely exceeds expenses. When it does, however (land leased to a farmer, for example, or a quarry), the income must be reported as ordinary income.

EXPECTED RETURN

Land returns are usually dependent upon demand and the potential use to which the land can be put. The following list forms a generally accepted use/return pyramid. The amount of land needed for a high return is smallest at the top, largest at the bottom.

industrial park
shopping mall
condominium development
apartment houses

hotel
small lots for single-family houses
large lots for single-family houses
manufactured home park
recreational vehicle campground
working farm
leased crop or pasture land

What does this mean in terms of the return on *your* dollar? Hypothetically:

- a tract unimproved in a high growth area can triple in value in five years.
- The same tract subdivided for residential housing could appreciate to ten times its original cost in the same five years.
- The same tract rezoned for a shopping center could easily bring twenty times its cost in five years.
- Or the same tract unimproved in a low-growth area might only bring a 20 percent profit in five years, just barely keeping pace with inflation.

And just think, if you find gold or oil on your land, you can become a millionaire overnight. Or, on the other hand, if an abandoned toxic waste dump is discovered just beneath the surface of your land, your best bet may be abandonment (with a tax loss).

KNOWLEDGE

Never, *never* buy land sight unseen. In fact you should walk every square foot of the land you intend to buy, get topographical maps (available from the U.S. Geological Survey) if it's a large tract and walk it all again. Look for dry streambeds that may becoming roaring rivers in spring, soggy swampland that will turn away developers, rock outcroppings that might be a hint that blasting will be needed, access to a road, and, most important of all, any evidence that the land may have been used as a dump site. Don't hesitate to call in experts— well drillers, septic tank companies, representatives from the local utility companies, soil experts, geologists, road builders, etc. These people can anticipate problems that should be taken into consideration in a decision to buy or not to buy, and at what price.

TOPOGRAPHIC MAPS

For a free index to maps available in the National Topographic Map Series write to one of the following addresses:

FOR MAPS OF AREAS EAST OF THE MISSISSIPPI:
Geological Survey
Distribution Center
Washington, D.C. 20242

FOR MAPS OF AREAS WEST OF THE MISSISSIPPI:
Western Distribution Branch
U.S. Geological Survey
Box 25286 Denver Federal Center
Denver, Colorado 80225

FOR MAPS OF ALASKA:
Alaska Distribution Center
U.S. Geological Survey
Box 12 New Federal Building
101 12th Avenue (Room 126)
Fairbanks, Alaska 99701

FOR MAPS OF CANADA:
Canada Map Office
Department of Energy, Mines and Resources
Ottawa, Canada K1A 0E9

If a river does flow through your land or if your land borders on a lake, check your state's riparian rights legislation before you buy. Riparian rights are rights to water and its use, and legislation differs from state to state. You might also inquire about mineral rights and air rights before you sign on the dotted line.

•   •   •

USING EXPERT OPINION

Almost everywhere in the United States there is an expert studying something. In the real estate marketplace, many of these experts are paid real estate professionals working for huge corporations. Others are demographers or economists. Almost all of them are evaluating sites. And if you keep your eyes and ears open, you can use their expert opinions without paying a penny for the information. While you hunt for investment land, watch out for news of the following possibilities:

- Proposed large shopping mall. Site selection for such a mall is usually the consensus of much expert opinion and based upon projections of probable population growth (demand). Residential land within an easy drive will almost certainly increase in value.
- Large corporations buying land in the area. Corporations buy land for expansion or relocation. Their new buildings almost always mean new jobs and a growing local economy. Residential and commercial land nearby is usually an excellent investment.
- Industrial or research park to be developed. Again more jobs = more people = higher land prices.
- Highway development or improvement or a new airport. Transportation facilities are usually improved *because* of growth, but improved transportation can also *bring* growth to an area.

BARGAINS AND NOT SUCH BARGAINS

GOVERNMENT LAND

Despite the fact that our government owns over 700 million acres in the United States, it is *no longer* in the homesteading business. There is *no* free land. Well, there might be a free piece or two in the outreaches of Alaska, accessible by airplane or dog sled. Today the government sells land and there is less for sale every year. What there is is sold at public auctions, but the prices are not bargains. The bidding is competitive (by mail and in person) and most parcels fetch a pretty penny.

If you're still interested in running down government land sales, you can get more information and periodic listings of what's for sale by writing to:

Bureau of Land Management
U.S. Department of the Interior
Washington, D.C. 20240

$ DOUBLE LOTS

Years ago it was quite fashionable when having a tract house built to sign up for the lot next door and mortgage it in with your house. The theory was that you could always sell the extra lot for a profit or have a house built upon it someday for one of your children.

In theory you can still do this, but in practice it gets more difficult every day. Builders do *not* want to sell improved lots (lots with road access and utilities brought in) because they can make a much greater profit by putting a house on that land. When they do agree to sell a lot, the price is usually prohibitive.

There *are* bargains here, however. You should keep a sharp eye out for houses advertised for sale on "double lots." Most of these houses will be fairly small and over thirty years old. Negotiate for such a property at a price that is at market value for the house on a *single lot*. You want to pay nothing or very little for the extra land.

While you are negotiating, *run*, don't walk, to the town hall, get out the tax maps, and check that the "double lot" is still a separate entity, a buildable lot. If you can't get positive verification on short notice, make your contract contingent on the "double lot" including a separate, legal building lot.

Mortgage the house on a *single* lot. Fix it up for resale, move into it yourself for a while, or rent it. At this point you own the open lot free and clear and that ownership can become the security for a construction loan.

Look into kit houses, modulars, and manufactured homes, choose a size and style that will fit in with the neighbors, and start building. As soon as there's something standing to take a picture of, list the property for sale. In good times you'll have a buyer before the construction is complete. There's good money to be made in this kind of sharp-eyed investment.

UNWANTED LOTS

Who wants to live next to the water tower, the telephone switching station, or the power lines? Developers sometimes leave such lots vacant and move on to another area. Would they come back to build for a buyer who showed up a year or more down the road? Very rarely. But they might sell you the lot for a relative pittance just to get it off the books.

Before you jump at such a property, however, check the deed restrictions. Is there a minimal square footage for all construction in the area? Is a certain style of housing specified? *Can* you build on this lot? If you can, you should buy *only* if you have the skills and motivation to do so, for the land alone will be worth little as an investment. And you should build the smallest, simplest house allowed by deed restrictions. The smallest, newest house in a neighborhood of fancier houses will usually bring a good return, even next door to the water tower.

LANDOWNERS IN TROUBLE

Ten years ago a developer had his backhoe man dig a trench from a soggy low spot on his land to the lake shore one hundred feet down the hill. The plan worked. The bog drained into the lake.

Unfortunately, the lake was community recreation property. That summer the bacteria count ran unusually high in the lake and the town fathers went on a witch hunt. They discovered the trench and stopped just short of drowning the developer.

Instead, they made life impossible for him. His petitions were tabled at almost every meeting of the planning board. And when they were considered, serious attention was paid to the most unusual objections and questions, always meriting further study. It was obvious that this man would not get preliminary subdivision approval in his professional lifetime.

This developer was in fact a spare-time player in the real estate game; his "real" job was in industry. During a coffee break one day, he told a fellow employee about his troubles. That man made the developer an offer. It was low, very low by cash price standards for land in the area, but it was a way out of an impossible situation. The developer took the offer and took back a purchase money mortgage for all but 20 percent of the sales price.

The new owner approached the planning board gingerly, with professional drawings based upon sound environmental research. Within ten months, he had preliminary subdivision approval and a contract of sale to another developer. The selling price was more than double the buying price and more than ten times the cash invested.

Does that sound fantastic? It's a true story. I witnessed it. And the moral is, if you hear of a developer or landowner in trouble, have a talk with him or her. If you can be rather certain the problems can be solved, be kind, bail the landowner out, at your price.

TAX SALES

The IRS can seize property and sell it without due process of law. Auctions are held periodically out of main tax offices and there are real bargains available. *But* (always there's a but or everyone would be running to these sales) you will receive only a bill of sale from the IRS for your land purchase. Can you turn the bill of sale into legal title eligible for title insurance? Maybe.

If you choose to go for a bargain parcel, get the advice of a good attorney familiar with this type of real estate sale. And do *not* build on the land until you are sure that your title is free of any clouds.

Municipal, county, and state government agencies can also seize and sell land for back taxes. These parcels sell at a fraction of their worth. *But beware!* In most states there is a period of redemption during which the former owner can pay up and reclaim the property. You, as a tax buyer, won't *really* own anything until this period passes. And it can drag on. The redemption time period in California, for example, is *five years*.

Still interested? Okay. There are also big bargains here for the gambler. But be careful. Try to find out why the land is being sold at a tax sale. *Can* it be developed? Is the zoning prohibitive? Is it sitting on a bed of black shale emitting high levels of radon gas? Or is the area an unpublicized Love Canal?

FARM FORECLOSURES

Many land dreamers think they can buy up a farm and turn it into an instant cash crop by subdividing for single-family houses. If this were so, don't you think the farmer would have thought of it? Or some experienced developer?

The fact of the matter is that most farms are not situated in locations appropriate for *current* tract development. If you're willing to wait twenty years and if you have the cash to carry your investment for that length of time, the land could very well become part of a high-demand area and ripe for development. Today's cheap farmland might make you a millionaire several times over, someday. Or it might not.

Landlocked Tracts

With a little creativity, perseverance, and guts, you can make big money on this investment. Landlocked tracts usually have access through a right of way over one of the bordering pieces of land. Something like this:

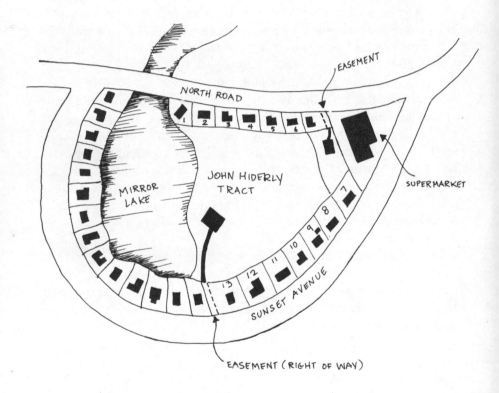

A right of way is almost never wide enough for a road, making further development of the landlocked tract impossible. Therefore, the tract usually sells at a price far below comparable land with road access or road access potential.

$ If you wish to speculate for big bucks, buy an option on the landlocked acreage. Get as much time as you can with renewals available. *Then* buy any piece of property that borders both the landlocked land and a road. (Any of the lots numbered 1 through 13 in the drawing of the Hiderly Tract would do the job.) If you're unusually lucky, something will come onto the market, but you may have to go door to door making inquiries and offers.

Once you own a lot that connects the landlocked tract and the road, have the landlocked tract surveyed and have a plat plan done for subdivision. With your plat plan in hand, go to the planning board. If you get preliminary subdivision approval, exercise your option and buy the landlocked tract. It's no longer landlocked! The road into the property will go through the connecting piece that you bought. If you do not get preliminary subdivision approval, don't exercise your option and resell the connecting property.

In a plan such as this one, you're risking the cost of survey and plat plan drawing and the transfer costs for the connecting piece of property. Your potential return from a developer looking for ready-to-go prime land is tremendous.

Land Specialists

In some areas of the country, land specialty real estate offices are opening. They're usually staffed by experienced personnel who offer to guide a buyer from acquisition through subdivision or rezoning and into resale, for a price. An inexperienced investor could find valuable guidance at such an office, but remember: there are commissions and fees involved. If you choose to use a real estate specialty firm, listen, then check everything. You have final say. It's *your* money.

SOME SUCCESSFUL INVESTORS

Changing Careers

Peter Lack graduated college with a B.A. in sociology and then took a job as a store manager with a national supermarket chain. But he wanted to be rich, and neither sociologists nor grocery store managers get rich on their wages.

Lack started his road to riches with the purchase of a small apartment building. He discovered, however, that he loathed the day-to-day demands of landlording. So he sold the building and bought a convenience store. Then another, and then still another. Yet his income grew but slowly, and Peter was impatient. He sold the three convenience stores as a package deal and with the profits bought a corner tract of land with commercial zoning.

Small though it was, the strip shopping center he had built there netted him $972,000. Lack was hooked. Today land investment, and sometimes but not always land development, in his professional occupation. Last year, his adjusted gross income was just over $3,000,000.

Does anyone go to college to become a land speculator? Hardly. This is a career that happens to people. Usually someone like Peter Lack stumbles upon a parcel somewhere, makes a profit, and discovers that he or she has an aptitude for the work. Do you want to be such a professional? My best advice: start with something small.

GROUPS AND PARTNERS

Tyrone Green is a real estate lawyer. Milton Silverstein is a civil engineer. Diana Lang is a tax accountant. Gerald Robinson is a heavy equipment specialist. Faith Hopper is a landscape architect. Stanley Racainski is a commercial real estate broker. What do they have in common? A piece of land.

They were equal partners in the purchase of a 168-acre tract which was recently approved for mixed development. On their land will be single-family houses, condominiums, a strip shopping center, two low-rise public housing apartment houses, a park, and a golf course, all planned to blend together into a community. It took the investment group three years and two months to get approval for this development and no time at all to sell it. A developer had signed a contract contingent upon planning board approval over a year before that approval was finally granted. Each member of the group netted just under half-a-million dollars profit from the sale.

But you don't have to be a lawyer or a civil engineer to join into an investment group to buy land. You simply need to bring to the group your talents, your patience, and a willingness to work. Oh, and, yes, some money to invest.

MOVING ON

Land investors with time, money, and knowledge can reap very sizeable profits without investing in heavy building equipment or becoming dependent upon numerous subcontractors or full-time employees. If you start out by buying a small piece of land and obtaining a minor subdivision approval, and you feel comfortable with the process, you may be in your element. Land subdivision is an investment vehicle that can be worked profitably while you pursue another full-time career. You will probably want to work on subdividing or rezoning only one or two tracts of land at a given time but you can "store up" as many vacant pieces waiting your attention (or their profit maturation) as you can afford to carry.

Long-term investors (those who plan to do nothing with their land for ten years or more) usually hold only one or two pieces of property because of the negative cash flow inherent in this vehicle. If you have more money to invest in no-time-required investments and already own a good deal of land, you might try condominium apartments, especially in vacation areas where they are sometimes available with rental pool arrangements that provide you with a vacation spot each year *and* a positive cash flow.

If you plan to make real estate your career, the next step after your first land investment or two is obvious: development. But *How to Become a Builder* is another book.

· C H A P T E R   7 ·

Vacation Homes

Oscar Dermann owns a group of five thriving convenience stores in a mid-sized city. He finds it difficult to take long vacations from his business, but he would like to provide a summer place for his family and a weekend retreat for himself. And he wouldn't object if the place appreciated in value while he owned it.

Helen Vite has four children under age ten. She wants a money-making opportunity that she can pursue at home or with the children along for the ride. She and her husband would also like a family-centered place to escape from their workaday world. Their investment vehicle of choice is a vacation home.

·   ·   ·

In America two types of vacation-property buyers are easily spotted: those who do *not* need extra income but very much want a place to get away from it all from time to time, and those who *do* need extra income and hope to get it from a vacation home in which they can also have some fun. There is a third type, as well, less recognized and far fewer in number: speculating investors. The category into which you fall will determine the type of property you buy, how many properties you buy, and how you (and the IRS) look upon rental of your property.

And *what* can you buy? Not so long ago, *vacation home* meant a cabin in the woods or a cottage at the shore. Today you can still buy the cabin or the cottage, but you might also consider a multifamily house, a manufactured house (formerly called a mobile home) in a planned community, a resort condominium apartment, a time share unit, a rental pool condominium, or even a farm.

Before we get into checkpoints for the investor in vacation property, let's examine each of these ownership options and consider their special characteristics and appeal.

DETACHED SINGLE-FAMILY HOUSES

Such a vacation house might be a two-room shack or a twelve-room mansion. In either case, it is a separate building on its own piece of land. It's most often sold by its owner or through a real estate agency. Maintenance work is the responsibility of the owner, as is liability insurance.

The single-family vacation house can be rented by the week during the "in" season and, if the structure is suitable to year-round use, for the entire "off" season for a reduced rate. Or it can be kept exclusively for the use of the owner.

Investors interested in detached single-family vacation properties should also read the chapter on handyman specials, since many of the same principles apply. In fact, the Vite family could summer in a different cottage each year while doing fix-up work and selling for a profit either at the end of the season or at the beginning of the next season. Single-family houses in good condition and good locations are the most common vacation home purchase of people like the Dermann family.

MULTIFAMILY HOUSES

Multifamily vacation houses range from a five-apartment converted mansion that resembles a slick condominium with separate entries for each unit and even garages on down to a weathered, two-story house with a sign near the door that reads ROOMS FOR RENT. Owner occupied, such properties provide a recreation place and an income source. All maintenance work, however, is the responsibility of the owner.

Investors interested in multifamily vacation houses should read the chapters on multifamily houses, handyman specials, and hammer-and-nails conversion. Helen Vite could well find her income-producing summer work in such a property.

MANUFACTURED HOUSES IN PLANNED COMMUNITIES

You've seen the full page ads for Shangri-la in your local Sunday papers. The prices are low, the interest rates are low, the houses are brand-new, beautiful, and fully furnished, and the resort amenities are fabulous. *Beware.* High-priced advertising campaigns and sales promotions are usually an effort to *create* a consumer attitude of desirability where there was once, or perhaps still is, only woods and green fields (or maybe a swamp that is now "the Lake"). Such man-made vacation communities may indeed become desirable areas, someday, if the builder's vision become a reality. But while construction is in process, the properties are often difficult to rent and difficult to resell. An investor like Oscar Dermann, however, might find exactly the place he wants in such a community if he buys when all facilities are near completion or on a resale in a completed resort area.

RESORT CONDOMINIUM APARTMENTS

These are usually slick, expensive and in the "best" resort areas. Each apartment owner pays a maintenance fee which covers just about everything outside the apartment, from keeping the swimming pool clean to vacuuming the hallways. Interior maintenance of the individual apartment is the responsibility of the owner.

There are many restrictions that come along with the freedom from outdoor maintenance chores in this kind of investment property, however. Most resort condo communities do not allow pets; some do not allow children. Often the condominium's bylaws restrict the number of rentals per year (some even allow only owner use or full-year rental).

Resale value depends upon the popularity of the resort area and the degree of new construction going on. Overbuilding can diminish value even in the finest vacation areas. Bad press (Miami Beach) or unexplained diminished popularity (Vail) can reduce both property value and rental income.

This type of investment property is not appropriate to the goals of either the Dermanns or the Vites. Its primary appeal is to upper middle class people in search of a retreat or an eventual retirement haven.

·   ·   ·

TIME SHARE UNITS

Time share apartments or houses are usually sold one week at a time. In other words, you own $1/52$ (or more likely $1/50$—two weeks a year are usually left open for refurbishing) of one apartment. The ownership style is that of a condominium with an annual maintenance fee and a set of bylaws. Most units can be rented by their owners or exchanged through international swapping companies for other vacation destinations. Resale, however, is a major problem. The real profit in time share resorts is for the sponsor or builder of the resort, who might make millions—quite literally. For the one-week owner, however, time share is simply *not* an investment. Most resale units sell for as little as half their original price, when they sell at all!

When you buy a time share unit, you're buying future vacations, a place to go away to. Such a purchase may save you money on the cost of your vacations, but it won't make you money in the real estate marketplace.

RENTAL POOL CONDOMINIUMS

This is a relatively new form of vacation property ownership that became a hot item in the early '80s, the time when *real estate* was synonymous with *tax shelter*. Essentially, you own a condominium unit at a particular resort that also functions as a hotel, renting out the individually owned units as though they were rooms. If you choose to have your unit participate in the rental pool (it is usually not required) you can use it only a specified number of days per year (usually twenty-eight days, but some resorts restrict to two weeks, or two weeks in season and two weeks out of season). During the remainder of the year, your unit will be available for rental. All income from the units in the rental pool is divided on a share basis annually among the owners (after management and maintenance costs have been deducted, of course). In most rental pool arrangements, your income does not depend upon how many times your particular unit was rented, but upon the number of shares assigned to your unit (its value) in the pool.

Most rental pool condominium apartments are very expensive. Before the Tax Reform Act of 1986, they created write-offs for the wealthy while guaranteeing them four weeks free vacation lodging per year. Today their paper losses cannot be deducted against ordinary income and highly leveraged properties have become very costly to carry. Many of these are for sale, some at bargain-basement prices.

 Buying such a unit for cash or with a mortgage small enough to assure positive cash flow, might be a good investment if the resort is in a prime vacation area and well maintained. In marginal areas or areas with essentially one good season (ten weeks or so), how desirable rental pool units will be after tax reform is a question that won't be accurately answered until the dust of post-reform reevaluation settles; probably about the turn of the decade in the case of this vehicle.

An investor like Oscar Dermann might be able to pick up a price bargain here that would provide some vacation time for his family with no maintenance work demands. The purchase is not ideal, however, since his use is restricted. They can't, for example, drop in for a sunny autumn weekend.

FARMS

 Around most of the nation, farm prices are low right now and a family looking for a weekend or summer retreat could make a good investment in this vehicle. Often use of the land and even the farmhouse can be leased back to the original owner or to another farmer and a new vacation cottage built upon a corner of the farm for the use of the new owner.

A farm vacation investment can produce income (which may or may not carry the property) and has some tax benefits reserved for farming. You'll have to see your accountant for these tax details, however, since federal, state, and local programs vary according to time and place and it would take another book to explain them all thoroughly.

Your farm vacation home investment may also turn out to be a long-term land investment (read Chapter 6) when, after twenty years of letting your children ride their horses and chase the new piglets, you discover that suburbia has crept up to the border of your farm. This investment might be suitable for either the Vite family or the Dermann family.

An obvious question comes to mind at this point: with so many very different kinds of vacation properties available, how can anyone possibly do a checkpoints analysis that has any meaning?

Well, I may have to digress with specific references occasionally, but in general I think you'll be surprised at how many investor demands are common to most vacation home styles.

CHECKPOINTS FOR THE INVESTOR

RISK TAKING

Housing experts and economists alike agree that vacation property responds more sensitively than any other form of real estate to changes in the economic health of the nation or the region in which it is located. In good times people pay top dollar for good rentals because demand far exceeds supply, but post a bad year or two and rents are driven down by the prevalence of vacant units when supply exceeds demand. Vacation spending along with eating out is usually the first cut most people make during times of tight money. A bad year may also make it difficult to sell your moderately priced vacation home, even at a reduced price.

There is an exception to the rule of volatility in vacation property, however. Very expensive homes are rarely affected by swings of the economy. It seems the rich can always find the money for a relaxing break.

If you purchase a vacation home for your own exclusive use, you can remain relatively oblivious to the swings of the marketplace. The general value trend of your property will be upward, unless area over-building or disrepair and unpopularity affect all the property values in the area. If you buy with the intention of renting enough time to make the unit self-sustaining, or if you intend to sell for a profit after refurbishing, you will need to watch economic barometers. It's most important to be aware of the financial risks in vacation property and to be absolutely certain that you can carry the property through a bad year or two.

On the positive side, the value of vacation property can also sky-rocket. If the area in which you buy suddenly becomes popular or if economic good times suddenly send masses of middle-income people in search of life's little extras, vacation home prices will far outpace comparable structures in a normal residential area.

NUMBERS, FINANCES, AND RATIONAL EVALUATION

Vacation homes are among the most enticing of real estate investments. People see them as self-supporting passports to pleasure. "We can spend a month a year here and rent the rest of the time. Or we can use the off-season for weekend getaways," they assure each other

INVESTOR DEMAND PROFILE

	1	2	3	4	5	6	7	8	9	10
1. Positive Action and Reaction										
2. Willingness to Take Risks										
3. Decision-making Ability										
4. Commitment—the Will to Follow Through										
5. Logical and Rational Evaluation of Options										
6. Ability to Deal with Numbers and Finances										
7. Ability to Deal with Legal Constraints										
8. Organization and Management Skills										
9. Foresight										
10. Imagination and Creativity										
11. Self-confidence										
12. Patience and Tact										
13. Self-control										
14. Social Contact										
15. Negotiating Skill										

and trot down to the real estate office to buy. Among the questions many buyers forget to ask are these:

- When exactly is the prime rental season? A long season or a double season (winter *and* summer) in a particularly desirable location such as Hawaii or the Canadian mountains can transform vacation home economics from self supporting to money making.
- What are typical rental rates, in season and off season? You can't figure carrying costs and profits unless you have some real figures.
- What do rental agents charge? What do they do? In some prime vacation areas, rental agents get as much as 40 percent of the rent. If you live near your vacation property there's usually no need to pay such an exorbitant fee. If you're a thousand miles away, however you must ask yourself who'll clean between tenants. Who'll supervise to be sure there are no wild parties. Who'll be certain the tenants don't bring their four cats along on vacation. Who'll collect rents and in fact *choose* the tenants. It is important that you decide *if* you need a rental agent, and if you do, that you calculate the commissions in your property evaluations.
- What is the cost of insurance? Some vacation areas need special high-cost protection against hurricanes, floods, landslides, earthquakes, forest fires, or other natural disasters. Others, especially those in isolated areas that are relatively unpopulated during the off season, need special vandalism protection.
- Are there any private association dues or club costs tied to the property? What services do you get in return?
- In the case of condominiums, what is the maintenance fee? Ask if it has remained relatively stable for the past three or four years. Ask if any major expenditures are anticipated in the near future. (New elevators, for example, can substantially affect the annual maintenance fee.) Ask if there's an established contingency fund to cover unexpected expenses. How much is in it?
- Are there rental restrictions imposed by a governing association, a board of directors, or bylaws? No children, no pets, no rentals under a month's term are examples of restrictions that might affect rentability. Racial and ethnic restrictions are, of course, illegal.
- What are the municipal taxes? Some vacation home owners forget that they are actually part of a working community.
- Is financing available? At what interest rate? For what term? These questions are essential to calculating your annual carrying costs.

* Are there property management or caretaker people available during the off season? How much do they charge?
* What special "closing up" procedures are necessary for the off season? Are there special problems with mice, raccoons, bears, ants, or other local wild animals?
* What's the cost of heat, air-conditioning, water, electricity, sewers or septic tank maintenance and refuse removal? *Can* you get refuse removal or even water during the off season?

I guess it's pretty obvious from the length of this list that income from investment vacation property is *not* the sum of the rents. Don't forget to calculate the minus factors! In good times, the bottom line is usually still very positive; in bad times, it can easily turn negative, since few of the cost factors go down in proportion to the lack of rental income.

Now you may be thinking, "So why bother with vacation property at all? I can get better or at least more certain cash flow from a multifamily house right in town."

True, but what you can't get in town is a stake in a rapidly appreciating marketplace. The baby boom population bulge is just beginning to move into a rather prosperous middle age, and with this movement the number of people looking for leisure property is increasing. Since demand is expected to exceed supply, vacation homes should prove to be an especially good investment during the next decade. The revised tax laws that still allow the deduction of mortgage interest on second homes won't hurt either!

LEGAL CONSTRAINTS

Many cottage vacation areas grew up more than fifty years ago in places where there were few if any legal constraints on building. Since then zoning laws and building codes have been enacted in most of these areas. The original buildings are allowed to remain in use, however, under grandfather clauses. All of which is well and good unless:

* you wish to add on either horizontally or vertically, since expansion of existing structures may not be allowed.
* you wish to renovate. In some locales, if you renovate any part of a grandfathered structure, you must bring the entire building up to

code requirements. This can be very expensive and might well require all new plumbing and electrical work, a new heating plant, and a new waste disposal system.

* fire or wind and water destroy your building. You may not be allowed to rebuild if your lot does not conform to the new zoning law. You can, however, apply for a variance under a hardship contention. The variance should not be unreasonably denied, but it may take several months to get through the board of appeals.

To be on the safe side when investing in cottage communities, you should go to the local municipal building and gather information on current building codes and zoning ordinances. Ask the town administrator what the policy of the town has been on rebuilding or upgrading vacation property. This information may well be a no-cost insurance policy for future reference.

At the opposite end of the spectrum, you may choose to buy vacation property in a condominium community. Here you will encounter a multitude of legal constraints, spelled out explicitly in the bylaws and house rules. You may not be allowed to have a garden or change the color of your front door, for example. Be sure that you read all the condominium documents carefully before you sign a contract to buy, and be absolutely certain that you can live within the rules as many of them cannot be changed except by unanimous vote.

Somewhere in between the cottage community and the condominium is the vacation home in a private association. Here rules may dictate the kind of house you can build, when you can use the swimming pool or the golf course, where your guests can park their cars, and even what type of boats are allowed on the lake. Again, be sure *before you buy* that the rule don't cramp your life-style. You may ask real estate agents or sellers for information on rules and legal constraints, but in general it's a good idea not to trust wholly anyone but yourself or your attorney.

DECISION MAKING

Owning vacation property comes with the usual real estate decisions: what to buy, when to rent it, for how much, to whom, when to do repairs, which repairs to do first, how much to spend. What many people fail to regard as a decision, however, is actually the most important decision of all: *where to buy*. Instead of critically assessing the relationship between location and their personal vacation preferences, they get caught up in a purchase because of family vacation traditions, or limited knowledge, or social pressure, or an excellent sales presentation.

If you intend to use your vacation home for *your* vacations as well as for investment return, try to choose a property that fits your recreation preferences. Use the chart on page 113 to test your needs and wants against the opportunities and facilities of a vacation area.

POSITIVE ACTION AND REACTION

Negative action may actually be the first positive step in choosing a good value vacation property. In hot areas with a good deal of development going on, you may find yourself under a lot of pressure from an organized sales team. Don't fall for the line "This special offer is good today only." Say, "Not today, thank you," and go out into the marketplace. Check the prices of comparable new property, the availability and prices of resale property, and the potential growth of the area. Are there environmental restrictions or local ordinances that will ensure limited development? If so, new and existing construction is or will be worth more. If there are no restrictions, overbuilding can greatly diminish property value.

The very tail end of the in season or the beginning of the off season is an excellent time for a little positive action that could result in a bargain. Taking the initiative to stop by and talk with an owner closing up his cottage might be a lucky break: that owner may be thinking of selling or he may know someone who is.

Times of disaster can also be bargain times for the ambitious investor in vacation property. Homes damaged by hurricanes, tornados, landslides, forest fires, etc., can sometimes be bought for minuscule sums. If your handyman skills are sharp and you have no fears of the disaster recurring in the foreseeable future, you might consider approaching owners who are "digging out." You may be more welcome than you think.

Weather problems can also be a blessing for the opportunist. Approach an owner at the end of a ski season that has had no snow or in a whitewater rafting area where there has been no rain and you may just find yourself with a strong negotiating hand. Remember, however, that next year's weather could be just as bad!

VACATION HOME LOCATION—A PERSONAL EVALUATION

HOW IMPORTANT TO YOU Rate from 1 to 10	WHAT'S AVAILABLE Rate quality from 1 to 10	
	ON PREMISES	NEARBY
Swimming		
Boating		
Golf		
Skiing		
Tennis		
Horseback riding		
Jogging paths		
Hiking trails		
Fishing		
Hunting		
Bicycle trails		
Casino gambling		
Track gambling		
Scuba or skin diving		
Night-time entertainment		
Good restaurants		
Live theatre		
Amusements for children		
Historic sites		
Museums		
Babysitting services		
Pets allowed		
Other		

COMMITMENT

A few vacation properties require no commitment other than cash: time share units, rental pool condominiums, and resort condominiums, for example. But, in general, owning a vacation property will make you very much aware of your role as property owner and landlord. Maintenance is a primary concern, especially near the ocean or in remote mountain areas, and the problems are *not* limited to the exterior. Most vacation properties are rented furnished, and you'll find that the life span of furnishings is short. (There's something about the combination of sand and suntan oil that absolutely destroys upholstery.) You will also be required to replace the dishes, ashtrays, decorative items, and other household paraphernalia that walks away during rental periods. And you'll almost certainly get some calls about clogged toilets or broken windows.

Unless you are willing to pay a property manager to handle tenants and maintenance, you should choose your vacation property investments in areas close to your permanent residence or in areas where you too will be vacationing. Lack of commitment to the maintenance of a vacation home will invariably bring about diminished value.

FORESIGHT

What will the future bring? Anyone who can answer with 80 percent accuracy will certainly become wealthy in our society. Experts are predicting a price/value rise in vacation homes. But how can you tell where a *particular* vacation area, *your* particular vacation area, is going? These indicators signal an upturn:

- Sale and rental statistics for the past three or more years show price increases well above the rate of inflation.
- Rent and sale prices are rising faster than in other nearby vacation areas, an indication of desirability.
- The vacancy rate for in-season rentals has been near zero for at least three years.
- Environmental restrictions and local zoning ordinances will prevent overbuilding.
- Older buildings are being renovated.
- Big-bucks construction nearby. A few large resort hotels, a corporate conference center, a PGA golf course, a marina, tournament tennis

facilities, expert ski slopes, an ice rink, all of these indicate that business has researched the area and found it desirable.

• Growth of support facilities. Check on restaurants, craft shops, gas stations, drug stores, etc. The new ones should be surviving; the old, established ones should be flourishing, even expanding.

IMAGINATION AND CREATIVITY

One of the best money-making investments for the creative person is the run-down vacation home in an area that is solid or being rejuvenated. Tasteful additions, paint and decorating, and a few "local charm" touches can transform a dog into a hot item. Sizable profits are a real potential with only a few month's work.

Charm, especially charm that captures the unique sense of a locale, is also a prime factor in renting at top dollar. Lobster traps that serve as coffee tables in a Maine cottage, specially designed racks for skis and poles in a Colorado cabin, a coral centerpiece in a Key West bungalow, all of these contribute to rental income and rentability (an especially important factor in not-so-good times).

ORGANIZATION AND MANAGEMENT SKILLS

The demands of a vacation house are moderate here. You'll have to keep records of rental income and costs (including the cost of replacing missing ashtrays, etc.) and you'll need to know the names and phone numbers of repair people whom you can trust. But you certainly don't need an MBA from Wharton to run one or even ten vacation homes profitably.

Management becomes simpler if you choose condominiums as your investment vehicle. In fact, there's practically nothing to it.

PATIENCE, TACT, AND SELF-CONTROL

Vacationers are somewhat more demanding and somewhat more destructive than ordinary tenants. They're paying top dollar for a good time and, damn it!, they *will* have a good time, or so the thought process goes. You may get more complaints from them and you may have more complaints about them. It's important to walk a fine line as the landlord of a vacation home. You don't want to lose you temper and become a growling ogre, but, on the other hand, you don't want to become a muddied doormat.

SELF-CONFIDENCE

This character trait quite naturally builds as you become more active and successful in the vacation home investment marketplace. Given the risk factor in this investment vehicle, you're bound to have a few sleepless nights over cash flow, cancellations, new construction in your area, and other factors. But once you get through a purchase and a sale or two, you will begin to put problems into perspective and trust your own judgment. In fact, the vacation home marketplace is an excellent training ground for bigger and more complex ventures such as multifamily houses, handyman specials, major hammer and nails conversion of one type of building use to another, ownership of small apartment buildings, and even the turnaround of faltering apartment buildings.

SOCIAL CONTACT

Knowing people in the community can do no harm and much good in the business of renting vacation property. For example:

- neighbors to your rented property can alert you to problems at the property before the police call you;
- contacts on planning and zoning boards can be invaluable in helping to get approvals for variances, additions, or renovations;
- the best tenants are often friends of friends;
- social contact in a condominium community can keep you abreast of rumors *before* they're listed on the agenda for the next owners' meeting;
- getting to know the people in the vacation community will enhance the time *you* choose to spend there.

NEGOTIATING SKILL

You will need only an average share of negotiating skill in your buying and selling of vacation property; it's much the same as buying your first or your fifteenth house. Dealings with tenants, if you decide not to use a rental agent, can call upon a bit more savvy, but nothing that good common sense can't handle. Usually the amount of rent for a one-week stay in nonnegotiable. Tenants staying for a month or more usually get something of a discount, and they may want to negotiate this a bit. Last-minute tenants coming in after a cancellation or in a down market where many vacancies exist will almost always try to negotiate the price downward. Don't reduce it, therefore, as a come-on; let them think that *their negotiating* reduced the price. You'll get the same amount of money, and they'll think they have a bargain.

TOOLS OF THE TRADE

WORKING TIME

Vacation property can consume as much or as little working time as you wish to allow. It can be an outlet for hammer and nails creativity or simply an investment that demands an hour or two a few months out of each year to keep records up to date. It all depends upon the type of vacation property that you choose. And, *for goodness' sake*, choose the type that best fits your life-style, your personality, and your wallet!

WAITING TIME

Waiting time in this investment vehicle is a variable of the market mood. A bargain bought in a hot market can sometimes be turned over within a few weeks of closing. On the other hand, the hottest bargain bought at the beginning of the off season might well have to wait for the start of the next in season before it can be sold.

For those buying for personal use only, there is no waiting time. As you use and enjoy your vacation home, appreciation just happens.

START-UP CASH AND CASH FLOW

Many people finance their first vacation home purchase by taking out a second mortgage on their primary residence. These loans are now easy to obtain: sometimes called equity lines, they come with no points charged to the homeowner. And they are being offered at interest rates that are almost competitive with first mortgage loans. Before you rush out to get one, however, you should be aware of a little surprise that Uncle Sam has in store for you.

INSPECTION CHECKPOINTS

WATER: If your vacation property uses a municipal water supply, it's probably acceptable. Check to see if the water is turned off in winter. If the property uses well water, ask how many gallons per minute the well pumps, how large the storage tank is, and how *old* the system is. Consult with a local well drilling company or two to determine how your statistics compare with those of surrounding houses. Also, and *most important,* have the water tested for purity. Some banks will not write a mortgage without a water test.

WASTE DISPOSAL: If there are municipal sewers, you need only concern yourself with paying the bill. If a septic system is used, try to get a drawing of the location of the tank and the leech lines or dry well. How long since the system has been cleaned or serviced? Walk the property where the effluent drains looking for soggy areas or clouds of tiny insects. Septic problems can be both difficult and expensive to correct.

TERMITES, DRY ROT, AND CARPENTER ANTS: A professional inspection is well worth the cost.

MICE, SQUIRRELS, AND BATS IN THE ATTIC: Check the attic area carefully with a large beam flashlight. Mice leave droppings. Squirrels shred anything they can get their teeth on to make nests. And bats will be disturbed by your beam of light and the noise you make. Get professional extermination help if you discover any of these pests. While in the attic area, also check for water stains on the beams, and be sure the attic is adequately ventilated.

THE ROOF: Shingles should have a granular surface. If they are smooth or have smooth patches on each one, you will soon need a new roof.

THE WATER HEATER: Age and size are most important. An 80-gallon tank will take care of a large family and guests. The life span of the average water heater is eight to fifteen years. If yours is on the older end of this spectrum, don't be surprised to discover a leak one day.

HEAT: What kind? What does it cost? How old is the plant? Does it indeed keep the house warm in winter?

ELECTRICITY: Is the house wired for an electric stove? A clothes dryer? Ask where the fuse box or circuit breakers are located.

WORKING ORDER: Check all appliances that are to be sold with the house. Check that the fireplace has a good draft (light a stick and hold it under the flu). You don't want a room full of smoke the first time you try to light a fire. Turn on the air conditioner. Will it really cool the whole house? Flush a toilet, turn on the shower, and open the kitchen faucet, all at once. Is there any water coming out of the faucet?

Tax law now limits the amount of home mortgage loan interest that can be deducted on federal income tax returns to a top limit of the *original* price of your home plus the cost of improvements. For example, if you bought your house ten years ago at $50,000 with a $40,000 mortgage and you have added $5,000 worth of improvements over the years, you can refinance or take out a second mortgage and deduct the interest on $55,000 of the principal—not a penny more, even if your house is now worth $150,000 and you just refinanced for $100,000.

This restriction makes a second mortgage on your primary residence or a refinancing less appealing as a means of purchasing your vacation home. What should you do? Don't give up! You can take out an equity line or a second mortgage that will bring your outstanding debt up to the original purchase price plus improvements of your primary residence and use this cash as the down payment for a mortgage on your vacation home. The interest on that vacation home mortgage *will* be tax deductible. The essential question of course, is: *will your income support all these mortgage payments?*

If your answer is *yes*, enjoy! If not, you may then want to consider rental of some time in the vacation home as a means of bringing in supporting income. Which brings us again to taxes.

TAXES

When our legislators began work on what is now the Tax Reform Act of 1986, they targeted the deduction of interest payments on home mortgage loans. The cry of protest from middle-class constituents—not to mention the National Association of Realtors' lobbyists—was so sustained and vociferous however, that the home mortgage interest deduction was soon restored to the proposed bill. With it, as something of a placator, the deduction of interest paid on the mortgage of a second home was also allowed. Now this addition was a considerate gesture, certainly, but when combined with the passive investment rulings, it was a concession that further complicated the already lengthy and convoluted vacation home tax laws.

Each and every year until the law is changed again, you'll have to decide if it's financially advantageous to treat your vacation home as a rental property or as a second residence. And if you own more than one vacation property, you'll be required each year to choose which of your properties, if any, you wish to designate as your "second home."

(You may designate a different property each year if you like, but only *one* property a year can be called your second home.)

The decision you make will affect how you calculate your taxes and therefore how much you'll pay the IRS. These are not decisions that can be made on the evening of April 14, however, since the IRS has established very specific rules to differentiate between a vacation residence and vacation rental property. Your occupancy and personal use of a vacation home *must* comply with the rules for the category under which you wish to be taxed.

Your vacation home is considered a residence if:

• you keep it exclusively for your own use, for the use of blood relatives (even if they pay you rent), or for exchange with other vacation home owners;
• you use it at least fifteen days a year, or more than 10 percent of the total number of days that it is rented at fair market value, whichever is greater.

Your vacation home is considered rental property if:

• you rent the property at fair market value, which means the going rate in the area;
• you restrict your use (and the use of your blood relatives) to fourteen days a year, or no more than 10 percent of the total number of days that it is rented at fair market value, whichever is greater.

These strict guidelines almost mandate that you make rental plans a year or so in advance in order to assure treatment in the category you choose. Now you may very justifiably be wondering, why all the fuss? The answer is money.

If your vacation home qualifies as a rental property, you're allowed to deduct losses in excess of the rental income as long as you actively participate in the management of the property, your adjusted gross income is under $150,000, and/or you have other profitable passive investments.

If your vacation home qualifies as a second residence, you are allowed to deduct all the mortgage interest paid, even if it exceeds your income from the property and even if the property stood vacant during most of the year. You are not allowed, however, to deduct other expenses, depreciation, or loss beyond the amount of rental income.

In both cases you must still allocate expenses to either personal use time or rental income. To do this, you multiply your total expenses for the year by a fraction: x/y. Here x is the total number of days you rented your property at fair market value. y is the total number of days the home was in use during the year (not the number of days in the year). In calculating the figure for y, do *not* count the days you spent at the property doing repair and maintenance work.

If you designate your vacation home as *rental* property, the expenses allocated to your personal use are *not* tax deductible, including even the mortgage interest you paid during that personal use time, but not including property taxes which *are* deductible even during personal use and vacancy time. Interest, expenses, and depreciation for the rental period *are* deductible against the rental income. This deductibility often produces a paper loss.

If you designate your property as your second home, the mortgage interest you pay during your time of personal use and during the time the property is vacant is deductible from your adjusted gross income. The mortgage interest allocated to the rental period is deductible against the rental income, but only up to the actual amount of that income. For example, let's say that mortgage interest cost you $1,000 during the two months the property was rented for $850. You will be taxed *zero* on the rental income, but you will lose the deduction of the $150 extra interest you paid and all other expenses except property taxes, since loss cannot exceed income when you designate a vacation property as a personal residence.

Is your head spinning with the numbers and the *if*s and *or*s? I know. Everyone loses track of what goes with what and what's the advantage of each designation the first few times he or she reads through vacation home tax law. I suggest that you gather your real numbers on your property together and sit down with a good tax accountant before you decide which option will work out to your financial advantage. Even before that, however, the comparison chart on page 122 may help you to sort out some of the plus and minus rules.

The Tax Reform Act of 1986 combined with the use and occupancy rules for vacation homes has created true negative cash flow in many ownership situations that were once negative on paper and positive in cash in the pocket. Many experts have therefore predicted that vacation houses will be dumped on the market in large numbers for several years to come. This unloading of unprofitable or no longer affordable properties will, they say, create a glut on the market and

VACATION PROPERTY

	SECOND HOME	RENTAL PROPERTY
Use	You, your spouse, or your blood relatives must use the property fifteen days or more than 10 percent of the total number of days that it's rented at fair market value, whichever is greater.	You, your spouse, or your blood relatives can use the property no more than fourteen days or 10 percent of the total number of days it's rented at fair market value, whichever is greater. Days spent in repair and maintenance work do not count as personal-use days.
Advantages	All mortgage interest for the year is tax deductible. If the property is rented for no more than fourteen days a year, no deductions for expenses may be claimed, but the income from the fourteen-day rental need not be reported on federal income tax returns.	Taxes, interest, all expenses, and depreciation that are allocated to the rental period can be deducted against the rental income and can exceed that income creating a tax loss.
Disadvantages	Property cannot show a tax loss.	Limited personal use Interest paid for the time allocated to personal use and the time the property is not in use is not deductible on federal tax returns. The total of tax losses for all rental property owned is restricted to a maximum of $25,000 per year, if you meet IRS income and participation requirements. Losses in excess of this amount must be carried forward to a profitable year or the sale of the property.
Number of properties	You may declare only one property as your second home. It may, however, be a different property each year.	You may own an unlimited number of rental vacation homes. In each home, you may spend up to fourteen days or 10 percent of the total number of days it's rented at fair market value, whichever is greater.

NOTE: Property taxes are fully deductible whether you declare your property a second home or a rental property. They must be allocated properly according to use, however.

result in a steep dive in prices. These predictions may be true, but I believe they will occur sporadically and in local pockets at different times in different areas of the country. All of which will create investment bargains for the investor in touch with both the local marketplace and the overall real estate and economic climate of an area.

 If you can structure your financing to carry a vacation property profitably under the new tax laws, you may well pick up a very fine investment during the next few years. Once the vacation home marketplace absorbs the tax-adjustment selling, prices should rise again, expecially since many baby-boomers will be comfortably settled into affluent middle-age about that time. Your profit potential should be very great indeed.

THE BOTTOM LINE

If you're Oscar Dermann, the bottom line is *how much pleasure does this property give me and my family?* You'll count the profit in dollars later.

If you're Helen Vite, however, you want to make money on your investment. To do this I suggest that you *spend* a little money. Before you sign a contract to buy anything (even the handyman special that you're *sure* you can refurbish in two months and increase its value by 50 percent), spend a few hours with a competent accountant. Check out the numbers and their probable effects on your budget and your tax payments. Discuss what seems to be the best approach to profits, *for you.*

KNOWLEDGE

Knowledge of the geographic area is *essential*, probably the most important aspect of investing in vacation property.

I know of one new buyer of oceanside property who was appalled to discover that the road connecting his cottage to the rest of the country routinely flooded at every moon tide.

"What's a moon tide?" he asked. And then after thinking a bit, "What happens if a storm hits during a moon tide?"

It was the $64,000 question. What indeed? No one will know for sure until that storm arrives at the height of high tide on a full moon. That new buyer, however, might have chosen a different piece of property if he had known the ways of the ocean better and paid closer attention to the lay of the land around him.

And how about mountain property? Can you *really* get to your ski chateau without chains on your tires or a tractor?

Before you invest in an area, spend at least a few weeks there during the peak of in season. And don't spend the time entirely as a vacationer. Keep your eyes open and ask questions of anyone who will talk with you. What happens in a storm? Is there well water during a drought? How does the town handle nonresidents using its recreation facilities? What about parking? Is there reserved space for guests of property owners in the municipal lot? Which recreation facilities are maintained by a private association, which by the town, which by the state?

If you're still up on an area after spending some time there, visit it several times during the off season. Is the area accessible? Are there enough support facilities (grocery stores, restaurants, gas stations, etc.) still open to make life pleasant and avoid long drives to meet basic needs? Is there danger from vandals in a practically deserted community with a minimal off season police force? Talk with some of the people who stay year-round. What's life like when all the tourists have gone? What's good and what's not so good about the off season?

Special Skills

All or any of the homeowner-type handyman skills can save you money when you become a vacation home landlord, but you must ask yourself if your time is worth this money. If not, then the special skills required might just be an ability to keep in touch with a good plumber, electrician, carpenter, exterminator, etc. On the other hand, some vacation home landlords find fix-up and remodeling to be a creative outlet that takes them far from the work world of the corporate office.

Location

Vacation homes are like all other residential real estate in that location essentially means town, neighborhood, and lot, and it is of utmost importance to value. In condominiums, it also means position in the building or complex.

Plus points for the town include:

- On or near a body of water.
- Historic character.
- Ample support and recreational facilities, including restaurants, golf and tennis, children's amusements, shops, and evening entertainment. Plus of course any specific attraction that makes the town a resort area—a national park, or caverns or a white water river, for example.
- Easy access by road or air travel.
- Low taxes. Low municipal property taxes do not make property more appealing to prospective tenants, but they certainly do help the profit margin of landlords.
- Friendly people. When the locals are antagonistic to the tourists, everyone feels uncomfortable.

 Plus points for the neighborhood include:

- Well maintained properties.
- Clean streets, beaches, walkways, etc.
- A sense of safety. You want to feel that you can allow your children to go for a bike ride or that you can take an evening walk alone without worry.
- Some homogeneity in housing value. Many cottage communities are a hodgepodge of architectural styles. They should be relatively close in price and rental value, however.

 Plus points for lots include:

- Waterfront or water access.
- Close to the central attraction of the area—the *best* ski slope, for example, or on the edge of the fairway.
- Views. It's amazing how much people will pay for a good view.
- Abutting forest, park, or other land dedicated to open spaces.
- Level.
- Good parking area or garage area.
- Play area—for volley ball, croquet, badminton, or just a sandbox for the children.
- Good drainage. The lowest lot in an area will become a sea of mud after a heavy rain.

- Privacy. A hedgerow or a stand of trees between houses adds to value. If houses are built very close together, the positioning of windows becomes important.

$ Plus points for condominium apartments include:

- High in a high rise. In fact, the higher you go in the building, the higher the price you usually pay.
- View. Whether it be ocean, mountain, golf course, volcano, or marsh land, vacationers like to *look* at something.
- Away from elevators or shared-space areas such as recreation rooms. No one wants the noise.
- Corner units. Only one wall is shared with a neighbor, which means less noise and more privacy.
- Close to parking.
- Close to the swimming pool.

SOME SUCCESSFUL INVESTORS

THE RETIRED OR ABOUT TO BE RETIRED

Despite their modest combined annual income of $40,000, Brian and Judy Klein had saved enough to put a down payment on a lake side house in the Ozark Mountains. He was fifty-six, she fifty-seven. They used the cottage on spring and fall weekends and rented it during the summer for six years, bringing in enough rental money to keep the property free from out-of-pocket costs.

When the Kleins retired in that sixth year, they took the $125,000 tax exemption on their primary residence and found themselves with a good deal of cash. Judy lobbied for investing that cash in real estate rather than money market funds. The couple paid off the mortgage on their Ozark Mountain home in order to provide themselves with inexpensive shelter for three-quarters of the year. They wintered in Hawaii.

"How?" you ask. "Hawaii is expensive and these people are *not* rich!"

They used the remaining cash from the sale of their primary residence to put a down payment on a condominium on the big island of

Hawaii. Each year they spend December, January, and February in their condo and rent it during the remainder of the year. Because Hawaii has a year-round vacation appeal—probably the highest in the United States—rental income not only supports the costs of the condominium but actually brings in a profit each year. Thus two lovely "vacation homes" came to provide year-round shelter for this retired couple.

ENTREPRENEURIAL HOUSEWIVES

In 1978, Muriel Mendoza found herself with time on her hands. She was in her mid-forties and did not want to venture back to college for that degree she never got, nor did she want to enter an employment marketplace without specialized training or skills. Her husband's income was sufficient, the youngest of their children had just married, and she was frankly bored with bridge groups and garden club meetings.. Self-employment seemed appealing. But what?

During a late fall antique hunting expedition in a seaside town forty miles from their home, she happened to see a FOR SALE sign on a waterfront property. Its lot was long and narrow, the cottage close to the beach, the two-car cinder block garage close to the road. Muriel saw possibilities.

She bought the property and spent the winter trying to get a variance that would allow her to build an apartment over the garage. The board of adjustment gave approval late in February, and Muriel then spent the spring supervising construction work on the apartment and fixing up the house. By summer, she had doubled the potential rental income of the property and was looking for another.

Today Muriel and her husband own six houses, one four-family building, a sandwich shop, and a parking lot in three coastal communities. Managing the real estate has become Muriel's full-time job, a job that leaves her free to structure her time as she wishes and which, by the way, bought her a full-length lynx coat last year as a bonus.

GROUPS AND EXTENDED FAMILIES

Three men I know, all partners in a law firm, recently bought a lakeside home thirty minutes from their office location. They were not investing for profit, however. They bought the house as an investment in pleasure. Each would occupy it with his family for four weeks of the summer, rotating the weeks each year so no one would get "stuck" with the end of June or the beginning of September forever.

This kind of arrangement *can* work for business associates, friends, or family members, but only if a set of guidelines regarding both recreational use and working time is established upon purchase. Otherwise, major fights are just about inevitable.

OPPORTUNISTS AND SPECULATORS

I watched from a house on high ground as Hurricane Carol hit the southern Connecticut coast in the mid-1950s and I came away with a lasting respect for the awesome and devastating power of wind and water. With the exception of one building, all the waterfront houses in the beach community were destroyed or damaged beyond repair. Two were actually moved from their foundations and deposited in pieces in the street.

The houses across the road from the waterfront were all still standing, but just. Their windows were broken, huge puncture holes dotted every roof, and interior walls were skeletons. One house had the beach community's twenty-foot-square wooden raft on its front porch and partially in its living room.

Two days after the storm, my uncle offered an owner $2,500 for what was left of his house, across the road from the then-calm ocean. They settled on $2,800. Today, thirty years later, the house stands on seven-foot concrete pillars to give it protection from rushing storm waters, but that protection has never yet been needed. Its value? In today's marketplace, $210,000. But you couldn't get my uncle to sell with an offer of twice that amount.

MOVING ON

If you really get into buying, selling, and managing vacation property and you get to know an area especially well, you may want to move out of individual cottages or condos and into some larger investments that will consolidate and focus working time and bring in larger profits. Think about:

- Converting a huge seaside mansion or an old hotel to condominiums.
- Finding a tract of land and working through a subdivision approval before selling to a builder.
- Not selling your tract to a builder but developing it with a manufactured home or modular home community, perhaps even using joint venture capital.
- Converting a rambling old house or a group of houses built closely together into a bed 'n' breakfast inn.
- Finding and taking an option on a site suitable for commercial use. With your option in hand, you might approach convenience store chains, fast food franchises, or a successful up-scale restaurant in a nearby community. If you're persuasive and your site is a good one, you might come away with plans for a building or the renovation of an existing building. Then exercise your option. Once the building is complete, you might just hold a very profitable lease!

Is that too much of a dream? Not really. Such investment success stories develop step by step and can very well start with a four-room cottage three blocks from the lake.

· C H A P T E R   8 ·

Condos and Co-ops

Rodney Mikimoto owns a home in a western Connecticut suburb of New York City where the median price of houses is the highest in the nation and appreciating at the second fastest rate in the nation. He has just received news of a transfer to Jacksonville, Florida, where the median price of houses is the fourth from the lowest in the nation. He is at first jubilant. He can buy a mansion! But it turns out to be not quite so simple. He may or may not be transfered back to the New York City business location within the next five years. No guarantees. He doesn't want the hassle of worrying about maintenance if he rents his Connecticut house and, besides, he needs at least part of the equity to buy in Florida. But if he sells his house and is later transfered back, he will have lost ground in the appreciation race and will have to move down markedly in housing. His investment vehicle of choice: a condo or co-op.

·　·　·

Owning a condominium or a co-op apartment or two can be a relatively worry free hedge against runaway prices for home owners temporarily leaving an area. The mortgaging on such property can be structured so that rental income more or less equals monthly payment of mortgage, taxes, and maintenance fees. Meanwhile the apartments, if well chosen, keep pace with the local market. When the investor-owner returns to the area, the profit from the sale of his apartments will be instrumental in keeping his housing standard intact. Such an apartment can also provide a place to live temporarily upon return while house hunting for the just-right property or while having a new house custom built.

Condos and co-ops are not just for transferees, however, and not just for doctors, lawyers, and corporate chiefs, either. Cab drivers, retired engineers, teachers, craft shop owners, you name it, this is an investment vehicle available to everyone with a little extra money to commit to a long-term investment.

Condominium and co-operative apartments are just about the fastest growing investment vehicle available in the real estate marketplace today, *and* they are one of the easiest to get into. In the apartment sector of the marketplace, it's not connections, big bucks, or special experience that will determine a good return, it's knowledge. And this knowledge is readily available, often free for the asking. To begin acquiring it, take a careful look at this investment's demand profile. Once you know what you don't know, you can begin to fill in the gaps effectively.

CHECKPOINTS FOR THE INVESTOR

LOGICAL AND RATIONAL EVALUATION OF OPTIONS

What's a condo? What's a co-op? We had best start right here, at the very beginning, since you can hardly be expected to make intelligent investment decisions unless you understand the ownership form into which you're putting your money. With but a few exceptions, in neither of these investment vehicles do you actually own any *tangible* real estate, no building you can point to and say, "that's mine."

In most condominium communities, you do own the air space *inside* the walls of your apartment and you own an undivided interest in the bricks and mortar, beams and boards, stairways, driveways, land, recreation facilities, and other shared space of the community. An undivided interest is one that cannot be severed or separated. In other words, you own, let's say, $1/100$ of the diving board, but you can't remove even a splinter legally. Condominium ownership generally means that you can decorate the inside of your apartment to your heart's delight, but you cannot plant a holly bush near your front door without permission and approval from the board of directors.

In a co-op, you don't even own air space. What you own is stock in

INVESTOR DEMAND PROFILE

	1	2	3	4	5	6	7	8	9	10
1. Positive Action and Reaction	▓	▓	▓	▓	▓	▓	▓			
2. Willingness to Take Risks	▓	▓	▓	▓						
3. Decision-making Ability	▓									
4. Commitment—the Will to Follow Through	▓									
5. Logical and Rational Evaluation of Options	▓	▓	▓	▓	▓	▓	▓	▓	▓	▓
6. Ability to Deal with Numbers and Finances	▓	▓	▓	▓	▓	▓	▓	▓	▓	▓
7. Ability to Deal with Legal Constraints	▓	▓	▓	▓	▓	▓	▓	▓	▓	▓
8. Organization and Management Skills	▓									
9. Foresight	▓	▓	▓	▓	▓					
10. Imagination and Creativity	▓									
11. Self-confidence	▓	▓	▓	▓	▓	▓	▓			
12. Patience and Tact	▓	▓	▓	▓						
13. Self-control	▓	▓	▓	▓						
14. Social Contact	▓	▓	▓	▓	▓					
15. Negotiating Skill	▓	▓	▓	▓	▓					

the corporation that owns the apartment building. That stock entitles you to a proprietary lease on a given apartment and a number of votes at the shareholders' meetings. In most cases, you must sublease co-op apartments that you purchase as investment property. Before you buy, however, be *absolutely certain* that subleasing is allowed, since some co-op communities want owner-occupants only. In other co-op buildings, subleasing is common and the purchase of blocks of rent-controlled apartments is an excellent investment opportunity for the long-term investor who can afford a negative cash flow. (More about this later.)

Both co-op and condominium communities are governed by boards of directors, almost always elected from among the owners in the building. Each apartment carries a given number of votes which can be cast in the election of officers or at meetings to decide issues such as *Should we raise the maintenance fee?* Owning a large number of votes, however, is not necessarily an indication of power in the government of the community. Most of the important rules for successful management are set out in the bylaws of the condominium or co-op and cannot be changed except by unanimous vote. If you really want decision-making power, you will have to serve on the board, and that usually means work without pay.

It's the job of the board of directors to enforce and adhere to the bylaws and house rules, to oversee the collection of maintenance fees, to decide how maintenance money is to be spent, to oversee the management company if one is used, to supervise maintenance workers if a management company is not used, and to issue an annual report on the financial state of the community.

 Be certain that you obtain a copy of the most recent annual report. It is a major tool in making an evaluation of the economic health of the community. If you don't understand the report, for the sake of your wallet, pay an accountant to go over it with you and explain the positive and negative figures and their likelihood of change. Such matters as the maturity date of a second mortgage on a co-op or the age of the roof in a condominium can measurably affect the annual maintenance fee that you, the apartment owner, must pay.

Engineers' reports on the condition and construction of a building are often available on condominium and co-op *conversions*, and they are a valuable tool in evaluating your potential investment. Be aware, however, that there are often *two* such reports, one commissioned by the sponsor of the conversion and one by the tenants' organization fighting the conversion, or fighting for lower prices on the apartments. And, funny thing!, the report from the sponsor always seems to read more positively than the report paid for by the tenants group. If you are buying into a conversion, try to get a copy of *both* reports and compare them. You can be fairly comfortable regarding those points upon which they agree, but you may have to do a good deal of detective work to come to your own decisions regarding the points upon which the reports differ.

If you are buying into an established condominium or co-op rather than a conversion or new construction, it's a good idea to hire a professional inspection firm to give you a written report on the condition of the apartments you wish to buy *and* the condominium or co-op structures and grounds as a whole. This type of professional inspection is more important in an investment apartment purchase than in a detached house purchase because you, as an apartment buyer, cannot always get access to working systems and common areas as easily as a professional inspector *and* because an incorrect evaluation or something you just happened to miss could be the breakdown that causes maintenance fees to jump by 30 percent in one year! That kind of escalation can cause painful negative cash flow and very real (not paper!) depreciation in the resale value of the individual units.

Reading and inspection are the best means to evaluating a condo or co-op community's condition (both physical and financial), but to make a rational judgment as to value you must do a little footwork in the marketplace. No one buys an investment apartment forever, and one day you'll want to sell at a substantial, even a remarkable profit if you can. To do this you want to buy at a bargain price, something substantially below the current market value, in an area that is appreciating or likely to appreciate faster than average.

This is where the footwork comes in. Resist the pitch of the guy in the sales office who tells you that his building is the best bargain and the hottest property in a 100-mile radius. Instead, go out hunting. Evaluate at least six other condominium offerings—a dozen is better— even if you are being offered an "insider's price" by the guy in the sales office. As an investor, you cannot take his word for worth. Is the insider's price really a discount or is the market value being inflated to make the offering look good? Use the services of other real estate agents in your search. Listen to what each has to say, pros and cons about the area, various buildings, prospects for appreciation, current

rent prices and vacancy rates. Ask about actual sales in the area. What did apartments similar to the one that interests you sell for recently?

To help you with this footwork, there's an evaluation guide on pages 136 and 137. Machine copy a bunch of these and fill one out for each investment apartment you consider. Having your evaluations on paper will keep emotional response from creeping into your decisions. It will also make the actual task of comparing easier.

LEGAL CONSTRAINTS

Liberty and freedom are important words in the United States. We like to think of ourselves as a nation of people free to do as we please. But in fact *none* of us lives in complete freedom. We stop at stop signs, pay taxes, take out marriage licenses, avoid trespassing on the property of others, and so on. In other words, most of us obey the rules that keep our society moving in an orderly manner.

It's just about the same in a condo or co-op community. Rules and procedures are created and enforced to enable a number of persons to live in close proximity and own considerable space and structures in common yet maintain a sense of privacy and autonomy. To own shared-space property successfully, you must be aware of these legal constraints and willing to abide by them.

Every condominium and co-operative apartment building in the nation has bylaws and house rules. Every state has condominium laws—sometimes called horizontal property acts—and the federal government, in the form of the SEC, the FHA, and the IRS, gets into the act, too.

If you choose to invest in condominium or co-operative apartments, you'll have to deal with the limitations imposed by the community into which you buy. If, for example, the bylaws state that apartments can be rented only under one-year leases, you can't rent month by month even if you own a penthouse overlooking the Gulf of Mexico that would bring twelve times the income with twelve monthly rentals.

But what if you want to change the rules? If, for example, the bylaws say no pets and you want to rent to your second-cousin and his Siamese cat, you must make your petition for change in accordance with the procedures set forth in those bylaws. You should be aware, however, that changes in the bylaws often require a unanimous vote, which is

EVALUATION GUIDE
TO APARTMENT INVESTMENTS

LOCATION OF THE BUILDING
Rank high if neighboring areas are good or improving.
Convenience to transportation and/or parking increases rank.
The health of the municipality (taxes, schools, land use, recreation facilities, economic growth, crime, etc.) affects the housing value.

PRICE
Rank 5 if the unit is priced at market value with comparable apartments.
Rank above 5 if the unit is priced lower than comparable, nearby units.
Rank below 5 if the unit is priced higher than comparable, nearby units.

MAINTENANCE HISTORY
Give higher ranks to units in communities in good repair, with a good maintenance history, relatively low monthly maintenance fees, and a healthy contingency fund for unexpected but necessary expenditures.
Also rank high if the condo or co-op community is well insured.

FINANCING
Rank above 5 for special financing at below-market rates.
Rank 5 for balloon mortgages, which can be a positive or a negative factor. Their value can change if the economy should change.
Rank below 5 for points that must be paid to obtain financing.
Rank below 5 for higher interest rates simply *because* your investment is a condo or co-op and not a detached house.

LOCATION OF THE UNIT
Rank according to your evaluation of the desirability of the unit in the building or complex.
A penthouse with an ocean view might merit 10.
The unit sandwiched between the super's free unit and the elevator might get a 1.
Corner units usually rank a few points higher.

(continued)

almost impossible to get. Changes in house rules (the hours the swimming pool is to be kept open, for example, or, sometimes whether or not you can keep pets) are easier to enact. They do require time, vote gathering, and formal approval, however.

EVALUATION GUIDE
TO APARTMENT INVESTMENTS

VACANCY RATE
The fewer the vacant units the higher the rank.

OWNER OCCUPANCY
Generally condominiums or co-operatives with a high proportion of owner-occupants are better maintained and thus tend to appreciate better. The higher the percentage of owner-occupants the higher the rank. The higher the percentage of tenants, the lower the rank. Ask a member of the board of directors for these figures.

SPECIAL FEATURES
Add to the ranking if any of these features are present:
Good recreational facilities
Amenities such as hot tubs, exercise room, meeting rooms
Good security systems
On-site shopping facilities
On-site medical or therapy facilities
On-site child care facilities
Views
Surrounding green acres
Nearby cultural centers

Take away points for these features:
No elevators (unless a one-level garden-style complex)
No facilities for the handicapped
Close to major highways, industrial areas, or other noise, air, and sound pollution generators
Lack of recreational facilities
Limited parking or no parking facilities

If all this sounds a bit stuffy and complex, don't be put off. Living within the rules on a day-to-day basis is not nearly as bad as reading about them in the law books. People accommodate themselves to a way of life.

In general, however, the best advice I can give to a condo or co-op investor is *look before you leap*. You *must* read those bylaws and house rules no matter how badly they treat the English language. And you must read them *before* you buy. Only then can you choose an apartment in a community where the rules are to your liking.

If you buy an apartment in a city where rent control is in effect, *legal constraints* will also mean a myriad of municipal restrictions and guidelines in the management of your investment property. These restrictions do not necessarily mark these urban apartments as bad investments, but they may bring about a number of years of negative cash flow before you can sell profitably, since rent control often precludes eviction without very substantial reason and it guarantees the rent-paying, law-abiding tenant lease renewals.

 If you decide to invest in occupied, rent-controlled apartments, choose those in which the tenants are either quite young or quite old. If you choose carefully (and with a little luck) it's likely your tenants will vacate their units within a reasonable time, under five years. Meanwhile you can think of the negative cash flow as money deposited in the bank, especially if you have invested in an area where housing is in short supply. Once you have a vacant co-op or condominium apartment, you can sell for a substantial profit, far, far above the total of your invested capital and the negative cash flow. And, by the way, all that negative cash flow through the years is tax deductible from the profit.

NUMBERS AND FINANCES

There's no escaping this item if you are considering the purchase of anything from a single studio unit in San Diego to a block of ten occupied, rent-controlled units in New York City. Calculate and study the numbers for the following:

- The going rate of rents in the area. Will the rent from your investment apartment(s) cover your financing costs, property taxes, and the maintenance fee? If not, can you handle the negative cash flow?
- Vacancy rates in the area. Can you carry a vacant apartment for three months without going broke? An area vacancy rate of less than 4 percent will almost surely mean quick rental with minimal vacancy time.
- Mortgaging. Should you go for a low-rate adjustable loan or a higher rate but fixed interest loan? How many points must you pay to get the loan? How long must you hold the unit before appreciation wipes

COMPARISON GRAPH

Name and Unit Number of Condo or Co-op:

Address:

Rank each factor on a scale of 1 to 10, 10 being the best, and place a dot at the appropriate point on the chart. When the dots are connected, really good buys will rank near the top of the chart on most factors and will contain few sharp dips in the line.

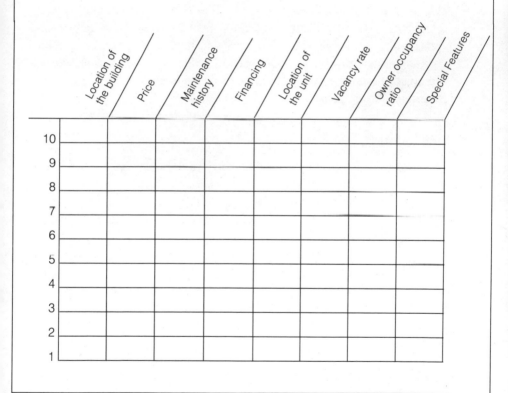

out the closing and loan procurement costs and your investment becomes genuinely profitable?
• Seller financing. Is it available? On what terms, at what interest rate? What is the length of the loan? Is there a balloon payment? Be

aware also that nonrecourse seller financing will protect your personal assets in the event of foreclosure but will also limit your deduction of tax losses to the "at risk" capital, that is, the amount of cash you've actually invested.

- Community solvency. Co-ops can go bankrupt. Condos can become so run-down that resale value plunges. Maintenance costs can soar. Can you gather enough evidence of good management and continued good management to warrant investing your money? Go back to those annual reports we talked about.

- Estimated costs in new construction. How accurate are the builder's estimates of future maintenance costs and even local property taxes? Have the costs of building condominium community amenities (the club house, tennis courts, swimming pool), which are usually completed last, been accurately estimated? These questions are difficult to answer accurately. The best safety device is to visit some recently completed communities in the area and get statistics on what these features *actually* cost.

RISK TAKING

Condos and co-ops share all the usual real estate risks, especially the value of location in terms of the economics of a local area. They also have two risk features, however, that are part and parcel of the investment vehicle, inescapable as it were. What are they? Management and maintenance.

As a condo or co-op unit owner, you are *obligated* to pay your share of maintenance and management costs. Your control of those costs, however, is limited to your voting power in the association, unless, of course, you volunteer to serve on the board of directors. Because of the importance of maintenance and management in determining investment return and resale value, your degree of risk in the condo and co-op marketplace varies with the type of purchase you make.

Safest is the resale unit in a well run, well maintained apartment community in an area that's appreciating. You can inspect maintenance and construction with your own eyes, or through a professional inspector; you can examine the track record of the board of directors; and you can hunt down sale prices on comparable units, thus pinning down market value. With a good conservative investment from among the resale units in your area, the likelihood of losing money is slim indeed.

Conversions are a bit more chancy. Although you can still compare apartment prices to comparable units that have recently been sold and you can still inspect the premises, you cannot anticipate how the community will be run once a board of directors takes control from the sponsor. The risk of maintenance cost spirals is high in a conversion because the building and its systems are not new and the sponsor has been keeping the records on maintenance practices and costs. Even with the best of professional inspections, unexpected breakdowns can occur. Some tenant groups negotiate with the sponsor for a repair contingency fund of several thousand dollars as a kind of insurance against rising maintenance costs.

 There are, however, bargain properties to be found among condominium and co-op conversion projects, especially in a soft, buyers' market. Sponsors wishing to get out of the entanglements of participating in the management of a partially sold building will often offer residents insider prices that represent real discounts of 15 to 20 percent off market value. In areas where rent control is in effect, offerings of occupied apartments to their occupants regularly run 50 percent and more off market value. Tenants in buildings where insider prices are being offered can be approached and deals made in which everyone profits. Unless, that is, the market remains soft long after your purchase.

If you choose to buy from an occupying tenant who has been offered an insider price, be certain that the subscription agreement or purchase agreement allows the tenant to assign his contract before closing. In that way, you pay the tenant and then step in line to purchase the unit at the tenant's price when the sponsor is ready to do the conversion. If the contract is not assignable, you will need to wait until the tenant closes and then pay closing costs when you buy from him. And one more word of caution: be sure to have the tenant sign an agreement to vacate the apartment once you assume ownership. You do *not* want long delays and court appearances trying to get an eviction when the tenant actually *sold out*.

In a buyers' market, some sponsors are also willing to sell blocks of occupied apartments at tremendously discounted "package deal" prices— as much as 75 to 80 percent off market value. Many are even willing to carry the financing on these purchases for a short term, usually three to five years.

There are fabulous buys in occupied, rent-controlled blocks of five or more apartments if you can afford to carry the negative cash flow until the units are vacated and available for resale. This was the investment vehicle of choice for the young neurosurgeon mentioned in Chapter 3. The time demands of this investment are negligible while the profit potential is tremendous. But remember, try to purchase those units that are likely to be vacated in the near term.

If you choose to purchase a block of units with seller financing, be sure that your agreement with the sponsor allows you to sell individual units before the maturity date of the loan. You will probably be required to pay off a proportionate amount of the principal with the sale of each individual unit.

Apartment investments in completed new buildings have less risk that breakdowns and repairs will cause an escalation in maintenance fees than in conversions, but they share with conversion investments the unknown factor regarding the competence of the board of directors. Until the apartment complex is on its feet and running independently for a year or two, no one will know how efficiently it will be managed. Despite this management risk, however, newly completed apartment complexes have an excellent chance for rapid appreciation during the first three to five years. Beware of boom areas, however, where overbuilding will depreciate value.

Unbuilt new construction—paper castles, as it were—is the highest risk investment in the condo/co-op marketplace. Why? You can't see what you're buying; you can't be sure that construction will be completed according to schedule and plans, or even completed at all if the builder goes bankrupt; you cannot judge the character of the community because there is no community; and you know nothing about the board of directors because it doesn't exist yet. Also, all estimates of maintenance fees and local property taxes are just that: estimates. But, if all goes *well*, profits can be very high just as soon as your unit is complete and ready for resale. If this option sounds interesting to you, read the chapter on preconstruction contracts, subscriptions, and options.

DECISION-MAKING ABILITY, COMMITMENT, AND MANAGEMENT SKILLS

There is little demand for these character traits once the condo or co-op purchase is made. Rent collection and remembering to meet your mortgage payments and maintenance fees are about the limits of your involvement. This kind of freedom from the hassles of being a landlord is a primary factor in the growing popularity of condos and co-ops as investment vehicles.

POSITIVE ACTION AND NEGOTIATING SKILLS

The primary *positive action demands* of condo/co-op investing occur in the finding, choosing, and buying stage. To find a good investment apartment, you will have to spend a fair amount of time in the marketplace. The following are some investment-hunt options:

• Proceed as you would if you were buying a single-family house. In most parts of the country, condos and co-ops are multiple listed and shown by Realtors. With resale units, you can negotiate on price just as you would on a single-family house. Prices on new construction are usually firm. Before you negotiate, let me warn you again to *be certain* that rentals are allowed in the condominium or co-op community.

• In a few major cities and some rural areas, real estate brokers do not use multiple listing services. To buy a resale in these areas you must make the rounds of all the real estate offices in the town or neighborhood where you want to buy. Ask to see what each office has to offer in your price range. Get copies of those listings that interest you and make comparisons.

• In areas where conversions are common, watch the newspapers for announcements and, even more important, put the word out to anyone who will listen that you're interested in an investment apartment or two. Tenants usually suspect a conversion long before it is actually announced, and you might be able to get an inside line on price and terms before units are officially listed for sale. Don't be shy about calling the sponsor's office and asking to talk with the person in charge of sales, even if you want to buy only one unit in a hundred-unit complex. These guys want to sell and every sale is important, especially at the beginning of a sales campaign when the staff is trying to generate momentum. In fact, early birds can sometimes negotiate a lower price. The sponsor is thinking about the newspaper ad that could read: *Seven Units Sold Before Listing! Don't Miss This One!*

• As you drive about in suburban areas, watch for sales office trailers in areas where ground is just being broken. Paper castles are a high-risk investment, but you can get in on rock-bottom prices.

• Stop in at on-site sales offices, whether the condos and co-ops are already built, under construction, or undergoing conversion. Get prices, fact sheets, engineers' reports, bylaws, house rules, and everything else that's being given away. If you are buying only one unit, you will probably have to make your offer through the sales agent on duty when you walked in the door. If you are interested in purchasing a block of units—five or more—however, ask for a face-to-face meeting with the sponsor or the builders. It's a little like buying wholesale: you should be able to negotiate a lower price when you buy "in bulk."

The secondary *positive action demands* of this investment vehicle come later, when you've owned your apartment for a while and are wondering if this is still the best of all possible investments for you. In many types of apartment purchase, new buildings especially, and apartments in recently revitalized areas of a city there is a time of fast appreciation and then a leveling off. Many investors, happy with the initial upward spiral, hold their investments too long.

 Keep close tabs on the resale value of your condos and co-ops and the value of comparable apartments in the area. If you see a leveling off, don't be lulled into doing nothing just because managing this investment takes so little time and effort. Put the unit on the market, sell it, and buy into other apartments or other investment vehicles that are on an upward wave.

If you live in an apartment building about to undergo conversion and are considering buying your own and several other units, you will face the need for some special negotiating skills and a heavy demand on your reserve of positive action skills. Generally speaking, tenants in a building undergoing conversion can get concessions in price, financing terms, fix-up allowances, and reserve funds against maintenance costs if they organize and negotiate with the sponsor as a group. The sponsor's professional sales agents will do better if the tenants act separately. They will negotiate privately with each tenant on a one-to-one basis and sell the units with one concession here, another there, but no major commitments.

SELF-CONFIDENCE AND SELF-CONTROL

Choosing to sell a money-making piece of real estate requires even more self-confidence than choosing to buy because you're not riding a wave of high hopes. You know exactly what the property has done for you while you held it, and you know pretty much what it will bring in the marketplace. Friends and relatives will also be there to help you with comments like, "What's the matter with you? You're doing fine. Why are you getting out?" They seem genuinely concerned about your making a mistake with *your* money.

And you probably will. Sometimes. You may well sell before the appreciation climb of a property has completely reached its peak. But take heart. When one of the world's most famous multimillionaires was asked how he made his millions, he replied, "I sold too soon. Always, I sold too soon." So if you sell too soon, count your cash, and vow to do better next time. Your growing net worth should provide plenty of positive reinforcement.

As in many real estate situations, there is a flip side to the appreciation question, however, and this one takes as much self-control as self-confidence. It's a matter of how you respond to the bad times, and believe me there will be some. When dealing in condos and co-ops, try not to sell in response to a bad year, a rumor ("rent control is coming!"), or a bad experience with a particular tenant. Get the facts and don't let emotions influence your decisions.

FORESIGHT

Foresight gets a 5 on the investment demand chart because it's about as important in apartment purchases as it is in other kinds of investment dealings. Yes, you've got to have a feel for the market. But as I've said again and again, the basic and essential ingredient for this Location is by far and away the best forecaster of future value. In apartment investment, the only other significant foresight that you'll need is the ability to evaluate maintenance and management. Will its direction be positive or negative?

PATIENCE, TACT, AND SOCIAL CONTACT

If you live in an apartment building in which you own several other investment apartments, you will need an ordinary supply of patience and tact, just about as much as people need to get along in any community. If you get involved in working on the board of directors, however, the demands for patience and tact will increase.

The amount of social contact you have with other owners and tenants will depend very much upon your personality and life-style. Don't try to change what you quite naturally are. There's room for every type of investor in this investment vehicle.

A good social network outside the condominium community, in the town, county, or even the state will help you to hear tips on apartments coming up for sale at bargain prices. Friendships with other apartment investors can also provide the listening ear or word of advice you may very much need when faced with a knotty problem.

IMAGINATION AND CREATIVITY

You might well be able to increase the resale value of your investment apartment by giving it a paint-and-wallpaper facelift after your tenants move out. Beyond this basic selling technique, however, there is little need or opportunity for creative expression in condo and co-op investing.

If you have beautiful ideas that you want very much to bring to reality, consider handyman specials, converting large old houses into multifamily houses, converting anything from a run-down apartment building to an abandoned factory into condominiums, or even trying your hand at becoming a builder.

TOOLS OF THE TRADE

WAITING TIME

Waiting time in this vehicle depends upon your choices, your goals, and luck. But that's a little too vague to mean anything, so let's look at a few specific situations.

- The purchase of a resale apartment to be rented. Usually there is a minimum waiting time of two to three years before appreciation wipes out financing and closing costs and leaves a margin large enough to be called a reasonable profit.
- The purchase of new construction available for occupancy. Appreciation is faster here and a unit may be ready for profitable resale in as little as eighteen months. Much depends upon housing demand

§ in the area and the desirability of the unit itself. The greatest likelihood of rapid appreciation occurs in units in the first completed section of a large complex still under construction. As the builder raises his prices, so goes the value of your investment apartment.

• The purchase of new construction not yet begun. Waiting time is dependent on how quickly the builder works and where your unit is located in the complex. In garden-type developments, choose first section units for fast turnover, last section units for maximum profit—you wait longer but the price has gone up more while you were waiting. If you're interested in these, read the chapter on preconstruction contracts, subscriptions and options.

• The purchase of unoccupied conversion apartments. In some states, conversion can take as little as six months from start to finish, in others as long as four or five *years*! Check with your attorney general's office to find how long the average conversion takes in your state. Many apartments contracted for at during-the-conversion prices have higher market value as soon as the conversion is complete. These can be sold immediately for a modest profit or held for a more substantial gain.

• The purchase of occupied conversion apartments. In areas where rent control laws prohibit eviction or where state laws protect elderly or handicapped tenants from immediate eviction in a condominium or co-op conversion, your waiting time can be long indeed. That's why these units are offered at prices up to 70 percent or more below market value. Can you afford the negative cash flow, and can you wait? You should be very certain about your answers here, because once into this investment there is virtually no way out until the apartment is vacated.

WORKING TIME

Negligible. Maintenance and management problems are under the supervision of the board of directors. If you choose to run for a position on that board, however, and you're elected, you'll certainly put in a good number of hours each month.

If you don't wish to pay outside workmen, there is also some working time required between leases to different tenants and before putting the apartment on the market for sale. It's the usual thing: paint, wallpaper, floor covering, soap and water.

START-UP CASH AND CASH FLOW

RESALE CONDOS: Throughout the country, condos are financed much the way detached houses are. The down payment requirements and the guidelines for buyer qualification vary from lender to lender, but they are essentially those that apply to detached single-family house mortgages or trust deed loans. If you buy and occupy a unit, you may be able to put down as little as 5 or 10 percent of the appraised value by using private mortgage insurance. If you buy for investment, however, you may be required to have a larger down payment, since private mortgage insurance is often limited to owner-occupied properties. Government-sponsored loans (FHA and VA) are available on condominiums, unless certain bylaws in the Condominium Declaration violate government policies. A clause that requires board of directors' approval of a prospective buyer, for example, would negate the possibility of FHA or VA financing on any of the units in the condo community.

When calculating your prospective cash flow, be certain to compare rental income against the *sum total* of mortgage payments, local property taxes, condominium maintenance fees, insurance premiums, and other miscellaneous costs such as sewer use fees or water bills. If your bottom line shows a negative cash flow too high to be easily assimilated into your life-style, you may have to make a larger down payment in order to reduce the mortgage payments due each month.

Since many condo buyers are first-time investors, I want to emphasize one warning: *don't overmortgage.* The old no-money-down or as-little-down-as-possible theories of the late 1970s and early '80s simply don't work anymore. If you mortgage so heavily that your rental income leaves you hundreds of dollars short each month, negative cash flow can become overwhelming, especially if you own more than one investment apartment! And if appreciation in your area is slower than you expected, selling may not be profitable. Instead of using leverage as a money-making tool, you'll find yourself in a negative leverage situation. In this case the cost of the borrowed money (the interest you must pay) could exceed the profit from appreciation. And that's *without* factoring in expenses. So please, be *sure* you calculate cash flow carefully before you buy.

"It's true," some people might be thinking right now, "I read about negative leverage in the early eighties when interest rates were so high. But tax benefits bail you out anyway, don't they?"

Not anymore! Before tax reform, an investor could experience heavy negative cash flow for twelve months of the year and then get all that cash back and then some when the federal income tax refund check arrived in the mail. Well, there won't be any such check to cover negative cash flow in the years to come. But I'm getting ahead of myself. We'll do taxes in just a bit.

CO-OPS: You do not take out a mortgage loan or get a trust deed on a co-op apartment since you don't really own real estate, you own stock in a corporation that owns real estate. The difference is a technicality, however, and most lenders in areas where co-ops are a common housing style make co-op loans that are structured in the same way as the prevalent forms of home mortgaging. Your stock in the co-op building is held by the lender as collateral for the loan. Down payment requirements may be somewhat higher, however, and some co-op bylaws require that as much as 50 percent of the purchase price be paid in cash without outside financing.

UNBUILT CONDOS: Signing a contract to buy an apartment in a yet-unbuilt community may require a deposit of only a few thousand dollars or it may require 10 percent of the purchase price. In either case, the contract should set the price with no room for changes. Do not accept what the builder may call an *escalation clause* or a *cost escalation clause* in the contract. This clause will allow him to raise the purchase price of your unit by a certain percentage (usually 2 or 3 percent, but sometimes as much as 5 percent) because of increases in the cost of labor or materials during the building period. If this clause is in the contract, you will usually end up paying the extra money no matter what the inflation rate has been. "Somehow, the builder's costs went up. Look, here are the figures. See?" This is price gouging in a legal gown.

You should also insist that there be a clause in the contract that allows you the right to assign the contract to another buyer at any time and for any reason before closing. For more information about the use of the right to assign, read the chapter on preconstruction contracts, subscriptions, and options.

When buying a paper castle, you might want to try negotiating for the following:

• that your earnest money be held in an escrow account rather than being turned over to the builder.

- that the escrow account be interest bearing and that interest be credited to you, the buyer. If the builder says *No* to this request, try to get the interest split 50-50.
- that earnest money be paid in installments. For example, $1,000 on signing and $3,000 on the first day of each of the three-month periods following. You will then have put down $10,000 over a year, just about the time your unit should be ready. This approach is much better than handing over $10,000 upon signing the contract because *you* get to keep at least part of your money longer. You're also risking less because you can monitor construction progress. Some builders will not accept installment deposits. Some will, however, because the arrangement does bring in cash even though it is distributed over time. A builder cannot touch the cash held in an escrow account until closing or until there's a mutual agreement for its release.

BLOCKS OF CONDOS OR CO-OPS: Investors who buy several apartments in a conversion—especially occupied apartments—can often negotiate financing directly from the sponsor with little or no down payment and excellent interest rates. Check the cash flow to be sure you can handle the investment, however.

TAXES

The government considers condominium and co-operative apartments a form of passive real estate investment. The purchase price of the apartment unit may be depreciated over 27½ years. The sum total of the annual depreciation figure plus the actual costs associated with maintenance and management, the local property taxes, and the interest paid on mortgage loans may be deducted from the rental income of the property. If the figure in this bottom line is positive, that dollar amount must be reported as ordinary income. If the figure is negative, however, it *cannot* be deducted against your earned income. It must be carried forward for deduction against a positive year in the future or against the profit upon sale, or against profit from other passive investments.

But there's an *unless* tagged onto this law. If your adjusted gross income is less than $100,000 and if you actually participate in the management of your apartment (choosing your tenants, collecting rents, etc.), you may deduct up to $25,000 a year in loss on your investment property. The $25,000 figure goes down gradually until we come to the investor or investing couple making $150,000 a year. They get no loss deduction. The investor who does not participate in the management of his condo or co-op (rental-pool condominium owners, for example) do not get any allowance for loss deduction against annual ordinary income.

In terms of local taxes, your condominium apartment will be taxed by the local municipality as real property, and you will pay these taxes either to your lender with your monthly mortgage payment or directly to the town. Taxes are *not* included in the maintenance fees of a condominium community.

In the case of a co-op, the local government assesses and taxes the entire building as one unit. This tax dollar figure is then divided among the shareholders. The monthly maintenance fee of a co-op, therefore, *does* include your share of the local property taxes.

In your apartment hunting, be aware also that the bylaws of some co-ops and a few condominiums allow for a so-called flip tax. The flip tax is a fee—usually a percentage of the purchase price—that the co-op or condo owners' association charges when an apartment changes ownership. The money is usually put into the contingency fund for major repairs and helps to avert maintenance fee increases. Either the buyer or the seller can pay this fee, by mutual agreement, or it can be divided between them. Ask if there is such a tax and who is paying it before you sign a contract to buy. Flip taxes can and usually do run into thousands of dollars.

EXPECTED RETURNS

There are two types of return in residential real estate investment: the annual return, which is the amount of positive cash flow for each dollar invested, and the return upon sale, which is the profit.

In the years before tax reform, highly leveraged mortgages and rapid depreciation schedules rarely created positive returns on paper. Instead investors got very positive tax shelters; their annual tax dollars remained securely in their pockets. That's gone. Today careful property selection and appropriate financing can give the investor in condos and co-ops a small positive cash flow each year or a small negative cash flow that can be carried forward until sale.

It's in the number of dollars you get to keep upon sale, however, that the new tax laws can actually be beneficial to the small investor. Oh, it's true, the capital gains shelter is gone and all income is taxed alike, but the real number of dollars in your pocket after you sell the property will probably be greater than that of the guy who bragged that he paid no income taxes in 1982. Why? In the first place, if you sell within the usual holding period of five to ten years, you will have depreciated less of the property's value than on the old fifteen-year schedule. The base figure from which you calculate your profit against the selling price therefore will be *higher*. As a result, you'll come up with a lower taxable profit figure. Not *less* profit, you understand, just a lower number upon which to pay taxes than if you had been depreciating on the fifteen-year schedule.

To this good news add the fact that you can deduct the losses that exceeded income each year that you owned the property from the profit figure. Again, we're lowering the amount that will be taxed.

I agree, it's not as good as it was, but it's not all bad, either!

"And what's the expected return?" you ask. "How much will I really make?"

Probably just a bit less than you would make by investing in a single-family house in the same area. Apartments are still a little less desirable to the general public than houses and therefore lag just a bit behind the rate of appreciation in single-family home sales. But it's not a bad deal for a no-work investment.

KNOWLEDGE AND SKILLS

Condominiums have become so widespread an ownership form that many people pay little or no regard to their legal complexity, an oversight that could be costly to a home buyer and devastating to an investor. If shared-space ownership is your investment vehicle of choice, you should take the time to obtain information on your state's condominium laws. These laws vary greatly from one state to another, from very strict, for example, in New York, Michigan, Florida, Virginia, and California, to almost laissez-faire in states where condos are less prevalent.

Co-ops are yet another story. They come under the rules of incorporation and under certain federal statutes. They are far less widespread, however. Most are found in New York City, upstate New York, in scattered towns in New Jersey, Washington, D.C., and Florida. Your state attorney general's office can help you to get information on state regulations.

Once you more or less understand regulations in your state, it's also important that you learn to read the particular condo or co-op documents associated with the property you plan to buy. If you don't trust your own ability the first time around, hire a good lawyer with experience in condo or co-op sales to go over the papers with you.

And finally, you will need market knowledge. To develop a sense of current market value and an eye for appreciation potential you must spend time, effort, and sometimes money in the marketplace. This is not to say that you can't carefully choose one or two apartments, keep them for a few years, and then sell for a substantial profit. You can. But if you intend to turn over property frequently or to speculate in preconstruction contracts or conversions, you must know what's happening around you, who's building, who's selling, who's applying for a variance, where new roads are being built, and what's happening in the business world—new offices, plants, closings, shopping malls, etc.

Which brings me to the final word of condo/co-op market advice: *stay local.*

Since shared space ownership investment does not demand landlord supervision and in fact requires almost no active working time, there's a temptation to invest in "a great buy in Xanadu" even though you know virtually nothing about Xanadu and rarely go there. This is a good way to make a big mistake.

Stay local, however, does not mean that you need restrict your investment purchases to the town in which you live. It does mean that you should invest in areas with which you have considerable familiarity. If you vacation regularly in a particular area, if you make frequent business trips to a particular city, or if you return regularly to the town where you grew up and still have relatives, you may well be or become familiar enough with the area to invest intelligently there. Intelligently is the "buy" word.

SOME SUCCESSFUL INVESTORS

VACATIONERS

Tony and Angela Napolitano stumbled upon a small motel that a speculator was trying to convert to condominium apartments. Of the thirty units, only eleven were sold. "The market is as soft as cotton candy," explained the sponsor. But a market as sharp as a samurai sword wouldn't have helped move the units much. They were dirty, musty, poorly furnished, and dark. Prospects for making money in this place seemed small to most people.

Tony saw differently, however. He had grown up poor, never having had a vacation, much less a vacation home. A one-bedroom apartment that looked out on Florida's Gulf Coast for less than $30,000 had tremendous appeal to him. He wanted to own it, dirt be damned!

It was a case of good luck and good location. In the first year, Angela and Tony spent their vacation cleaning and painting their unit. Then they put it into the hands of the condo-manager who doubled as a rental agent. Of course, this agent rented his unsold units first. Angela and Tony collected seven weeks' rent in nine months.

In the two years that followed, however, all the condo units were finally sold. The new owners cleaned and decorated their units and took charge of the owners' association. The dilapidated motel suddenly took on an appealing new look. In their fourth year of ownership, the Napolitanos' unit was rented 70 percent of the time available and cleared a profit of $8,800.

More recently, two major hotels have been built nearby and Long Boat Key has become an "in" spot to vacation. Tony and Angela spend three to four weeks a year in their unit, but they have to reserve their time in advance. Yes, rental demand has become that great.

And the current market value of this condominium? About $130,000. A $100,000 increase in six years. Not bad, especially considering that they only put $10,000 down.

SPECULATORS

When New York City was near bankruptcy, David Shapiro bought ten occupied, rent-controlled co-op apartments for $80,000. Four are still occupied and under rent control but their income almost meets expenses now.

The other six? David has sold them off as each became vacant over the years. To date, he has made slightly over $1,300,000.

NEWLYWEDS

Pearl and Terhune Jackson never rented. They saved up enough cash to make the down payment on a new one-bedroom condominium unit before they were married and moved in right after the honeymoon.

It wasn't always easy to meet both mortgage payments and monthly maintenance fees, but they kept telling themselves and each other that it would be worth it.

It was. In three years the newly completed units in the complex were selling for $35,000 more than the Jacksons' purchase price. Pearl and Terhune sold and moved into a two-bedroom unit, one of the first available in a new complex going up across town. This apartment was almost twice the size of their former home, but it cost them $5,000 *less* than their selling price.

"Impossible!" you're thinking. "Or just a lucky break."

Not at all. The first units to sell in a condominium complex where construction has just begun almost always go at bargain prices. Evidence of occupancy is well known in the business as an important stimulus to sales, so the owners want to sell units even if they don't get quite the price they'd like. They make up for it later. Early occupants therefore get the bargains. Those that sell just before construction is complete and buy first available units in another complex are on their way to successful real estate investment.

RETIRED PERSONS

Stanley and Margaret Timoshenko bought the condo in Phoenix purely as an investment (good annual return, good appreciation, no work), but a year later Stanley suffered a heart attack. Suddenly the lawn maintenance, gardening, and fix-up chores that he had enjoyed became a serious burden in the eight-room single-family home where the couple lived. They moved into their condo.

For years afterward, Margaret would say to people, "The condo saved Stanley's life." They bought three more units with the money from the sale of their house. The income provides several luxuries each year.

COLLEGE STUDENTS' PARENTS

John Apelles was accepted at Stamford University but without provision for on-campus housing. It was his first choice school and he begged his parents to let him go. So quite by chance, John Apelles, Sr., and his wife Stephanie became property owners in California.

They bought a two-bedroom condominium and John Jr. took in three roommates. The rent the roommates paid fell a little short of meeting expenses, but, in all, the cash that the Apelles family had to contribute was considerably less than dorm charges.

They sold the condo after John's graduation for a net profit of $23,000, more than a year's tuition.

SINGLES

Eric Kainer graduated from the University of Connecticut in 1985, took a job at a computer firm in Massachusetts, and bought a small single-family house six months later. Real estate was the way to wealth, he thought. But he hadn't figured on the grass cutting, hedge clipping, weeding, downspout repairs, and water heater replacement, among other things. Eric wanted his weekends free and he resented the house he'd bought. He sold for a modest profit and bought a condo ten minutes from work.

MOVING ON

Expansion in this investment vehicle tends to be horizontal. Because working time does not increase proportionately with the number of owned units, it's possible to expand your investment base widely and rapidly. Negative cash flow is the most common problem in condo or co-op apartment investment, however, and often sets limits on the number of units an investor can carry at one time.

If you and your life-style are right for this investment vehicle, don't be too quick to jump ship. Some investors assume that the logical next step after owning ten condo apartments is owning a ten-unit apartment building. It's simply not true. Apartment building evaluation and management require different skills and different time commitments.

The other common faux pas that successful condo or co-op investors make is a jump into the conversion process. The thought is: "If I own ten condos now and I'm doing great, why not sell them, buy an apartment building, and convert *it* into condos? Then I can make a fortune selling off the units!"

Well, you might. Or you might be buying yourself a hair mattress. Condo or co-op conversion is a *very* different ball game from condo or co-op investment ownership. There are legal entanglements on every level—federal, state, and local—and the time commitments, and the time delays . . . but that's another book.

There is, though, another type of condominium or co-operative investment that you might like to investigate if you're doing well with this vehicle: vacation resorts.

Holding a condo or two, or three, in prime escape areas such as Sanibel Island in Florida or Scottsdale, Arizona, can be a break-even cash flow investment for the present and a paid-up retirement haven for the future.

If you'd like a vacation area investment but want to devote absolutely no time to its management, you might also consider a rental-pool investment. Condominium units with rental-pool arrangements have been sold in this country quite successfully for almost a decade now. Co-op ownership of hotel rooms with share interest in all resort facilities and income is a newer idea that is rapidly gaining a following. The Mariner's Inn on Hilton Head Island in South Carolina has been one of the most successful of these ventures. If you're interested, you might want to read the previous chapter on vacation homes and then talk with real estate agents in areas that you personally know.

CHAPTER 9

Small Apartment Buildings

During the past fifteen years, Edna and Tim Halloran have, at one time or another, owned four multifamily houses, three single-family houses, and five condominium apartments. They have just sold a tract of land which they bought and subdivided in eighteen months for a profit of $100,000, after taxes. Edna is an exuberant, enthusiastic risk taker (and a marketplace huntress). Tim is a careful, practical organizer and record keeper. Their investment vehicle of choice—a small apartment building.

In this investment vehicle's marketplace, that sign should be heeded as carefully as the one that reads THIN ICE at the end of the road to the shore of Lake Opportunity. A small apartment building can be a relatively low risk, positive cash flow, inflation-hedging, money-making investment for the knowledgeable and well prepared real estate buyer. Or the same small apartment building might become the decade's biggest money-loser for the inexperienced real estate buyer out to get rich quick. Why? Read on.

CHECKPOINTS FOR THE INVESTOR

LOGICAL AND RATIONAL EVALUATION OF OPTIONS

The old real estate saw that says *there are three important factors in real estate: location, location, and location* needs a little revision when an investor takes on small apartment buildings as the vehicle of choice. It should read: *there are three important factors in successful small apartment house investment: location, structure maintenance, and management.* Overlooking any one of these three can make an investment go sour. A poorly managed building in the best location will lose money. A building with the most conscientious management but serious structural and maintenance problems will lose money. A structurally sound, well managed building in a poor location will lose money.

"So how does anyone make money in apartment houses?" you ask. "Do you have to find the perfect place every time?"

No. Well, not exactly. You do have to choose very, very carefully. With the new tax laws and with rent control looming in many areas, there are experts saying that residential real estate as a money maker is dead. But there are just as many experts saying that with the documented housing unit shortages in most parts of the country, with the increasing number of single-person households, and with lower interest rates or at least stable interest rates, apartment buildings are today's best bet for high-return investments. Who's right?

Actually, both, because the investment potential of apartment buildings is *local* and you cannot judge local investment potential by national standards or averages. In some places a small apartment house investment will bring in a higher return than anything else you might

INVESTOR DEMAND PROFILE

	1	2	3	4	5	6	7	8	9	10
1. Positive Action and Reaction										
2. Willingness to Take Risks										
3. Decision-making Ability										
4. Commitment—the Will to Follow Through										
5. Logical and Rational Evaluation of Options										
6. Ability to Deal with Numbers and Finances										
7. Ability to Deal with Legal Constraints										
8. Organization and Management Skills										
9. Foresight										
10. Imagination and Creativity										
11. Self-confidence										
12. Patience and Tact										
13. Self-control										
14. Social Contact										
15. Negotiating Skill										

choose; in others it will break even if you're lucky year after year until appreciation, caused by higher demand or some other factor, makes it profitable to sell. And *you*, the investor, must decide which conditions prevail in your area. Not an easy job and certainly not for someone without previous experience in the real estate marketplace.

In making the decision to choose or not to choose investment in small apartment buildings, ask yourself the following:

• What is the economic temper of the area? Most parts of the country are *not* overbuilt in residential units, but what about yours? Are major employers moving in or out? Is there a diversity of employers rather than a single giant? Is the population growing? Faster or slower than the national average? Are young people moving in or away?

• What are the current and projected housing needs of the community? Remember, rental housing is a *commodity*, its price is a function of supply and demand. Is there a current housing shortage? What is the apartment vacancy rate? Anything under 5 percent is a tight market that tends to force rents up, unless rent control is in effect. How much new construction is under way? Projected for the future? A tight market one year can sometimes stimulate overbuilding and a very loose market three years later. Sit in on a few planning board sessions in your town and get a feel for what's going on.

• What are transportation facilities and options in the area? Good transportation or improvement of transportation often precedes growth.

• What is the municipal tax rate? Is it low enough to attract business? Is there space for new businesses? Will good schools, recreational facilities, and other features attract prospective residents? Is police protection adequate?

• What, in fact, does a particular community have to offer that will attract new people? Would *you* choose to live there?

If, after working through all these test questions, you come up with an answer something like: *yes, there's a high demand for housing and a good economic base to support its continuance*, a small apartment building could very well be an excellent addition to your investment portfolio. Now, however, you must choose which one to buy, and that will call upon all the real estate experience you have. Let's go back to basics. Here's what to look for in a property:

Location

- Near public transportation
- Good residential area
- Marginal area with likelihood of a turnaround
- Parking available
- Desirable community near employment centers
- No threat of rent control

 Structure Maintenance

- Relatively new building in good condition
- Older building with major working systems (wiring, plumbing, roof, furnace, etc.) recently updated or certified by a professional inspection firm to be in good working order

$ *Management*

- Currently being well managed with a less than 5 percent vacancy rate. Talk with some of the tenants. What do they think of the way things are run?
- Sloppy record keeping and management but still a low vacancy rate and tenant satisfaction with the area. (This situation is easily redeemable by the new owner.)
- Marketing desirability is high. Buildings with a large number of efficiencies and one-bedroom units rent most quickly. The ratio of rent income to space being rented is also greater when a building contains a large number of smaller units.

ABILITY TO DEAL WITH NUMBERS AND FINANCES

In the good ol' days, many investors used the rule of thumb that the purchase price of a building should be approximately eight times the gross rental income. *Forget that rule.* Today's marketplace is far more complex. Investment success is not a matter of the ratio between purchase price and gross rent. In fact, gross rent should not be the factor of consideration in a purchase. Much, much more important is *net rental income.* You must ask yourself therefore *how does rental income compare with operating expenses?* And that's just step one.

Almost equally important is the debt structure of the purchase.

Before tax reform, rapid depreciation allowances and therefore excellent deductions could make a building a valuable investment asset even though it was in a state of constant negative cash flow. Many investors bought with little or no money down. They congratulated themselves on the leveraging that would bring fabulous profits upon sale with only a small amount of cash at risk; and they extolled the wonders of tax shelter. Today some of these same people are selling their buildings at prices below market value because their negative cash flow is cutting into, well, not the bread on their table, but certainly the number of evenings they're enjoying at the town's finer restaurants.

Debt on an investment *must be structured carefully*, for there is now no tax shelter to erase the pain of more money going out than coming in. This fact will undoubtedly mean that most real estate investment will be purchased with higher down payments: It will be necessary to invest more cash in order to bring about an acceptable cash flow.

Which of course brings up the question of *return* on that cash investment. A wise purchase is the result of careful calculation of the projected cash flow and the probable return upon sale. Some people rely on their own bookkeeping skills for these figures, with or without the help of a user-friendly computer. I urge you not to count yourself in this group. Before you sign a contract to buy, spend as much time as it takes going over all the figures you've gathered with a competent accountant or financial adviser. When a million dollars is a common price tag in the real estate marketplace, you're dealing with *big* numbers and those numbers stand for real dollars! You do *not* want to make a mistake. Professional assistance therefore is usually well worth its cost.

The numbers you'll want to gather to bring to your accountant are these:

- gross rental income
- other income, such as that from vending machines, laundry facilities, etc.
- management expenses, including advertising for new tenants
- maintenance expenses
- property taxes
- debt service cost, that is, the monthly payments you expect to make to the lender

- vacancy rate, current and projected
- nonpayment of rent and eviction cost losses

If you *must* have a rule-of-thumb number by which to gauge asking price against value, many investors use a capitalization rate approach. They usually take net income times ten, although some high-priced accountants are recommending that net income times nine works better with the new tax laws.

Let's stick to the ten figure for our example. Using capitalization rate method, if the net annual income of a property (that is, gross income minus operating expenses) is $100,000, the approximate worth of the building is $1,000,000. But please do not agree to pay $1,000,000 for a building because you read this rule of thumb. Remember, the value of your investment property is determined by a combination and interaction of factors. Study them. Rank their importance *to you*. Use professional help.

SELF-CONFIDENCE

Having just advised you to use an acountant to evaluate the return on your investment, I must now warn you that *no one*, not your accountant, not your lawyer, not your brother-in-law, will look after *your* money as carefully as you will (or should, anyway). The final word on your investment decision is yours, and you must have the confidence to follow your own judgment, after weighing and evaluating all the advice you can get.

In apartment house investing, however, there's a demand upon the investor's personality even beyond self-confidence. Self-confidence must stretch here into self-reliance, and sometimes even into stubborn perseverance.

What am I leading up to? A job that may sound simple until you try it: *getting the facts*.

Since negotiations on price for an apartment building are based upon rental income, expenses, and the condition and location of the building, some sellers try to highlight the entire picture with rosy tints and make getting accurate information very difficult. Some building owners, just prior to putting a property up for sale, will fill their apartment house's vacant units with friends and/or relatives who hand over the rent check each month and are handed back a like amount of cash or a week's supply of groceries. Some owners "forget" to list certain expenses, or they might make a "mistake" in an entry. And it's funny how that pile of boxes got put over the sump pumps in the cellar. Angry buyers will tell you of instances where rent rolls were knowingly falsified, or they'll tell you how they were shown five apartments, all in excellent condition, only to find, after ownership, that the other fifteen were in need of new everything.

Before you buy an apartment building, you have got to be sure you have accurate information on all aspects of that building. And "the books" the owner shows you may not be accurate. One way to be sure that expenses are not being minimized and rents maximized is to have your lawyer request copies of the seller's past two years' federal income tax returns pertaining to the ownership of the apartment building. No one wants to list more income than necessary on a tax return, and no one wants to claim expenses lower than they are.

Regarding the condition of the building: the seller may not be willing to show you every apartment while you're still in the considering or negotiating stage. That's okay. But don't accept, "Oh, Thelma's apartment is just like Birdie's downstairs." Include a clause in the contract stating that your purchase is subject to a professional inspection of the building and all units within the building. *Then go along with the inspector when he does the inspection.* There's nothing quite as good as a see-for-yourself evaluation.

RISK TAKING, COMMITMENT, AND FORESIGHT

Why only a 5 for the risk taker on this investment demand chart? From what I've said so far, one would think apartment houses are pretty risky business. In fact, it's common knowledge that most pension funds and trusts are *not* interested in investing their money in this vehicle. That's a sure sign of high risk, isn't it?

Not so. Pension funds and trusts avoid apartment house investment because this vehicle is too *management intensive*, which is a business jargon way of saying that positive returns are too dependent upon good and relatively constant management of the property.

And that's exactly why this vehicle gets a 10 in commitment and a 5 in risk taking. If you buy wisely and manage carefully, the risk of actually losing money on your investment is relatively small. There may indeed be some years of negative cash flow or a major expenditure which will generate a loss for a particular year, but the tax losses can be carried forward to be used against profitable years or against the reported profit upon sale of the property. Careful selection of property, good debt structure, and a commitment to good management will keep loss years to a minimum and will weigh the odds heavily in favor of your apartment building being a real money maker.

There are no sure things, however, so you must be aware of the risks that be. In small apartment building ownership watch out for these:

- local economic depression because a major employer leaves the area or a major industry undergoes cutbacks
- rent controls
- municipal problems such as high crime, poor schools, overcrowding, or government corruption and high taxes, which create an undesirable image for the community
- overbuilding of similar residential rental real estate or condominiums
- poor management

Of these, poor management can be corrected by you, the new owner. All the others can usually be anticipated long before they happen, *if you know your local area well*. Foresight therefore gets only a 5 on the investment demand chart.

There are three ways to manage a building. You can live in one of the units yourself and oversee everything. You can hire a live-in superintendent. Or you can hire a management company. A few, determined-to-save-money owners try to manage their buildings in absentia without any supervision on the premises. With frequent visits this can work for two- to six-family houses, but once you get over six units and into the apartment house category, it usually costs more than it saves.

Of the usual management methods, the owner live-in is least expensive but most time consuming. Commitment here requires a 10 + (along with patience and tact high up on the scale), for you'll not only hear about every dripping faucet but also about the skateboard left in the hallway and the late-night party with the loud stereo. And, worse yet, you'll be expected to *do something*, and immediately, since you are, after all, the owner.

If you hire a live-in super but handle most of the management decisions yourself (choosing tenants, selecting when to do repair work, paying the bills, etc.), you'll be ridding yourself of some headaches but still holding close control of your investment. This method cuts down tremendously on your personal time commitment but it does, of course, increase operating costs slightly.

Hiring a professional management company to act as your agent is the least time consuming but most expensive management method. Control is the issue here. Keeping in touch with your building may require more self-discipline than you think, but it's essential not only to assure good maintenance and management but also to qualify you for the $25,000 federal allowance for tax loss against ordinary income if your adjusted gross income is less than $100,000 a year. If you're within the income guideline, you can qualify for this deduction if you "actively" manage your property. The government will allow you to call yourself an active manager while using a management company or management agent if *you* set the rent, approve new tenants, decide upon or approve major expenditures for repairs or renovation, and so on. In other words, if you stay in control.

Organization and Management Skills

"I don't need to read this," you're thinking. "I've already decided on option three, hiring a management company."

Well, you're wrong. *Even* if you hire a management company, you need management skills to run an apartment building successfully. The management company is simply your agent. If your attitude toward the property is uncaring and disorganized, it leaves space for disorganized and uncaring management, which is a sure-fire way to lose money. You, as the building owner, should have an organized schedule for checking through management reports, auditing income and expenditure figures, and visiting the building. You should also present the management company with a list of house rules and policies to be enforced.

If you choose hands-on management, time spent in the set-up process for an organized management approach to your building will be returned a hundredfold in time saved when problems are anticipated and solutions are therefore at hand. People in general, not just tenants, get frustrated when they don't know what to do in a given situation, and frustration is a first cousin to anger. You can avoid many problems by providing your tenants with a well written handbook spelling out house rules, what-to-do-ifs, what-will-happen-ifs (like if you don't pay your rent), and listing some community and building resources (baby sitters, for example). You can also avoid problems by giving your super explicit directions regarding his duties and providing blank forms for keeping written records of all necessary items.

And, of course, *you* must be available. Everything goes downhill when a manager doesn't have time to manage, which, first of all, means time to listen. *Listen* when someone from your apartment house calls you!

POSITIVE ACTION

Once you set your building in order, you must be willing to keep a finger on its pulse. If that pulse becomes erratic, the successful investor cannot pull his hair and cry, "Woe is me!" Something must be done, and, believe me, when something must be done all heads turn toward the person who *owns* the building. You are then indeed the *landlord*, a designation that carries not only rights but also responsibilities.

You can work with your tenants or you can fight against them, but you cannot sit back and "see what happens." Apartment building ownership requires an active, positive, it-can-be-done outlook.

DECISION MAKING

Of course, the major decision is to buy or not to buy. Once the decision to buy is made, however, it gives birth to litter after litter of little decisions. When to raise rents; when to do repairs; choosing a super; do I give this out-of-work tenant an extra month, she *is* trying to find work; do I allow a sublet for six months? Apartment building ownership means questions, sometimes quandaries. If you're not prepared to make decisions and set out policies and then stick to them, you'd best try another investment vehicle. Condos aren't bad; there the board of directors runs the place. But remember, you don't have as much control, and in the real estate marketplace control is often a key element of success.

IMAGINATION AND CREATIVITY

The business of apartment building ownership doesn't call upon human creativity very heavily. Yes, you can enhance appearance with a little paint and decorating, but unless your plans include a renovation or restoration, you should keep the changes simple. Clean and comfortable are your watchwords for most apartment buildings.

PATIENCE, TACT, SELF-CONTROL, AND NEGOTIATING SKILL

You will certainly call upon these social graces while you're in the apartment building buying process, but you will not get to know your skills and limitations in each of them until you take on the role of apartment building owner.

Think about it. Your building affects two aspects of the lives of its tenants: *home* and *money*. Exempting *love*, are there any two issues more emotional and provocative? To this explosive mixture, add the element of living in close proximity with a diverse group of individuals. It's no wonder residential real estate management is as much a people management business as a building and financial management business.

I don't mean to imply that you, as owner, should settle every squabble between your tenants. But I do want to warn you that you will be called upon to handle problems with a good degree of tact, patience, and even some negotiating skill. Tenants are active and savvy people nowadays. You may discover yourself in contention with a well organized tenants' rights group.

Before you respond in anger or call in your lawyers, try listening to their problems. Try a little role playing—how would you feel in their shoes? And try to let them see the situation from *your* shoes.

Some building owners attempt to protect themselves from this kind of "bother" by using a corporate holding company and remaining invisible behind its shield. What happens? Tenant dissatisfaction builds with no vent. There's usually a high turnover rate, which, by the way, adds significantly to operating costs. Graffiti, vandalism, complaints to the municipal housing board, complaints to the board of health, complaints to the police, nonpayment of rents—the resulting problems list goes on and on. Better to listen and attempt to come to some fair compromise.

LEGAL CONSTRAINTS

They exist, and on every level: federal, state, and local. So *Be Prepared*, as the Boy Scout motto goes, know the laws and stay within their limits. Also *be aware* of how much compliance will cost you in dollars spent on both paperwork and physical improvements.

On the federal level: The Fair Housing Act (Title VIII of the 1968 Civil Rights Act) prohibits discrimination in housing on the basis of race, sex, religion, or national origin. When you choose among tenant applicants, you must therefore substantiate your decision on a basis other than the above factors: income qualification will do, or employment stability, but you must apply the same criteria to all applicants equally.

On the state level: Many states have fair housing legislation of their own which supplements but does not override federal law. Among the discrimination factors prohibited by some states in addition to those named by the federal law are *age, marital status, the presence of children in the family, the receipt of welfare aid payments, income dependency upon child support payments from a divorced spouse, color, and mental or physical handicap.*

You will need to check with your own state's office of landlord/tenant affairs (or whatever the department is called in your area) to obtain information on its specific legislation regarding fair housing practices. If you have trouble finding the name of the bureau that has jurisdiction over rental policies, call your state attorney general's office and ask for information and direction.

Often getting rid of undesirable tenants is more difficult than choosing good ones. Evictions are handled by specified local jurisdictions in each state, *but* the procedures for eviction are usually set out in state law. Again, check with your attorney general's office for information regarding eviction procedures.

On the local level: Fair housing laws have also been enacted by county and municipal governments. Among local issues are sexual preference (gay rights legislation) and rent control rules that allow or disallow apartment leases to be shared by move-in relatives.

Local jurisdictions also control minimal housing standards (health and safety rules), housing inspections, and evictions.

Currently, rent control legislation must be state-approved in eleven states. Twenty-five other states now have municipalities where local rent control laws are in effect or being considered.

SOCIAL CONTACT

As a landlord facing tenant complaints or problems month after month, you may get to feeling a bit lonely occasionally, something like the lone knight in a tournament where new opponents just keep coming. Fortunately, however, you're landlording in the late twentieth century, the age of networking.

Many communities, sometimes even neighborhoods, have apartment owners' groups. These can be helpful, especially to a beginner trying to solve recurring problems for the first time. Seek out whatever groups there are and talk with the members. Join if you feel compatible.

Many larger cities and metropolitan areas also have Community Housing Resource Boards (CHRBs), called "cherubs," like the angels. These are private, nonprofit corporations comprised of members from the community and members from local government agencies interested in fair housing. Among the ten to twenty or so participants in a CHRB organization you might find a Realtor, a designated representative from the local apartment owners' association, a member of the municipal planning board, a buildings inspector, a representative from the community's ministries, and a representative from fair housing groups. Many CHRBs are funded, at least in part, by grants from HUD.

Hot local issues and tenant grievances can often be discussed and resolved by the local CHRB without going to court. Find out about your local group, what it does, and the predominant bias of its rulings.

On the national level, owners of small apartment buildings might consider joining the National Apartment Association, 1111 Fourteenth Street N.W., Suite 900, Washington, D.C., 20005. This active group is made up of owners and developers of residential rental properties. Among its functions are the support of a professional lobby in Congress and numerous educational seminars and conventions held in various locations across the nation.

TOOLS OF THE TRADE

Many investors who buy one small apartment building go on to own two, three, six, or even dozens. Which means that despite all the problems and demands of this investment vehicle, it must work pretty well, or why would these people stay in and expand? Why? Because becoming a millionaire is a common occurrence in this marketplace. Let's look at how it's done.

WAITING TIME

Before the Tax Reform Act of 1986, both individual investors and groups (primarily syndicates) bought apartment buildings as tax shelters. On the day they closed on their purchases, they were planning to sell in seven years or so, just about the time that their tax shelter benefits became significantly diminished. The old tax law therefore stimulated relatively frequent turnover activity.

That's over. The rush of sales activity in late 1986 and early 1987 was stimulated by highly leveraged tax shelter owners who could not afford the negative cash flow they had structured into their purchases without the tax write-offs of the old law. Many of these properties were sold and are still being sold at bargain prices.

"But how long after the day of purchase must an investor wait to cash in one of these bargains?" you ask.

That depends. It depends on your investment goals and the debt structure of your purchase. Purchases structured to produce good positive cash flow will probably be held *longer* than the old seven-year maximum since there is now no tax incentive to sell a money maker.

Purchases recognized as bargain properties—properties that are being sold at below-market prices because of excessive leveraging, negative cash flow, and a glut of such buildings being dumped into the marketplace within a relatively short period of time—might well have a *shorter* waiting time than the old seven-year period. How much shorter? Well, the speculating investor who can structure a purchase so that it will produce a small positive cash flow or a negative cash flow that he can afford to carry for a while might figure that three or four years will be sufficient for the turmoil generated by tax reform to subside and realistic market appreciation to reestablish itself. In a good building and a good market, a 50 percent increase in value over five years is a conservative estimate. The investor not particularly interested in long-term monthly income would probably be inclined to take the money and run at that point.

WORKING TIME

As I've already mentioned under Risk Taking, Commitment, and Foresight, how much of your time your apartment house demands will depend on the management style you choose. Apartment houses can be a source of extra money at which you work nights and weekends, if at all, or they can become your full-time job and primary source of income. The choice is yours.

· · ·

START-UP CASH AND CASH FLOW

Can you buy a place with nothing down? Yes. Would you want to? I doubt it.

In the past, apartment houses were financed with multiple mortgages and often heavy seller financing. Tax shelter, not positive cash flow, was the primary objective. Today, you've got to be more careful if you want to survive financially. *More careful* usually means a bigger down payment, which in turn means carrying a smaller debt.

CHECKLIST FOR APARTMENT BUILDINGS

Before you buy, get accurate information about all of these:

rent roll
local property taxes
water, sewer, and utility costs
maintenance and repair costs
management expenses
cost of adequate insurance coverage
income from vending machines or other sources
expected vacancy rate
grounds maintenance costs (including swimming pool, playgrounds, etc.)
probable amount of mortgage needed
interest rate and probable debt service costs
condition of the building:
   Check:
   roof
   elevators and stairwells
   basement
   individual units
   smoke alarms and sprinkler system
   locks, video monitors, and other security systems
   window guards and windows
   building frame and exterior
   parking area pavement
   working systems (heating plant, plumbing, electrical, air conditioning)

Does that mean that leveraging is dead? Not at all. Leveraging, the ability to buy a building with less than its full purchase price in cash down and thus bring about a higher rate of return on investment capital upon sale, was and still is a primary factor in the outstanding performance of real estate as an investment. Just think through this oversimplification: You buy a $100,000 building with a $20,000 down payment. In five years you sell the building for $200,000. You've doubled your money, right? No. You have changed your $20,000 into $200,000. That's ten times your invested capital—the leveraging principle at work.

But you realize, of course, that these numbers are not real. You must factor in interest on the debt, income from the property, operating expenses, and taxes. And that's where *nothing down* goes out the window.

First of all a building's negative cash flow and paper losses can no longer be deducted from your ordinary income. And second, too much debt at too high an interest rate can put you into a negative leverage situation.

Negative leverage usually occurs in times of high mortgage interest rates, low rate of inflation, and small down payment requirements. You have negatively leveraged a property if the interest you paid out while owning it exceeds the appreciated value when you sell. You have then, in fact, *lost money* by borrowing.

In today's marketplace, you want to avoid negative leveraging and you also want to avoid positive leveraging that causes heavy negative cash flow. You must, therefore, carefully calculate the cost of your debt on the property. Ideally your annual total mortgage payments should be less than the gross income minus all operating expenses (i.e., the net income). Look at these numbers as an example:

INCOME FROM PROPERTY:	$500,000	The total of 12 months'
OPERATING EXPENSES:	200,000	mortgage payments is
NET INCOME:	$300,000	$280,000.

An investment debt structured this way would give you a positive cash flow of $20,000, which depreciation allowances might just wipe out for tax purposes.

Now $20,000 in positive cash flow is operating on the proverbial

shoestring. Think what the cost of a new elevator might be. (A refinancing job for sure!) Or, more likely, think how a higher than anticipated vacancy rate or a bad debt loss on an eviction or two could cut
into your shoestring of a positive cash flow. And how about putting a
little aside as a contingency fund? Or putting in that improvement
you've been postponing?

Yet this kind of shoestring is exactly the way even careful investors
usually start out in today's marketplace. As the years pass and rents
go up, the positive cash flow increases. And if, as every investor hopes,
appreciation occurs at a higher rate than inflation, your down payment
is indeed positively leveraged. You then are on your way to your first
million.

TAXES

Let's review the key points again.

- All income is taxed as ordinary income; there's no longer any special
  treatment for capital gains.
- The depreciation period for residential real estate is 27½ years.
- All rental real estate is treated as "passive activity," which means
  that losses generated by it cannot be deducted against earned income.
- Nondeductible losses can be carried forward, however, to be used
  against passive income in another year or profit upon sale.
- There is an allowable loss deduction of up to $25,000 for investors
  who *actively* manage their real estate and whose adjusted gross
  income is less than $100,000.
- For every dollar an investor makes over $100,000, fifty cents is
  deducted from the allowed $25,000 maximum loss deduction. At an
  adjusted gross income of $150,000, the loss allowance reaches zero.
- Interest paid on mortgages on rental property is deductible against
  the income from the property but not against your ordinary earned
  income or your portfolio income.
- Loss deductions on investments held prior to October 22, 1986 (the
  date the new tax law was signed by President Reagan), are to be
  phased in over four years in order to bring them into line with the
  treatment accorded to investments purchased after that date. The
  phase-in reads as follows:

Tax year	Percentage of passive losses deductible against ordinary income
1986	100
1987	65
1988	40
1989	20
1990	10
1991	0

• Loss generated by one passive investment (a recently purchased apartment house, let's say) can be deducted against profit from another passive investment (a condominium apartment purchased ten years ago, for example, or your interest in your brother's shoe repair business in which you do not actively participate).

• Suspended losses that are carried forward year after year will be allowed first against the net income from the sale of that investment, then against the net income from the sale of other passive investments, and finally against income from other passive sources.

All of these new provisions require careful record keeping and a good calculator. Some professional investors and entrepreneurs have renamed the Tax Reform Act of 1986 the Accountants and Lawyers Support Bill. Need I say more?

EXPECTED RETURN

In recent years the Consumer Price Index for residential rents has increased about 50 percent faster than the Consumer Price Index for all items. Since the value of apartment buildings ultimately depends on the rental income they can generate, this fact should help to support and even increase the appreciation rate of residential buildings in areas that are not grossly overbuilt or under rent control legislation.

Many experts are predicting a dip in the price of buildings during the period that overleveraged investors dump their properties on the market and then a sharp rise in prices as the continuing short fall (in most areas) of new residential rental construction in relation to housing need pushes rents higher.

$ To translate: in most areas of the country, this is an excellent time to buy the right building at the right price with the right debt structure.

KNOWLEDGE AND SKILLS

The most important knowledge you can bring to an apartment house purchase is an intimate familiarity with the local area, its demographics, its politics, and its economics.

The most important single skill necessary for success in this investment vehicle is careful, accurate, and comprehensive record keeping.

INVESTOR GROUPS

Since debt structure has become significantly more important in the viability of apartment house purchases, many investors will find themselves cash short when all other indicators say *go* on a prospective deal. The obvious answer to such a problem is to pool available cash with friends and relatives. You can form an ordinary partnership or you can form a limited partnership with yourself as the general partner (read the next chapter). In both cases your profits will be diminished somewhat by being shared, but you *will* have a chance at those profits.

SOME SUCCESSFUL INVESTORS

EXPERIENCED AMATEURS

Tim and Edna Halloran, this chapter's profile couple, did buy a small apartment building. It consisted of twenty-two units, was fifteen years old, and carried a price tag of $1,300,000. They negotiated down to $1,000,000.

The couple put down $250,000 and took out a $750,000 mortgage with a twenty-five-year term and an interst rate of 8.75 percent. The average monthly rent was $550 per unit. That's $550 × 22 = $12,100 a month multiplied by twelve months = $145,200 a year gross income. Operating expenses for the building were $50,000 in the first year;

interest and principal payments on the mortgage were $75,000. There-fore, approximate figures were:

Total income	$145,200
Total expenditures	125,000
Positive cash flow	$ 20,200.

The Hallorans' $20,200 positive cash flow represents a pretax return on their investment of 8 percent. Not bad, but the news is even better when you take depreciation into account, and the punchline is still to come. After 4½ years of ownership, the Hallorans sold the apartment house for $2,300,000! They were out looking to buy two more before the check even hit the bank.

PROFESSIONAL MANAGERS

Kenneth Pettigrew specializes in turnarounds. Like a lifeguard in a coastal patrol boat, he searches the waters for people (or perhaps buildings) in trouble and he pulls them out.

When Pettigrew hears that a building owner is losing money or having tenant and vacancy problems, he studies the financial facts and the location of the building. If both are to his liking, he makes the owner a below-market offer. About two-thirds of the time, he makes a deal.

Then Pettigrew and company move in. They improve the exterior appearance and the landscaping, paint interior hallways and staircases, fix everything that's broken, and *raise the rents*. The written notifi-cations of the rent hikes are always accompanied by an announcement of new management (with the names and contact phone numbers listed) and a handbook for the tenants which lists the new rules and states that they will be strictly enforced. Some tenants always move out at this point, which pleases Pettigrew because he redecorates their apart-ments and rents them for even higher figures. His goal is always to improve the image of the building and attract the finest tenants.

Pettigrew's median holding time for an apartment building is four years and two months. His median net profit is $980,000.

Besides the apartment buildings that he buys and sells, Pettigrew owns a condo on St. Croix, a house on Hilton Head, another house in La Jolla, California, and a ski chateau in Utah. And, by the way, he dropped out of high school in his senior year.

MOVING ON

Most investors who are successful with one small apartment building buy another and another, often each being larger than the last. Some go on to become syndicators, others move into investment in commercial real estate. But still others pull back to focus their investing on handyman specials, multifamily houses, or condominiums.

In truth, small apartment building investment is the connecting link between part-time investment for a little extra income and full-time investment as primary income. It's the crossover vehicle between the marketplace of the amateur and the marketplace of the professional.

· CHAPTER 10 ·

The Friends-Only Syndicate

Since her children went off to college, Margaret Ruby has become something of a real estate whiz kid. In three years she's bought and sold seven pieces of property very profitably. Now something even bigger has caught her eye, a 200-unit garden apartment complex, poorly managed but ripe for a turnaround. All her available cash, however, is tied up in another apartment building she recently acquired. She wants therefore to start a privately organized limited partnership to raise the cash she needs in order to structure the garden apartment deal so as to bring in a positive cash flow within two years. And Margaret Ruby wants to be the general partner. Her investment vehicle of choice is a friends-only syndicate.

· · ·

If someone says *syndicate*, do you think of limited partnerships in which multimillionaires shelter their income by investing in overpriced Caribbean hotels or perhaps Arabian stallions? That's the way it *used* to be. Today it's a brave new world after tax reform, but a new world in which the savvy, creative investor can still use this well-established investment form to put together deals that will produce honest income and very sizable profits upon sale.

"Wait a minute!" you cry. "Did you say *limited partnerships?* Those things have to be registered with the Securities and Exchange Commission and there's all kinds of state laws and regulatory commissions in on the act, too. This is a big-bucks ship in legal rough water. Definitely not for me."

Don't close the book, please. There's a big difference between a public limited partnership and a private limited partnership, and beyond that there's still another fine line between the small group, private limited partnership composed strictly of friends, relatives, and acquaintances and the one offered only to accredited investors with or without a relationship other than their investment interest. In this chapter, I'm talking about the "friendly group" out to buy something together. In most cases, neither the state nor the federal government will create undue restrictions on or expenses for such a business arrangement.

If you have had some successful experience buying and selling real property during the past several years, read the demands of this investment vehicle carefully. It might provide the opportunity for a one-time shot at a particularly profitable piece of real estate that you otherwise could not afford to buy, or it might be the first step to a new full-time career.

CHECKPOINTS FOR THE INVESTOR

LEGAL CONSTRAINTS

The governing statute for limited partnerships is the Uniform Limited Partnership Act of 1916, which was revised in 1976. The problem, however, is that it is not uniform in every state. Some states still subscribe to the original act of 1916 without the revision, others have accepted the revisions and/or added revisions of their own.

Generally, a limited partnership consists of one or more general partners who are responsible for complete control and management of all aspects of the business. Theoretically there can be any number of limited partners who have no share or say in management and control. The number of limited partners, however, *is* a factor in determining whether a particular limited partnership is regarded as a public or a private limited partnership. (More about this in just a bit.)

The general partners can bind the partnership to responsibilities and

INVESTOR DEMAND PROFILE

	1	2	3	4	5	6	7	8	9	10
1. Positive Action and Reaction										
2. Willingness to Take Risks										
3. Decision-making Ability										
4. Commitment—the Will to Follow Through										
5. Logical and Rational Evaluation of Options										
6. Ability to Deal with Numbers and Finances										
7. Ability to Deal with Legal Constraints										
8. Organization and Management Skills										
9. Foresight										
10. Imagination and Creativity										
11. Self-confidence										
12. Patience and Tact										
13. Self-control										
14. Social Contact										
15. Negotiating Skill										

are personally liable for the partnership obligations. The limited partners have no financial responsibility beyond their capital investment— the amount of money they put in.

"Sounds pretty much like a corporation to me," you say. "Why not just call it a corporation?"

Because it's not a corporation, it's a *partnership*, and that's very important to you, financially.

Limited partnerships have become the most common form of group real estate investment in the country because they have special tax advantages even in this age after tax reform. Corporations are currently taxed at higher rates than individuals. The corporation pays this higher tax rate on its earnings, then it distributes dividends to its shareholders. If you invest in a corporation, therefore, you experience double taxation, once at the corporate rate and then again at your individual rate on the dividends you receive.

The partnership escapes this double taxation. In the eyes of the IRS it is a nontaxable "ghost," and its earnings and losses are passed through to its partners. This structure therefore works well both for a knowledgeable, experienced real estate investor who wants to raise capital by taking in limited partners and for the limited partners who either do not wish to participate in the management of property or simply do not have the time available to do so. So how does someone like Margaret Ruby go about starting one?

The Uniform Limited Partnership Act requires that a new limited partnership make a public filing of a certificate of limited partnership that sets forth its name, the character, location, and term of its business enterprise, and the names of capital contributors and the profit share of the partners.

Now this doesn't sound too complicated, does it? It isn't, except for one small hitch. The specific procedure and the filing place is different from state to state. To establish your friendly limited partnership, you *must* employ the services of a local attorney. And be sure to choose one who knows something about limited partnerships. Your cousin-in-law who specializes in divorce cases might just lose you more money than he saves.

Perhaps you're feeling a bit incredulous just now. You're sure it couldn't be that easy. You *know* you've heard about SEC registration and state regulations.

They exist, but not for everyone. Starting a limited partnership is just about as easy as registering if:

HOW NOT TO BE A CORPORATION

If the IRS decides that your limited partnership is really a corporation, you'll lose the partnership pass-through benefits. If the issue comes up, the government will test your organization against four corporate characteristics. To be considered a partnership, no more than *two* can apply to your syndicate. Let's look at them.

CENTRALIZATION OF MANAGEMENT

Since the general partner or partners take complete control of management and the limited partners have no say or responsibility, virtually all limited partnerships have this corporate characteristic.

LIMITED LIABILITY

If a corporation loses a million dollars and declares bankruptcy, each stockholder loses only the purchase price he or she paid for the shares. Here again the limited partnership structure conforms to that of the corporation. The limited partners are liable only to the extent of the value of their share holdings.

CONTINUITY

A corporation exists forever. The death of a major shareholder or of the chief executive officer may cause a ripple or two, but the corporation goes on. To differentiate itself from a corportion, a limited partnership should provide that the partnership is dissolved upon the death, insanity, or withdrawal of any one of the general partners. Most limited partnership agreements, however, also provide for the ability to reorganize and reform the limited partnership once a departing general partner leaves.

TRANSFERABILITY OF INTEREST

In a corporation, you can elect to sell your interest (shares) at will. To distinguish itself from a corporation, a limited partnership will usually require that share interests cannot be transferred except back to the general partners or with the general partners' permission.

•   •   •

- you limit your offering to a small group of relatives, friends, and associates,
- you do business in the same state as the property you intend to buy,
- you make your offering of limited partnership shares only to residents of the state where you do business and the property is located,
- you do not advertise your offering publicly,
- you comply with the laws of your state concerning fraud and equity.

"Still sounds too good to be true," you say. "Where do the SEC and state laws come in?"

The Securities and Exchange Commission gets its jurisdiction from interstate commerce as set out in the Securities and Exchange Act of 1933. If you cross a state line in making your limited partnership offering, the SEC can step in on the basis of your selling securities interstate. As a "friendly syndicator" you will want to avoid the necessity of registering with the SEC since the procedure is complicated, time consuming, and expensive—$50,000 would be a conservative estimate.

In addition to the registration requirements of the SEC, some states have so-called blue sky laws which get their authority from state police powers and are designed to protect investors by requiring registration and disclosure of certain information in a certain format. These laws are nonexistent in some states and rather stringent in others. Among the states with extensive state regulations regarding limited partnerships are California, Illinois, New York, Ohio, and Texas. It's essential that you use a local attorney since laws and procedures are not uniform across the nation.

Generally, however, you can avoid blue sky regulation if you keep the number of investors in your private limited partnership under thirty-five. You should also be certain that you can show some prior relationship among the investors, one to another (friends and friends-of-friends is acceptable, so is offering to all members of a club, church, or synagogue). In addition, you should offer limited partnership shares for sale on a one-to-one basis, or at most in a group small enough to fit into someone's living room.

There are some SEC guidelines for expanding your group beyond thirty-five investors if all those who increase the number beyond thirty-five are "accredited investors." According to the SEC, an accredited investor is one who has a net worth of $1,000,000 or more, who has a yearly income of at least $200,000, and who's purchasing a syndication unit of $150,000 or more. (These are rare birds in most social circles, so you might just as well focus on the number thirty-five.)

Above all, remember that although you can avoid SEC regulations and "blue sky" regulations, you cannot avoid the local court system and its laws concerning fraud and equity. Be open and honest about your offering. Make your figures and projections as accurate as possible and disclose every pertinent fact to every member of your investor group. *And use a local attorney.*

POSITIVE ACTION

Okay, a limited partnership can be formed with minimal expense and some help from a local lawyer. But what good is that to Margaret Ruby? *All* her spare cash is tied up in that new apartment building she just bought.

The most exciting thing about becoming a syndicator is that *you don't need any cash*. Or not much, anyway. What you need is expertise, experience, a good track record, and the ability to inspire the confidence of others. Here's how it works.

Because it's overleveraged and poorly managed, the apartment complex that interests Margaret Ruby can be purchased for $1,000,000. After doing some careful calculations, she estimates that she can turn the complex into a positive cash flow investment within two years while carrying a mortgage of $500,000. She therefore needs $500,000 cash down payment plus closing costs.

Margaret decides to sell thirty limited partnership shares at $20,000 each, which will bring in $600,000. She will use the extra $100,000 for closing costs and renovation.

You nod. "Yes, she can buy that way. But what's in it for her?"

The general partner, in return for expertise and the responsibility of running the limited partnership, gets either an up-front fee and a portion of the operating income (called a free lease) or, as in the case of Margaret Ruby, a share in the ownership of the property (called a free piece). Or both.

Although Margaret Ruby has accepted capital from thirty investors, she will structure the limited partnership with thirty-five shares. She, the general partner, will hold five shares. In other words, her expertise in finding this property and creating and managing the limited partnership will be worth the equivalent of an investment of $100,000.

When the profits or paper losses are divided, each limited partner will receive $\frac{1}{35}$ share while Margaret Ruby will receive $\frac{5}{35}$.

But what if the losses are not paper? What if the complex needs more cash to survive during the turnaround? Margaret Ruby can take out a second mortgage. She can ask for an additional cash contribution from each limited partner. Or she can loan the partnership some of her own money.

What a way to make money! Is that what you're thinking? *A $100,000 share for free! It's hard to believe.*

Believe it. These figures are relatively conservative. Some syndicators have made many times this share.

RISK TAKING

"Well, she deserves that money," some readers will say. "Look at the risk she's taking. If the complex goes under, she is *personally liable* for half a million dollars, and that's just the mortgage. She's liable for repair bills, and management costs, too. She could lose everything she's worked so hard to build up."

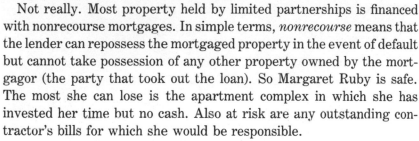

Not really. Most property held by limited partnerships is financed with nonrecourse mortgages. In simple terms, *nonrecourse* means that the lender can repossess the mortgaged property in the event of default but cannot take possession of any other property owned by the mortgagor (the party that took out the loan). So Margaret Ruby is safe. The most she can lose is the apartment complex in which she has invested her time but no cash. Also at risk are any outstanding contractor's bills for which she would be responsible.

COMMITMENT

Now consider this risk taking from the shoes of a limited partner. It's a bit frightening, isn't it? *The general partner has nothing to lose.* But she does. Think about:

* Her time. If the building complex goes under, her $100,000 worth of shares is worth nothing. And she has therefore worked for nothing.
* Her potential profit. If she succeeds in doing a profitable turnaround, she has one-seventh of the profits coming to her.
* Her reputation. The ability of a syndicator to raise money is de-

pendent upon that person's track record. The more successes, the more people willing to trust the syndicator with their money in another venture, and another. One major failure, one instance of walking away, however, and the syndicator's career sinks as fast and as permanently as the *Titanic*.

NUMBERS AND FINANCES

It's the numbers that scare off most people from the syndicator's marketplace. The dollar signs all seem to have too many zeros after them and there are so many other long numbers with both plus and minus signs thrown in. And then there's the people. When you're the general partner of an investment property and you have thirty-five investors, two hundred tenants, the buildings inspector, the super, the neighbors, the local CHRB (Community Housing Resource Board), and the community board of health to answer to (not to mention your Uncle Sam), you must keep records. (More numbers!) You must also publish the results of your record keeping for your limited partners.

 My advice to the numbers dilemma: Hire a good property manager or property management firm and a good accountant. By the time you're far enough into real estate investment to become a syndicator, you simply will not have enough time to do these chores yourself. You *must* delegate them to others, competent and trustworthy others.

ORGANIZATION AND MANAGEMENT SKILLS

Delegating does not mean giving up responsibility, however. The efficiency and productivity of your manager or management company will very much depend upon your input. If you wish to improve management, *you* will have to formulate the new guidelines under which you want the management company to work. You might well create a complete set of written forms for their use, for example. Think about:

- Application forms for prospective tenants. What specific information do you want? What factors, in your experience, indicate prospective "good" tenants?
- A welcome booklet for tenants that sets out rules and procedures for the use of the property, the parking lots, the shared space and

recreation facilities, and also provides information on community resources and where to complain if such-and-such happens.

- Entering and vacating inspection reports that tenants will fill out upon taking possession and (with the super present) upon vacating the property.

- A management agreement between you, the general partner, and the manager or management company you hire. Responsibilities should be listed. Salary or fees should be specified.

- An "under new management" letter to be sent to the tenants in residence when you take possession. This should include the name of the manager or management company, the name of the super, the name which the rent checks are to be made out to, where to mail or deliver rent checks, and an emergency telephone number.

- Forms for maintenance requests by tenants. Forms for tenant complaints.

- Agreement forms for contractors who will be doing work on the property. Be certain they have adequate insurance coverage.

- Forms for prioritizing work in and around the property. Large investment properties cannot be effectively managed on a crisis-response basis.

- A budget.

- Forms upon which the management company will report monthly activity (financial and otherwise) to you.

- Form letters for a rent increase, overdue rent, a management complaint to a tenant, lease expiration, guidelines for returning a security deposit.

DECISION-MAKING ABILITY

You may hire the finest management company in town and provide them with a complete set of working guidelines, but the decision making associated with your investment will still rest with you, the general partner.

- You will decide which renovations will be done when.
- You will decide if and when to raise rents.
- You will decide to evict a tenant.
- You will decide if the management company is doing its job.
- You will decide when to sell the property and for how much. (Unless

a specific time of sale is indicated in the limited partnership agreement.)

The limited partners will decide nothing.

But what about the limited partner (there's one in every group) who calls you once or twice a week to make "suggestions"? "I was in the building yesterday and I noticed a crack in the plaster in the ceiling of the hallway of the second floor. Don't you think we should have that repaired? We don't want a suit if the plaster falls, you know." And then the following week: "I was by the complex and noticed that the swimming pool looked awfully cloudy. Don't you think we should add a little more purification chemical or something?" Or simply, "Why haven't you . . ."

The solution to this headache is an easy one. Simply remind this zealous investor that he or she is a *limited* partner who is not allowed by law to participate in managing the investment. And then mention casually that if a limited partner does partake in management of the investment property, the law states that he or she gives up the limited liability of a limited partner and becomes personally liable for the partnership debts.

It will be a rare limited partner who will call you after that little conversation.

RATIONAL EVALUATION AND FORESIGHT

When you become a syndicator, you're acting not only for yourself but also for others. In a sense you take on a fiduciary role: you are the trustee of your limited partners' money. You therefore have a responsibility to choose investment property that will appreciate and prove profitable to all. So how do you do that?

Again, it's easier than you might think. There are only a few basic guidelines:

- Do not attempt to become a syndicator until you have had considerable experience and success in the real estate marketplace.
- Work locally, where you know not only the geographic area but also its economics, demographics, and politics.
- Use only investment vehicles with which you are thoroughly familiar and in which you have had extensive experience. For example, don't

try to syndicate a land development investment if your success has been in apartment houses. And don't try to syndicate an apartment house complex if your experience has been in handyman specials. Without expertise in the vehicle that you're syndicating, you could lose your shirt. And your reputation.

• Apply all the standard evaluation guidelines to your limited partnership property that you would apply to a purchase for yourself alone.

• Hire the best professionals available—lawyers, accountants, residential management companies, surveyors, engineers, whatever it takes.

• Be absolutely honest in selling your limited partnership shares. Don't overinflate expectations.

• Structure financing very carefully. The new tax laws do *not* encourage maximum leveraging. It will probably be necessary for you to raise more capital and finance less of the purchase price. This may mean taking in more investors and splitting the profits further than you'd like, but do so if you must. It is important that cash flow from your investment be positive or have the potential of becoming positive within a year or two.

CREATIVITY

"A rating of ten in creativity? A *ten* for putting together a group to buy a piece of real estate! How can that be?" you ask. "Deal making is about as creative as selling vacuum cleaners door to door."

I disagree when the "deal" is a limited partnership. Creativity is the making of something where there was nothing. It takes a creative eye and a creative mind to identify an appropriate piece of real estate, to gather the investors, and to structure the debt and cash flow. The creativity of the syndicator shapes and forms the syndicate. In fact, some syndicators get too creative. The biggest tax avoidance schemes of the early '80s were the product of the creative efforts of syndicators, lawyers, and tax accountants.

Beyond creating the limited partnership itself, syndicating calls upon yet another aspect of human creativity. Not the creativity of the poet, painter, or musician, but the creativity of the actor. Much of the syndicate's success depends upon the general partner's "stage presence": his or her ability to present the property and its potential to a prospective investor clearly and completely and, at the same time, to inspire confidence and credibility.

Creativity gets a 10 not only because it's the force that brings the syndicate into being but also because the inability to project oneself as a dependable, money-making agent for an uninvolved and sometimes uninformed investor can be a road block to syndication success.

AN OUTLINE FOR MARKETING YOUR FRIENDS-ONLY SYNDICATE

PRESENT THE PROPERTY
Use pictures.
Use maps: where is it located? What is it close to?
Use data sheets: how many apartments? How much land, etc.

DISCUSS THE PRICE
At what price have you negotiated an option or a contract contingent upon the formation of a limited partnership?
Use comparables or other information to document your opinion that the property is fairly priced or a bargain.

EXPLAIN THE CONCEPT OF LIMITED PARTNERSHIP
Point out limited liability.
Point out freedom from management or decision making.
Point out share value in all profits.

EXPLAIN HOW YOUR LIMITED PARTNERSHIP CAN BUY THIS PARTICULAR PROPERTY PROFITABLY
Tell how many limited partners there will be and the cost of each share. Explain the principal of a free piece for the general partner.
Show the proposed debt structure and probable cash flow.
Explain federal tax laws regarding the limited partnership.
Discuss the prospects for appreciation, the expected profit, and the currently projected holding time before selling.

"ASK FOR THE ORDER"
Ask your prospective limited partner if he or she would like to join you in this venture.

PATIENCE AND TACT

These heavenly gifts line up after creativity as positive attributes for the syndicator, and I might add teaching skill as a caboose. Remember, by the time you're ready to syndicate you'll have become something of an expert in your field but you'll be explaining your plans and projections to investors who know little or nothing about it. You'll be asked the same foolish (to you) questions again and again, and you must answer them sincerely and thoroughly, as though you were hearing them for the first time.

Once you have your syndicate up and running, tact will replace patience in the forefront. You cannot be overly patient with delays and incompetence, but you will surely find that tact will get the job done more quickly than anger.

SELF-CONTROL

In doing a syndicate, self-control should probably read self-dicipline. There are no time clocks to punch; no bosses looking over your shoulder. If you want to get the job done, you've got to get up each morning, kick yourself in the ass, and get going.

SELF-CONFIDENCE

Things *will* go wrong. Something always does. The small items—a broken sewer pipe, a deadbeat tenant—can be dealt with as easily as extinguishing small fires. But what about the catastrophes? Interest rates soar and the market plays dead; the zoning board denies you application for a subdivision; the town's major employer announces that the corporation is moving to Yazoo City, Mississippi. Suddenly your projections are popcorn. Your limited partners begin to call you in the late evening: "Hey, Margaret, how are you? Ah, I was just wondering about . . ."

When you handle other people's money in a field as subject to the winds of fortune as real estate, you've got to believe in yourself. Historically, real estate has performed better than any other investment vehicle over the long term. So you've got to believe that you can pull your syndicate out of the catastrophe, and because of your belief, you've got to try.

I recently met the general partner of a large limited partnership heavily invested in apartment houses in Houston. On the day we met, Houston was one of the worst places in the nation to own apartment buildings, and the government had announced a tax reform program two weeks earlier that would eliminate the tax shelter that was the remaining thread of life for his syndicate. Was he down? Not at all. He believed Houston would recover and meanwhile he was looking for passive money-making investments (he mentioned a shoe store) against which he could write off the losses of his apartment buildings and return his investors some positive cash flow. I admired this man. His was the self-confidence, the determination, and the creativity that draws Success into its arms like a docile mistress.

If *you* run into major problems, your syndicate may take a little longer to show the profit you expected or, you may have to alter your plans. But you must continue to believe that you *can* find a way to handle the problem. Look into yourself for the support you need.

Negotiating Skill

It takes the same tried-and-true negotiating skills to put together a $2,000,000 deal as a $50,000 deal. By the time you're ready to become a syndicator, you should have your own style down pat.

Social Contact

Yet another 10. Really a 10+. When you start out to form your limited partnership, the kind and number of people you know in town and your reputation there will make or break you. If you think you might syndicate some day, get involved in your religious group, scouts or your children's favorite sports groups, golf, tennis, a theater group, a professional group or two, run for mayor, put out a community newspaper, whatever interests you. This is the time to keep a high profile; you want people to recognize you and have positive thoughts when they do.

TOOLS OF THE TRADE

START-UP CASH

You will need some pocket change to print brochures and the like, but essentially you, the general partner, need invest no capital in your syndicate. You'll raise the cash you need by selling limited partnership shares.

Most lenders are receptive to making loans to limited partnerships if they know the general partner and consider him or her reliable, if the investment vehicle is sound, and if the debt is well structured. Large thrifts and commercial banks will probably be your best bet for your beginning venture, especially if you stay in town with a lender that knows you or your reputation.

 You will want to be sure that your mortgage or trust deed is written as a *nonrecourse loan*. That's important for your personal financial protection. When you use nonrecourse financing, however, you cannot offer a share or shares in the limited partnership to the lender as an incentive to making the loan since the federal government prohibits any lender who writes nonrecourse financing on a property from holding an interest in that property.

CASH FLOW

Many of the nation's largest limited partnerships (they like to call themselves MLPs, Master Limited Partnerships) are restructuring their holdings in order to offer positive cash flow and potential appreciation as the primary incentives to investing. Many are even putting together all-cash purchases of income-producing properties to guarantee the highest possible return on the investment dollar.

In structuring your syndicate, use your accountant to help you calculate carefully the amount of debt you can carry and still yield positive returns. There are no rules of thumb here. Each deal is truly unique and must be judged of itself.

WAITING TIME

The waiting time before you can sell for a sizable profit varies according to the investment vehicle you choose, the particular piece of property, the local and national economies, and luck.

Forget the *sell in seven to ten years* rule that prevailed in the early '80s. Tax reform has made that advice meaningless and worthless. You should sell when you are ready and the property can offer substantial profit. Or when you agreed to sell in the original limited partnership agreement.

WORKING TIME

At the outset, syndicating may require a twenty-five-hour day. Finding the right property, putting the deal together, gathering the investors, buying the property, and setting up its management all demand and consume time like a hungry baby. Once you have your syndicated property operating, however, you should find that the people to whom you've delegated authority and responsibility are doing an excellent job and you don't really have much to do. I suggest you take a vacation. And then, if you're like most syndicators, you'll be ready to start another syndicate.

TAXES

Under the Tax Reform Act of 1986, limited partnership shares are considered *passive investments*. As such, losses generated by the investment cannot be deducted against ordinary earned income or against portfolio income such as stock dividends.

As a syndicator, therefore, you should inform your prospective limited partners that their investment is *not* a tax shelter. Your goal is to make money, not to hide it.

The rules, however, are not all negative. The losses (paper or otherwise) that a limited partnership records each year can be forwarded indefinitely to be deducted against future years with positive returns or against the profit upon sale. Losses from a passive investment can also be deducted against profits from another completely unrelated passive investment in a given tax year. For example, a $1,000 loss from a limited partnership share can be deducted against a $1,400 gain from your passive ownership share in your nephew's gas station.

· · ·

EXPECTED RETURN

Since you, the general partner, invest little or no cash in your venture, the cash-on-cash return potential of this investment vehicle is phenomenal. The cash return on time, effort, responsibility, and expertise, however, is a little more realistic. And *that* is what you are paid for. Nevertheless, syndication is definitely a potential road to riches. A million dollars a year is not an uncommon income even for a "small-time" syndicator working six or seven "friendly" syndicates, let's say a woman working quietly in central Massachusetts whom no one beyond the state line has ever heard of.

KNOWLEDGE AND SPECIAL SKILLS

The special skills required to start a syndicate are almost all professional skills, and you'll find your days more pleasant if you simply hire the qualified lawyers, accountants, engineers, etc., that you need. Knowledge, *your* knowledge, however, is the *sine qua non* of this investment vehicle. It's your knowledge of the area, of the type of property to be invested in, and of the real estate marketplace in general that will be the single most important factor in the success or failure of your limited partnership venture.

SOME SUCCESSFUL INVESTORS

LAND SPECULATORS AND DEVELOPERS

Todd Phyfe not only had had experience in land investments, he had served as a member of his town's planning board for eight years. When he was told about the tract for sale near Sante Fe, he wanted it so badly he could almost taste it! He knew the area well, it was a favorite vacation spot, in fact he had often thought of retiring there. Here was opportunity at his doorstep, *but without seller financing.*

It was $475,000 for the tract, cash. Todd could raise, maybe, $100,000 himself, but that didn't stop him. He got in touch with a builder of modular houses and got good news. Yes, they would be pleased to work with him on the tract and at volume discount prices that were lower than those offered to the general public. He checked out zoning regulations, utility costs, road building requirements, drainage patterns. Everything seemed to say *go!* And he did. He took a six-month option on the land, hired a technical writer, and put it all into print.

With brochures in hand, Todd Phyfe started out to form his first friends-only syndicate. Share price was $25,000. There would be thirty-five shares of which he would receive three free. Thirty-two shares at $25,000 would bring in $800,000, good start-up money. Of the thirty-two shares to be sold, Todd would buy three, one in the name of each of his three children.

His accountant had helped to figure the costs and bought the first two shares. Forty lots could be created on the land, allowing for road space, without needing a zoning change. With the modular houses he planned to place on them, each lot would be worth approximately $150,000. At that price, gross revenues would be in the $6-million range. He would buy the modulars, delivered, for approximately $50,000 each, which would still leave him with $4 million to work with in calculating the potential return on the limited partnership investment share.

Estimating $2 million in development costs would leave him $2 million in profit. The modular company was willing to finance part of the road building costs; a local lender was willing to finance the remainder plus construction costs for foundations and utility hookups. Phyfe sold out his limited partnership in 3½ months and exercised his option on the land.

Because prices escalated faster than costs during the construction and marketing period, the actual profit from Phyfe's venture was $2.8 million. Divided by thirty-five shares it yielded a return of $80,000 per share 3½ years after purchase. This return represented a $55,000 pretax profit from the investment of $25,000.

Todd Phyfe did well. His three free shares brought him $240,000, his profit on the three shares he bought for his children another $165,000, a total return on his venture of $405,000. Not bad for part-time work.

One of the problems of investing in land is the difficulty of borrowing. Syndication therefore becomes a very appealing means of raising cash. In fact, the *Crittenden Real Estate Syndication News* reported early in 1987 that raw land syndicators "led the pack" among the leading money-raising syndications in 1986.

. . .

Conversion Specialists

David and Martin Green, brothers, had represented both sponsors and tenants in co-op conversions during the seven years they had been practicing law together. It was no wonder then that they heard about the thirty-two-unit apartment building before it was offered in the marketplace. Rent control was keeping the return down, some repairs were needed, and the owner wanted out. There was a $460,000 principal balance on the assumable mortgage on the property and the seller was asking $1.3 million. The Greens negotiated the asking price down to $890,000 (they knew how much the seller wanted to unload this property) and made their contract contingent upon their being able to raise $500,000 through sales of shares in a limited partnership they would form. The Green brothers would be the general partners.

The brothers sold thirty-three shares at $21,000 each, receiving two shares free and charging a 15 percent general partners' fee. Each share sold therefore represented $17,850 in available cash, a total of $589,050. The Greens bought the building and started the conversion process. Their law firm, quite naturally, represented the sponsor (their limited partnership) and collected the customary and usual fee for such work.

A second mortgage loan in the amount of $250,000 was required for repairs and renovation work. The conversion's legal and engineering costs ran to $300,000.

The apartments were first offered to their tenants at insider prices averaging $72,000 each. Only nine tenants bought ($648,000). Eight apartments became vacant during the conversion process and were sold after the conversion was complete at $128,000 each ($1,024,000). The remaining fifteen apartments were sold as occupied units at an average price of $75,000 each ($1,125,000).

How did the venture turn out financially? Let's take a look, keeping in mind that these are approximate figures which do not take into account taxes or the profit/loss profile of the building during the three-year conversion/marketing process.

Costs

purchase price	$ 890,000
repairs and interest on second mortgage	300,000
conversion costs	300,000
marketing	100,000
	$1,590,000

Income from sale	
nine insider-price apartments	$ 648,000
eight vacant apartments	1,024,000
fifteen occupied apartments	1,125,000
	$2,797,000

From the gross income from sales ($2,797,000) you must subtract the costs ($1,590,000) to get an approximate profit figure of $1,207,000. Dividing this figure by 35 gives you a return per limited partnership share of $34,485. Subtract the original $21,000 invested and each limited partnership share yields $13,485.

Each limited partner therefore increased his investment by more than 50 percent, without factoring in taxes. Virtually all were satisfied with this return, especially considering the relatively short (three-year) holding time.

But what about the Green brothers. How did they do on this enterprise? Again the figures are approximate, but you'll get the idea.

Two free shares at $34,485 each	$ 68,970
Fifteen percent of thirty-three shares	
($3,150 each share)	103,950
	$172,920

Each brother therefore made over $86,000 having invested *not one penny* of his own money and having spent but little time beyond what they were being paid for as attorneys for the sponsor.

If that seems like a good return to you, you should bear in mind that this example was only a modestly successful conversion. Some co-op or condominium conversions make a great deal more money, especially in areas where they are not hampered by rent control. And remember also that you don't have to *be* a lawyer to do a profitable conversion, but you should know one.

MOVING ON

Beware! Syndicating is addictive. Those who are successful in one small friendly syndicate often start another and another. Many move on to larger and larger groups of limited partners and to multiproperty holdings within a single limited partnership. They learn to comply with state blue sky laws and they register with the SEC. They hire sales people and form companies. Some even move into the huge public master limited partnerships.

If you're successful at syndication and you like the work, it is very likely to become your full-time career, and a most profitable one at that.

· CHAPTER 11 ·

Limited Partnerships

Ronald Freid is an airline pilot with cash to invest but little time to look after his investments. He'd like to buy into something that would give him a fair annual return or a paper loss and a future payoff that would be a good deal better than the usual safe harbor investments such as bonds, or CDs. He'd like to have a few tax benefits thrown in too, as a bonus. Investment vehicle of choice—a limited partnership.

· · ·

Most real estate specialists agree that the flagrant tax avoidance schemes of some limited partnerships were responsible for the bludgeoning of real estate in the Tax Reform Act of 1986. As a result, limited partnerships as an entity received a direct hit.

Their chief attraction had been the pass-through of paper losses to their members. These losses could be deducted against each member's ordinary income. This, of course, resulted in smaller and smaller payments to Uncle Sam. In the early '80s, there were many millionaires, heavily into real estate limited partnerships, who paid little or no federal taxes. Then Congress (and the nation) screamed *halt!* Today the losses (paper or otherwise) generated by limited partnerships *cannot* be deducted against ordinary income.

In September 1986 when the proposed tax law changes were first made public, newspaper financial pages across the nation featured headlines that read something like this: LIMITED PARTNERSHIPS KILLED BY NEW TAX LAW. But limited partnerships, or at least some of them, have risen from the dead and are now structured as an investment vehicle that may not rate five stars but certainly deserves a *good*.

If you have cash to invest but little time to manage your investments, a limited partnership might be just right for you. The key to success, however, is in choosing the *right* limited partnership, and that will take a little research on your part.

Before you read any further, go back and read Chapter 10, The Friends-Only Syndicate. That chapter explains the concept of a limited partnership from the general partner's point of view. It will provide you, the would-be limited partner, with a perspective that will sharpen your evaluation techniques, for you'll understand the goals and rewards that motivate general partners. It will also serve as a kind of primer for your further reading, since the basic principles of limited partnership organization are the same for a group of twenty friends buying an apartment building or for a billion-dollar company owning sixty properties and having thousands of investors from across the nation. If you can understand the friends-only group, you can work your way through the glossy pages of a public offering prospectus or listen to the smooth, well rehearsed presentation of a syndicate salesperson without being overwhelmed or led blindly off to la-la land.

CHECKPOINTS FOR THE INVESTOR

After you understand the general principles of limited partnership organization, you must then sift through the advantages and disadvantages of the various types of offerings and choose the one specific limited partnership most likely to achieve your goals. To do that you should understand the demands made upon the investor who steps into this marketplace.

LOGICAL AND RATIONAL EVALUATION OF OPTIONS

If you've heard about Securities and Exchange Commission registration requirements and the individual state regulating bodies that supervise syndication and you're feeling rather protected, stop! Compliance with the rules of these bodies in no way guarantees the quality of an investment offering. A general partner who meets every rule to the letter can choose the most miserable properties for syndication and *no one will stop him or her*. It's you who must judge the quality of an offering. To some extent your choice will be limited by the amount

INVESTOR DEMAND PROFILE

	1	2	3	4	5	6	7	8	9	10
1. Positive Action and Reaction	▓									
2. Willingness to Take Risks	▓	▓								
3. Decision-making Ability	▓									
4. Commitment—the Will to Follow Through										
5. Logical and Rational Evaluation of Options	▓	▓	▓	▓	▓	▓	▓	▓	▓	▓
6. Ability to Deal with Numbers and Finances	▓	▓	▓	▓	▓	▓	▓	▓	▓	▓
7. Ability to Deal with Legal Constraints	▓									
8. Organization and Management Skills										
9. Foresight	▓	▓								
10. Imagination and Creativity										
11. Self-confidence										
12. Patience and Tact										
13. Self-control										
14. Social Contact	▓	▓	▓							
15. Negotiating Skill										

of money you have available to invest and the degree of risk you wish
to take. To a lesser extent, it will also depend upon whom you know
and what you hear. Let's take a look at the options.

PUBLIC LIMITED PARTNERSHIPS: These are the giants. Do names like
Balcor/American Express; Consolidated Capital; Merrill Lynch, Hub-
bard; and the Fox & Carskadon Group ring any bells? These and other
public limited partnerships make their offerings either directly (from
the syndicator) or through stock brokers, life insurance companies,
financial advisers, or smaller syndicators who also act as agents for
the large companies.

The minimum investment in these large syndicates is usually $5,000
and virtually all of them are registered with the Securities and Exchange Commission. An expression of interest will bring you a prospectus filled with facts and figures. Also, if you are buying into an
established syndicate, you can usually obtain a list of property holdings.
Bear in mind, however, that the general partners can sell and buy,
or in fact make any decision relating to the business, *without consulting the limited partners*. So a particular property that catches your
eye as valuable might just be the one currently under negotiation
for sale.

Newly formed public limited partnerships are usually "blind pool"
organizations: you turn over your money without knowing where it's
going. Once the general partner has collected the cash, he or she or
they go out and buy the investment properties they think best. If
you're gasping at the risk, let me assure you that this is perfectly legal.
In fact some financial advisers will tell you it's the very best way to
go since the general partners have maximum flexibility and can snap
up good value properties (bargains) whenever and wherever they find
them. More cautious advisers will tell you that the value of the blind
pool public limited partnership lies *completely* in the expertise of the
general partners.

As you can see, investing in a public limited partnership is very
much like investing in the stock market. You're putting your money
on what you think is your best bet, but you have no control over how
it's used. There is one major difference, however. In most cases, you
cannot sell your shares in a limited partnership without the permission
of the general partners. This restriction protects the limited partnership from being classified as a corporation. Some limited partnerships
have buy-back provisions in their sales agreements, others allow their

CHECKING OUT A LIMITED PARTNERSHIP

THE REAL RATE OF RETURN

Put aside all paper-loss and tax-shelter ideas and look to find the rate of return generated by the properties, without financing as a factor. To do this, look at the figures provided in the offering literature or ask sales reps for the information you need. Annual reports are a good source. Take a year's *net operating income* and divide it by the price paid for the property or properties. If you don't get something in the 7 percent or better range, you had better dig a little deeper to see what's going on or look at some other offerings. (To get *net operating income,* take a years' rental income plus income from vending machines, washing machines, etc., and subtract operating expenses, local property taxes, and management fees.)

NET CASH FLOW

Before tax reform, most limited partnerships were structured to produce paper losses for their members. And even now a certain amount of paper loss is acceptable if the property is really producing a large enough income to cover its expenses.To check this, take the partnership's bottom line (their net taxable income or, more likely, their loss) and add to this figure all the year's depreciation allowance, the amortization, and any other noncash expenses that were declared. This is the *real* net cash flow and it should *not* be a minus figure. If it is, the property income is not great enough to meet its expenses.

SOURCE OF DISTRIBUTED RETURN

In a limited partnership that distributes cash to its members rather than a tax loss, check to see where that cash is coming from. Buried deep in the records of some limited partnerships are borrowings that contribute much to their "looking good" in the annual reports. General partners have been known to contribute their own funds to the partnership (for return later, of course) or to defer their fees to be collected in later years. Others have dipped into reserve fund in order to come up with a cash distribution, or sometimes they have refinanced one or more of their properties. All of which means that no real *income* was distributed.

A good means of checking for the source of distributed funds is to gather the annual reports of the past two or three years and compare them one to another. Look for larger than normal fluctuations in the same figures on each item. Avoid limited partnerships that are receiving these intravenous feedings to maintain life!

•   •   •

limited partners to "assign" their shares, which the lawyers say is different from selling them, but the result is about the same.

Now I admit choosing from among the nation's limited partnerships is not as difficult as choosing from among the stocks listed in the *Wall Street Journal*, but it's pretty close. To help you get started on the evaluation process, I have ten questions you might ask about any limited partnership you are offered.

$

1. How long has the *general partner* (this could be an individual, a group, or even a corporation) been in business? Successful experience, in fact a damn good track record, is what you're looking for. You might ask about other limited partnerships that were sponsored by this general partner. How did they perform? What did the balance sheet look like when they were liquidated?

2. Where is the property to be invested in? Most, though not all, limited partnerships (even blind pool groups) concentrate on specific geographical areas. You want to know growth projections and economic health in those areas.

3. What kind of property is (or is to be) the primary holding? Different investment vehicles can expect different returns and different forecasts. Office buildings, for example, are now over-built in many parts of the country. Bad investment. Or is it? If you buy at a bargain price now, and the builders stop building because everyone *knows* office buildings are overbuilt, will they still be overbuilt in three years? The experts say not. Then your office building will be a bargain. Ask representatives of the general partners *why* they choose to invest in a certain type of real estate.

$

4. How long will the limited partnership exist? Many if not most have at least target liquidation dates. If you think you may need your investment money in ten years for college tuition and your limited partnership is slated to liquidate in eight, you're probably okay. And even if you don't know exactly when or if you'll need the money, it's nice to know when you can get it.

5. Can you sell out (get your invested money back) before the projected date for liquidating the partnership? Ask specifically if the general partners offer a buy back and *at what price*. Some buy-back offers are at a good deal less than the invested dollar amount. Can you assign your limited partnership shares?

6. What is the projected cash flow? In a syndicate owning several rental buildings, the cash flow might well be positive. In a construction project, it will certainly be negative and may even require that the limited partners continue to invest additional funds for several years.

7. How much of your investment dollar is the general partner getting as a fee on the day you sign up? Average is about 15 percent, but I've seen some as high as 25 percent. Does the general partner receive an annual management fee? And will the general partner share in the profits when the limited partnership is liquidated? How many shares will the general partner take from the profit?

8. Will there be financing (borrowing) above and beyond the contributions of the limited partners? If so, how much? How will it be structured? At what interest rate? What terms? The amount and structure of financing is a key issue after tax reform. Too much leverage can mean disaster.

9. Is there a limit on the number of shares to be sold? Advocates of limited shares say a finite number prevents the syndicator from spreading the cash flow thinner and thinner while lining his or her pockets with general partner fees. Opponents say a limit on the number of shares prevents the general partner from raising capital and expanding without borrowing. Who's right? It depends. This is a factor that you must consider in light of all the other data you collect.

10. What are your state's regulations pertaining to limited partnerships? Call your attorney general's office to find out. Is the limited partnership you're considering in compliance?

If all this sounds to you like a lot of risk factors for a small return, you may be surprised to learn that most financial advisers consider public limited partnerships less of a risk than private limited partnerships. Why? Well, the general partners, they say, can spread their risks among many properties. In other words, a half-vacant office building can be carried for a while by a full-to-capacity shopping center. Secondly, the financial people will tell you that the risk to the individual investor is small because the price of each share is small and only that money, not your home and car, are at risk in the deal. And finally, provisions in the new tax law allow loss deductions from one passive investment against the profits from another. To stay afloat, therefore, some heavily leveraged limited partnerships might sell some of their *buildings* and move their money into income-producing businesses which they do not operate (a 40 percent share in a fast food place, for example). The paper loss from the buildings the partnership still holds can be deducted against the profits from the fast food place and perhaps a small cash distribution made to the shareholders.

This is big-bucks wheeling and dealing, done by professionals with the help of staff accountants and lawyers. The people who do it will tell you that they're offering the little guy a chance to share in the profits of their expertise. Maybe.

PRIVATE LIMITED PARTNERSHIPS: If public limited partnerships are the giants of the real estate marketplace, private limited partnerships are its rich guys. Buying a single unit in such a partnership usually costs somewhere between fifty and a hundred thousand dollars. In cash.

"Wow!" you exclaim. "Why so much?"

Because the investments are large—shopping centers, skyscrapers, resorts, etc.—and there are fewer investors, each of whom therefore gets a larger piece of the pie. Being asked to join into one of these luscious "opportunities" is a little like being asked to join an invitation-only club. There is no advertising of the offering. Information about it is not disseminated to the public. And there are minimum-income requirements which one must meet before being allowed to buy in. Both the SEC and individual state laws determine the minimum income for an "accredited investor" in a private limited partnership of more than thirty-five members.

If the private limited partnership crosses any state line in its membership or promotion, the SEC guidelines apply. These are a net worth of $1 million or more, an annual income of at least $200,000, and the purchase of a syndication unit of $150,000 or more. If the private limited partnership has more than thirty-five members but all business is within one state, state rules apply. These vary from one state to another. You can get information on your state's rules by calling the attorney general's office.

Most private limited partnerships are specified property syndicates. No blind pools here. The property or properties to be purchased are presented in tasteful brochures. You can even inspect the buildings yourself if you're so inclined. Or you might get a carefully drawn architect's rendering of what will be after the limited partnership collects its capital and gets construction underway and then completed.

Generally there are three reasons for forming a private limited partnership.

1. To build something (a resort, a shopping center, a condominium community, an office building, etc.)
2. To buy something and convert it to something else (a rental apartment building to condos, for example, or a warehouse to an indoor specialty shop mall)
3. To buy a property for its current cash flow and/or its future potential appreciation.

Of these three, new construction is the most risky. Things always go wrong. There are always delays. Too much of this, and you become cash poor. Either the limited partners then chip in a bit more, or the general partner goes to a lender. (Both bad.)

The risk factors in conversion are time and state and local laws. The start of the conversion process or even of cosmetic construction and refurbishing can be held up for years by state conversion laws and/or local zoning and fair housing laws. Meanwhile, there's always the chance that the market will change from red hot to ice blue. Were that to happen, would the converted apartments sell? Maybe. But at *what price*? Profits from a limited partnership specializing in conversion are dependent upon the selling price of the apartment units.

Buying a building for income and potential appreciation is the safest option. But also the least glamorous and sometimes the least rewarding. Buying land for potential appreciation is a little better than rolling dice.

If you are asked to join a private limited partnership (one on the grand scale, not a friends-only syndicate), you're probably wealthy, but you may or may not have previous real estate experience. In either case, be cautious. Before you put down your money and sign on the dotted line, try to judge the proposed purchase by the standards of its own species. That is, judge an apartment building by apartment building standards, as though you were going to buy it alone. You may spend hours poring over numbers to do this, but it's your only safety net. If you're not good with numbers or simply don't have the time or patience for all this calculating, hire an accountant or a lawyer to do the work for you and give you an opinion of value. Their fees will be but a drop in the bucket of cash you'll be investing.

If the proposed property purchase passes muster, turn to pages 207 and 208 and test the private offering against the ten questions for a public offering. If you still come up positive, go ahead. Returns are usually greater in private limited partnerships, but so are the risks.

THE FRIENDS-ONLY SYNDICATE: Do *not* join into a friends-only limited partnership because you're a nice guy and you want to help Harry out. Buy in because you see an opportunity to make money. Test the investment offering against the standards for that type of vehicle and test the limited partnership by the same standards that you would use for a giant public offering. In fact, you may want to hire a lawyer (*your* lawyer) to go over the limited partnership agreement, since mistakes can be made when general partners and their lawyers are just starting out, as it were.

DEALING WITH NUMBERS AND FINANCES

Think about these numbers:

- Income from the property
- Operating expenses
- Management fees
- Local taxes
- Depreciation
- General partners' fees
- Projected return on your investment
- The investment's impact on your federal income taxes

Too many numbers you say? But they are all essential. If you can't handle all these factors, you can't adequately judge a limited partnership offering. Either don't buy or consult an accountant or financial adviser before you buy.

ABILITY TO DEAL WITH LEGAL CONSTRAINTS

Most of the legal research, organization, and compliance will be up to the general partner, but you, as a limited partner, should be aware of the state and federal regulations that apply to the particular limited partnership into which you're buying. You should also ask the general partner or his representative if the limited partnership is in compliance.

You certainly don't want to lose money because someone forgot to register with the proper agency!

And be aware of the new federal tax laws regarding limited partnership income. (More about that in just a bit.)

RISK TAKING

The amount of cash you put into a limited partnership is the amount you risk. If the partnership goes broke, no creditor can lay claim to your house, goods, or salary in order to pay the syndicate's debts. Theoretically, the general partners take on full financial responsibility for the debts of the limited partnership, but actually they also risk little. Most general partners are quite savvy in the ways of the law (or have very good lawyers), and they structure their involvement in the partnership and its debts to be quite safe from potential disaster. Some use corporations as the up-front general partner; others use only nonrecourse financing.

Essentially then, limited partnerships are not risk free, but if you can afford to lose the money you've put in, they're pretty much headache free.

POSITIVE ACTION AND DECISION MAKING

Probably the most difficult positive action you'll be required to take while involved in limited partnerships is a negative action. Once word gets out that you have money to invest, you'll surely be invited to seminars, cocktail parties, and luncheons where slick-as-new-ice professionals will present you with opportunities to join in their ventures. Your positive action will be learning to say "No, thanks," and mean it until you are ready to invest. (It *is* a good idea to attend several of these meetings, however, before putting down your money.)

Then follows the only decision you will be required to make: *which one?*

FORESIGHT

It is in deciding *which one* that foresight comes into play. Does your knowledge of demographics hint that apartments will be scarce within two or three years? Or perhaps the shortage will be in retail outlets, or in retirement communities. If you follow your hunches, you'll want to choose limited partnerships with strong holdings in the type of building you think will be appreciating. But remember, predicting the future is a guessing game in which specific knowledge may put the odds in your favor but nothing will guarantee a win.

Just to illustrate, think back to the early '80s. Savvy experts (the demographers, the economists, the sociologists), all of them were predicting that the Northeast was dead. Low population growth, an aging population, and few new employment opportunities characterized the entire area. Go south and southwest, said the experts.

Today the Northeast is the hottest territory in the country. Housing prices are going through the roof, unemployment is low, and high-paying jobs are abundant.

What happened to the South and Southwest? They tell me it's a buyer's market there. Real property is selling for less than people paid for it, apartment and office buildings are standing half empty, young people are moving out in search of better jobs.

So who can tell what will happen in 1998?

TOOLS OF THE TRADE

WORKING TIME

None required. Or, more accurately, none required *after* you make the decision to put your money into ABC or XYZ and company.

WAITING TIME

The life span of a limited partnership is usually determined at conception, the key question being: *how long will it take to get maximum benefit from this purchase?* In the good ol' days of tax shelter structuring, most limited partnerships lasted seven to ten years. The new positive-cash-flow, appreciation-oriented partnerships may be written for longer (or perhaps even shorter) terms depending upon the prognosis for the particular vehicle or vehicles invested in.

Be sure to ask about liquidation dates before you sign one of these deals. Limited partnership shares are not easy to sell and you will probably be in for the duration (unless, of course, you want to get back a good deal less cash than you put in).

Start-up Cash

The limited partnership may need $80 million to start up, but the start-up figure for *you*, the limited partner, is the cost of a unit share. Ask, however, exactly how much of the money you pay in is designated as the fee to the general partner. This fee is tax deductible against income from the property. In the event that there is no distribution of cash during the lifetime of the partnership, the fee can still be deducted from the profit upon sale of the property or properties held by the partnership. This takes a bit of bookkeeping work, but it's worth the trouble.

As I mentioned earlier, most general partners' fees are in the range of 15 percent. If you're approaching anything much higher than that, ask why. Some general partners take fees as high as 25 percent and then skim profits before distributing cash to limited partners. Read your prospectus carefully and ask (several times of different people, if you must) *how much is the general partner getting on this deal?* It's one thing to pay an expert for his or her services, yet another to be robbed.

Cash Flow

Any annual distribution of real money to shareholders was a rare happening in the limited partnership marketplace of the early '80s. At that time, virtually everyone was selling tax shelter paper losses. These sometimes amounted to three or four times the amount you invested.

Today positive cash flow is the goal of most of the general partners who want to stay in business and *cash on cash* is the sales-peg phrase of the year. What the salespeople are talking about when they say *cash on cash* is the cash return on the amount of cash you invested. It should not be less than 7 percent unless there are extenuating circumstances such as fix-up costs or the potential of very great profit upon sale.

The Bottom Line

You won't know this for sure until the partnership is liquidated, but the prospectus will give you some estimates. Remember, you don't want *just* a hedge against inflation from your limited partnership investment, you want to *make money*. Look for partnerships that will invest in property likely to appreciate at a rate that is higher than the rate of inflation. Or look for partnerships that expect income from the properties to be high, high enough to exceed the rate of return you could get on more traditional and more liquid investments. But remember also that limited partnerships (when you are a limited partner) are *not* a quick-rich road.

TAXES

Limited partnerships are considered *passive investments*. Income from them is taxed at the same rate as your ordinary earned income. It is reported to the IRS also, so don't overlook it when filing in April. Losses, however, *cannot* be deducted against your ordinary income. They can be handled in one of two ways:

1. Carried forward. You can carry your limited partnership losses forward indefinitely, waiting to deduct them against a cash distribution or against your share of the profit upon sale of the property.
2. Deducted against other passive investments. If you own units in more than one limited partnership, you can deduct the losses from one against the cash distributions from another. If you own rental property (considered a passive investment), you can deduct the losses generated by your limited partnership units against gain from the rental property. If you own a share in a business and you do not participate in the management of that business, it too is considered a passive investment and limited partnership losses can be deducted against your gain from the business.

Even taxes, however, are relatively work free when you invest in a limited partnership. When you sit down in March or April to begin your tax calculations, you'll have your limited partnership figures at hand. Depreciation, operating expenses, local property taxes, etc., are all calculated by accountants for the limited partnership. You'll get a figure (your share of the gain or loss), and that's the number you'll use in calculating your own federal taxes.

Some limited partnerships have been designated as tax shelters by the federal government and are required to register as such under Section 6111 of the tax law. If you own or buy into one of these, you'll receive a copy of Form 8271, Investor Reporting of Tax Shelter Registration Number, and other tax shelter information. I wouldn't forget to report these numbers, and I wouldn't try to handle this data on an individual tax return until talking with an accountant well versed in the new tax law.

KNOWLEDGE AND SPECIAL SKILLS

You study the prospectus, you listen, you gather all the information you can, you make comparisons with other investments, and you make a decision. If that decision is to buy into a limited partnership, all your knowledge of real estate (or anything else) will have no bearing on the fate of your money. As a limited partner nothing you say or do can or will affect the management of the partnership. The knowledge and special skills needed therefore are evaluation skills and, perhaps I should add, the self-restraint to say "no" to sales pressure until *after* the evaluating is complete.

SOME SUCCESSFUL INVESTORS

WELL-INFORMED PROFESSIONALS

Robin Naughton heard about the private limited partnership at a neighbor's cocktail party in Pontiac, Michigan. With $50,000 to invest, she had been looking for some good real estate but nothing seemed to be appreciating at a satisfactory rate in the geographic areas she knew personally. This limited partnership was being formed to develop a tract of houses and a small strip shopping center near San Diego, an area of the country she knew was doing well in its overall economy and in the housing arena in particular.

She put her money in, and the decision turned out to be a good one. During the first four years, she showed loss figures on her tax returns. Then small gains for two years. The partnership was dissolved when all the properties, including the fully leased shopping center, were sold. Robin received $140,000 on her $50,000 investment in just over eight years.

Holding a mortgage for that length of time would have doubled her investment with the interest payments being made at regular intervals over the course of the holding period. In such a case, she could have reinvested the money being paid to her and thus increased her return beyond the doubling figure. But she probably would not have tripled her original investment. The limited partnership came close to doing that, while requiring no time or work from Robin.

RETIRED PERSONS

Clyde and Harriet Vizettly sold their home, took the $125,000 over-fifty-five homeowner's tax exemption, bought a retirement condo, and had just over $100,000 left. They knew this money wouldn't last long if they started spending it, but they knew little about investing. Their insurance agent suggested an appointment with their life insurance company's financial advisers.

Clyde and Harriet bought into a public limited partnership that was being sold through the life insurance company. "It was advice well taken," they told their friends in the years that followed. Their $100,000 earns them between $9,000 and $11,000 each year. Money which they spend happily, without guilt or worry, and without responsibility for managing the principal.

A FEW DON'TS

DON'T invest money you might need before the date upon which the partnership is to be dissolved. Shares can be very difficult to sell or transfer.

DON'T invest to avoid paying federal income taxes. Tax shelter days are over.

DON'T put your money into a limited partnership if you want to participate in real estate management or decision making.

DON'T expect to get rich from your investment in a limited partnership. You can often do about as well in more traditional investments (a money market fund, for example, or treasury notes). It's the general partners who get rich in limited partnerships.

A DISASTER STORY

Charlie Higgins could charm the scales off a snake. I remember him sitting on the fireplace hearth, a drink in his hand, his shoes off, his hair tousled and his eyes sparkling as he told the handful of party guests who had stayed late about the joys of entrepreneuring.

"Watch me!" he challenged. "I'll be driving a Porsche 928 before any of you trade in your station wagons."

Charlie's office was professionally decorated and lavish enough to assure anyone who might enter that he was indeed making a good deal of money. But most of his selling was done away from the office. A birthday card and flowers to a widow of eight months. (She later invested most of her husband's insurance money in one of Charlie's limited partnerships.) A tip on some vacant land about to go up for sale to a man who saw real estate as the way to wealth. (This man and Charlie became equal partners in another, highly leveraged, land deal.) A $10,000 contribution to his church's fund to build a gym for its school. (The pastor invested $35,000 he had recently inherited in another of Charlie's limited partnerships.)

In fact, Charlie was so smooth, so professional, so obviously competent and knowledgeable that a local savings bank invested over $1 million in one of Charlie's projects. And the owner of a local hardware store mortgaged his building to come up with $500,000 for the same project (a shopping center in Texas).

Charlie drove his Porsche for exactly eleven days before he was arrested. He was the first person I ever knew to get his name in *The New York Times* and the only one to serve time in prison.

Some of the properties Charlie showed to his prospective investors didn't exist, the Texas shopping center included. Others were bought with other people's money that was committed, supposedly, to entirely different investments (which Charlie never purchased). You see, Charlie knew a very good printer who would print everything or anything Charlie wanted or needed. And Charlie always looked good on paper. He even paid returns to some of his early investors by using money given him by new clients.

You might say that Charlie's real talent was in moving money, a kind of borrowing from Peter to pay Paul and then from Saul to pay Peter, while lining his own pockets on the way between each person. He overreached his limits, however, when he took in the savings bank. A sharp executive with some money behind him found Charlie out.

What happened to Charlie's clients? The widow went to work as a secretary, even though her children were still young. The land investor lost $45,000. He was implicated in Charlie's schemes and found blameless, but the association cost him dearly. He, his wife, and family were excluded from many local social functions for several years, until people began to trust again. The hardware store owner had to scrap his plans for early retirement and is still working at age sixty-three. The priest and the savings bank survived.

Do I need to supply a moral to this tale? Some pithy statement about watching out for yourself or remembering that nothing is risk free . . . No, I think I'll let you make up your own moral.

MOVING ON

The only limitations to the holdings you can have in limited partnerships are your income and net worth. Some people, particularly those who are wealthy enough to plunk down $100,000 for a share in a private limited partnership, favor this investment vehicle above all others. And, you must admit, the no-work aspect *is* attractive.

If you're not happy with the relatively modest returns, the general partners' fees, and the lack of liquidity, however, and you want to stay in a real estate related field, you might look into real estate investment trusts (REITs), which are traded on the stock exchanges and over the counter. Or you might explore mortgage-backed securities. That kind of trading, however, is another book. An investment banker, your stock broker, or a financial adviser can get you started in gathering information. And remember, don't buy anything until you feel confident of your understanding of the investment vehicle and until you've made some comparisons with other opportunities in the same vehicle.

•   •   •

ABOUT REITs

Here we're stepping into the stock market, for buying into a real estate investment trust (acronym REIT, pronounced reet) is exactly like trading in General Motors: you do it through your stock broker and pay the standard commission. The difference for the investor is that REITs do not pay corporate taxes as long as 75 percent of their assets are in real estate and 95 percent of their income is passed directly to their shareholders. Like corporations, however (and unlike partnerships), they cannot pass losses to their shareholders for tax purposes.

There are three types of REITs:

- mortgage REITs, which basically lend money secured by real estate;
- equity REITs, which buy, sell, and manage income-producing property;
- hybrid REITs, which do both.

Their attraction in today's economy is *cash on cash,* i.e., a good return on your invested capital. The typical yield is usually 7 to 13 percent.

REITs are *not* a guaranteed safe harbor investment, however. They *can* go under (many did in the early '70s). Explore each offering prospectus very carefully, looking for a good track record. It is also advisable to consult with several experienced investors in this type of vehicle before jumping in. Those investors who favor REITs will tell you they are a liquid investment in an illiquid field. Which is true, but not necessarily good.

Bear in mind also that under the new tax law, REITs are regarded by the IRS as *portfolio income.* Losses generated by rental property are *not* deductible against gains from portfolio investments. In other words, the government doesn't really think of REITs as a real estate investment at all.

· CHAPTER 12 ·

Preconstruction Contracts, Subscriptions, and Options

Irene and Bud Pindar live in an area of the country where growth is tremendous. If you drive on a road you haven't taken in three or four weeks, you're almost certain to discover a new office building or condominium community going up, or so it seems. The Pindars have lived in the area for fifteen years and know it well. They recently sold an investment property and have $40,000 in after-tax profit. Their investment vehicle of choice: preconstruction contracts, subscriptions, and options.

· · ·

There are a number of men and women enjoying the sun on Maui each February who have created wealth by signing real estate contracts upon which they never close. These are individuals of foresight, positive action, and another quality that some of us would call brass. If you were to engage one of these nice people in a friendly conversation over piña coladas at poolside, he or she might just tell you, "It's easy. You hardly need any money at all to get started and you can make a bundle with no work and practically nothing to lose. Try it . . . you'll like it!"

Should you?

Maybe.

Speculation in contracts, which is what you are doing when you sign an agreement to buy something that you intend to sell for a profit before you actually buy it, is a very rewarding occupation in a booming real estate marketplace. But it can become rather stressful if either the economy in general or the local real estate market in particular goes sour. Yes, there is the fail-safe of actually going through with the deal, buying the property and renting until things get better, but you'll be standing hat-in-hand before lenders to do so. You'll also need both qualifying income and excellent credit, not to mention financing savvy to rival that of your highly paid investment banker and negotiating skill on a par with Mr. Kissinger's.

"Hold on," you say. "You've got me interested, but I've never even heard of this game, much less played it. How about backing up a bit and explaining how these things work?"

Now there's a good idea. Let's take each of the most common types of contracted-future speculation separately.

PRECONSTRUCTION CONTRACTS ON HOUSES AND CONDOMINIUMS

It's no secret that builders offer the first few houses in a new development for sale at prices lower than they expect to get for later construction. *Sold* stickers on schematic maps of an area tend to stimulate action by other prospective buyers, and down payments on future construction help to raise cash for road building bonds, salaries, subcontractors' fees, and building materials.

In single-family-house developments, many speculators will sign up to buy a house on a lot far into the development. They know full well that it will be a year or more before the builder gets the road in to the point they have selected. The speculation here is on a rapidly escalating base price for the selected model once some construction is complete and a few families take occupancy. The risk is the down payment money and the return it might have earned in another investment vehicle.

The amount of down payment required is usually 10 percent of the price of the house. Think of this money as your pile of chips on the table. You're betting that you will be able to sell your contract for a profit shortly before completion of the house you signed up for. Here's how it works:

> You put down $10,000 on a $100,000 house. Nine months later, the house is still three months from completion and possible closing but the builder's price for the same model is now $135,000. You offer to sell your contract to purchase to a nice young couple for $25,000. If they take it, you get your $10,000 back plus $15,000 profit. The nice young couple gets to buy the house from the builder for the $90,000 you owe on your contract. The total cost of the property for these assigned buyers then is $115,000, a $20,000 savings. Everyone is happy except the builder, who would prefer to sell at the $135,000 price.

"Sounds great!" you say. "But why do you classify this as a high-risk investment? It seems so easy."

It is in theory, but you can lose all or most of your $10,000 if the builder goes bankrupt before he gets to your house. And home builders *do* go bankrupt. They're on the high-risk list at most lending institutions. Or, equally unpleasant, you may not be able to sell your contract if the economy (national or local) goes sour or if the building is shoddy and unappealing when complete.

Exactly the same principles apply in low-rise condominium speculation. Some investors actually sign up to buy six or more condos in one complex. *All at the same price.* They choose one in each of six different buildings, calculating that the sixth will have the greatest profit since it will be finished last.

Why not buy all six in the last building scheduled for completion? Because builders are no fools. "One in each building" is almost always a part of the negotiating process for multiunit speculation, but more about this later.

In high-rise units, the game is a little different. In most cities, no unit can close until the entire building is complete and a certificate of occupancy issued for each apartment. Speculation therefore is best pursued in the preconstruction stage, *before* the first shovel of earth is dug out from the ground. Many builders will accept deposits on paper plans at special preconstruction prices. Once the construction process begins, however, and the building is being actively marketed by real estate agents, prices go up and the ability to negotiate a deal goes down.

SUBSCRIPTION AGREEMENTS

Again the theory is the same: put down some cash to guarantee your right to purchase at a given price some time in the future and then sell that right to purchase for a profit. But the problems and risks are a little different.

In the real estate marketplace, the term *subscription agreement* usually refers to the sale of apartments in a co-op conversion. Essentially, the sponsor contracts to sell you an apartment (really stock in a corporation with a proprietary lease on the apartment) for a named price before the conversion actually takes place. In states where the conversion process is a long one (over a year in New York, for example) your "insider" preconversion price can indeed bring about a handy profit. In a good market, the apartment appreciates in value during the time the sponsor is working on the conversion. As the conversion date approaches, most sponsors then begin to advertise and actively market the unsold units in the building. Prices invariably rise as the professional marketing begins and the process itself brings prospective buyers to your door.

The risk is somewhat greater than house or condo speculation, however. Think about these questions: What if the conversion is never completed? Will you get your money back? Will the co-op be desirable to the general public once conversion *is* complete? In other words, will there really be buyers for the apartments? And if you can't sell your subscription agreement before closing, can you afford to close? Will rent from the unit cover your costs? Will rent control come into play? How well will the co-op be managed once the sponsor pulls out? What stabilization is there for monthly maintenance costs?

This is big-city business, not for the faint of heart. But the preconversion prices offered by sponsors of co-op conversions are usually well below market value for a similar *condominium*. So while speculation in co-ops may be more risky, it is often also more rewarding.

OPTIONS

An option secures for the investor the *opportunity* to purchase at a named price within a named period of time, but it carries *no obligation* to purchase. Options are most widely used in commercial real estate and land development, but there is a way to use them in the housing marketplace—*if* you can negotiate the deal.

Sometimes home owners or investors who are unable to sell a house in a soft market will settle for rental of the property. With a little coaxing, some of these sellers (the ones who are not too well informed in the ways of the real estate marketplace) will include an option to buy at an agreed-upon price and a right to sublet in their lease agreements.

The procedure for the speculator who finds such a seller is to enter into a two-year lease agreement with an option to purchase the property at the market value on the day the lease is signed *and* the right to sublet the property. Here you're speculating that the price of comparable houses (and therefore *your* house) will be considerably higher in two years. Once you sign the two-year lease, you sublet to a tenant who will pay *you* rent equal to or better than the rent you owe the home seller.

Twenty months later or so, *if* the house has appreciated as you expected, you *sell your option*. This works exactly the same as the price speculation in under-construction house or condo contracts.

But here's the good part. If prices have *not* appreciated as you anticipated, you simply move out your sublet tenant and allow the seller to have his house back. You have lost *no money*.

Well, almost always no money. There are some risks in deals such as this. Perhaps the sublet tenant doesn't pay his rent and has to be evicted. Or leaves in the night. You may be out income for a time while you are still obliged to pay the seller the rent you agreed to. Or you just might get a sublet tenant who damages the property.

Overall, however, the odds are excellent for excellent profit. So why aren't more investors into such deals? *Because they are hard to find.* This is one of the types of investment activity "taught" by so many of the Quick-Rich TV seminar salesmen. It works in theory. It works if you can find the situation. But sellers desperate, uncaring, or uninformed enough to accept such terms are rare indeed.

Preconstruction contracts, subscription agreements, and options, each is distinctive in the investment marketplace but each is also very much like playing futures in the commodity marketplace. To be a part of it, one needs a spirit that delights in the roll of the dice. To win at it, one needs knowledge of the marketplace and the particular commodity in question. Let's run through some checkpoints.

·   ·   ·

CHECKPOINTS FOR THE INVESTOR

POSITIVE ACTION AND REACTION

Since it's the early bird that gets the best prices in this game, you've got to be out there in the marketplace. You should know what's going on in every corner of your town, what subdivisions are before the planning board, who's applied for building permits, what new businesses are coming to town and what businesses are closing up or leaving town. Remember, everything that happens in a town affects its future property values. And future property value is what you're betting on in this investment vehicle.

Beyond getting out there to know what's going on, contract speculation also demands initiative. *Don't hesitate to approach a builder before the sale of his lots or condominium units is announced to the public.* The time while a developer is waiting out planning board delays is exactly the time that your negotiating skill might cut you in for a big share of future profits.

In subscription agreements for co-op conversions, however, positive action may mean *not* jumping at the initial offering price. Here *reaction* comes into play. As a tenant being offered an "insider" price, you must respond to offers and suggestions that you know are structured to the benefit of the sponsor. My best advice? Organize! Form a tenant group and negotiate *only* in the single voice of that group. If you can get really good offers at the preconversion stage, you can hardly help but make money when the actual conversion is imminent.

RATIONAL EVALUATION AND FORESIGHT

A well-developed sense for real estate activity in your area and a thorough knowledge of real estate's timeless principles will do much to enhance your ability to predict the future. Don't leave home without them. When you do leave home and go out to trade in the marketplace, check out:

- Location: Nothing is more important. Think about accessibility to workplaces and transportation arteries, the value and nature of the surrounding properties, terrain, and (believe it or not!) the view— what will prospective buyers see when they inspect the almost completed building in a year or so?

INVESTOR DEMAND PROFILE

	1	2	3	4	5	6	7	8	9	10
1. Positive Action and Reaction										
2. Willingness to Take Risks										
3. Decision-making Ability										
4. Commitment—the Will to Follow Through										
5. Logical and Rational Evaluation of Options										
6. Ability to Deal with Numbers and Finances										
7. Ability to Deal with Legal Constraints										
8. Organization and Management Skills										
9. Foresight										
10. Imagination and Creativity										
11. Self-confidence										
12. Patience and Tact										
13. Self-control										
14. Social Contact										
15. Negotiating Skill										

- The town: Schools, taxes, government services, government *honesty*, recreation opportunities. As a speculator, you will want to sign contracts to buy in places where people will want to live. The most elegant development of houses being sold at relatively low prices will not bring a good return in a town known for government corruption, high crime rate, or poor schools.
- Local industry: Growth is a key word if you choose contract speculation as your investment vehicle. If you see economic growth happening, the odds are good that population growth is right behind it, and behind that, of course, are good odds for making money.
- Reputation of the builder: Don't put your money on a Johnny-come-lately with rose-colored glasses, no matter how good a deal you are offered. Choose developers with experience and expertise in the kind of property you are investing in. A person's reputation for building a fine single-family house is but a modest recommendation of his or her ability to complete a condominium community or a high-rise building, and vice versa. In real estate development, experience, what you know, and who you know count most heavily.
- Character of the construction: People want to live in beautiful surroundings. Choose properties that will have architectural style and character in line with the latest trends. Good taste (yours) and your ability to judge the direction of trendy features will add many dollars to the sale price of your contracts, subscriptions, or options.

RISK TAKING

Many investors who deal in contracts see their at-risk factor only in terms of the down payment money they've turned over to the developer. And, quite rightly, they invest only money which they can afford to lose.

But it's not quite that simple. In good economic times (when property is selling well), the failure to find a buyer for your contract and your inability to go through with the deal and actually buy the property will usually result in the loss of your deposit money. The developer or sponsor will simply pocket *your* money and then put the property up for sale at the current market value. A very profitable move.

When times are bad, however, you may not be able to sell your contract and the developer may resent the long wait for another buyer for the property that *you* signed up to buy. Some developers will then sue for specific performance, *your* specific performance. And they might just add some "damages" (emotional and financial) to their suit, too. That this could be painful to you is an understatement of the first order. Which is *why* contract speculation is risky business.

LEGAL CONSTRAINTS

When speculating in contract resales, do not use the standard printed contract that the real estate agent pulls out of the supply closet. Find yourself a good lawyer who has experience in real estate deals and have that lawyer draw up the contract so that you have maximum protection under the laws of your state.

When all other elements of the contract are the best that you and your attorney can negotiate, the most important clause for you as speculator is the right to assign the contract, subscription agreement, or option. (The right to assign means the right to transfer all the conditions and responsibilities of the contract to someone else, with or without a consideration, which is usually money, changing hands.)

In most jurisdictions across the country, it is considered that a contract which does not *forbid* the right of assignment *allows* the right of assignment. *But do not rely on the absence of words to guarantee* you anything. Have the right to assign your contract, subscription agreement, or option written in.

In a few of the country's real estate hot spots, some builders are currently charging from $2,000 to $20,000 to have the right to assign written into their sales agreements. Negotiate over this clause. You might be willing to go for the $2,000 figure if you expect to make $20,000 in six to twelve months, but ideally you want no fee for the right to assign.

As another means of protecting their clients, some attorneys try to negotiate a clause in the contract which will hold the down payment money in escrow until closing. If you can get this concession from the developer, it's a fabulous safety net against his declaring bankruptcy at some point in the future. But you should be aware that most developers object. They want (and often need) deposit monies to help defray construction costs and to provide income (for the bread on their own tables) while construction is in progress.

Mortgage contingencies are another trouble spot in speculation contracts. If you're signing up to buy a property that will not be completed for a year or more, you will have great difficulty finding a lender willing to make a commitment for so long a period of time. Many such contracts are therefore written without mortgage contingencies. This does not mean that you or your assignee can't use a mortgage to buy the property, it simply means that the contract is not *dependent* upon getting a particular kind of mortgage in a particular amount.

And finally, in multiunit deals (in which you sign up to buy more than one unit or house over an extended period of time) be absolutely certain that you have *a separate contract for each unit*. It is complicated and difficult to sell the right to buy one of several units named in a blanket contract.

Numbers and Finances

It doesn't take a lot of space on the paper to subtract the current asking price of a piece of property from the probable market value in a year or so. The figure you get is your *maximum profit*, an amount very difficult to achieve in contract speculation. Ahhh, but sweeten the pie a bit. Divide that profit in half. Now you're still making money, but the buyer of your contract is also saving money. Very tempting. If you're good at negotiating, you'll *make* more than your assigned buyer *saves*. But even 50-50 isn't a bad deal.

Before you cover the remainder of your calculations' page with fatuous smiley faces and hand-drawn variations on the dollar sign, stop to do a few more calculations. Answer these questions:

- What are your attorney's fees? Deduct them from the anticipated profit.
- Is there a cost escalation clause in the contract? Many developers write in a statement that the buyer will agree to a 2 to 4 percent increase in price in the event that materials or labor costs rise during the period of construction. If this clause is in your contract, be assured that you or your assignee will have to pay very close to the full amount allowed. (The builder always seems to be able to document cost increases in everything.) Negotiate to have the entire cost escalation clause struck out. If the builder won't buy that, try to negotiate a very low percentage or a maximum fixed amount. Then deduct this number from your potential profit since your assignee or his or her attorney is sure to stumble over the clause and refuse to pay the extra.

• What would it cost to close on the property if you could not sell the contract? Add in lawyers' fees, title insurance, mortgage application fees, points, tax escrow, and insurance. If you add these numbers to the price named in your purchase contract, how much must you sell the property for in order to show a profit? (Don't forget to factor in the real estate commissions at this new asking price.)

When you have finished doing these calculations, you'll see quite clearly that the object of this game is *not* to close title on a property. If you must close and resell immediately, your profit will be small indeed—if there is one.

COMMITMENT

"What's the commitment?" you ask. "All anyone has to do is sign a contract, wait for the place to be almost finished, and then sell the contract."

Not quite. If you wish to protect the down payment money you've invested, you'll keep your eye on activities at the construction site. Long delays may mean trouble, and if a little investigation does indeed reveal that the builder is "having some problems," you may wish to sell out early, even for little or no profit. Rapid progress, on the other hand, may bring you your financial rewards earlier than you anticipated, *if* you know your building is nearing completion and it's time to sell the contract.

If you're a contract speculator who is dealing in a number of properties with several different developers, it's usually a good idea to keep a reminder calendar. When you first sign the contract to buy, indicate inspection dates and the builder's name or the property address at certain dates on your calendar throughout the coming year. It's essential that you don't lose contact with this investment vehicle. And, believe me, losing contact is easy when the vehicle makes no demands on your presence, or your decision making, or your wallet.

DECISION MAKING

There are only two decision times:

1. Buying: what to buy, when to buy, and for how much.
2. Selling: when to sell, and for how much.

Imagination

I gave this personality trait a 4 in the investment demand profile because imagination is an important factor in foresight. You don't have to be the kind of creative person who can fabricate something from nothing in order to speculate in contracts successfully, but you do have to be able to visualize how things will look when paper plans are turned into bricks and mortar. The person who can stand at the edge of a muddy field crisscrossed with the tire ruts of construction vehicles and sprinkled with empty soda and beer cans and imagine, no, *visualize*, where his or her condo unit will be in the complex is more likely to choose an easily salable unit. Which means he or she will be more likely to sell a contract quickly and profitably.

Social Contact

It is not necessary to work in or with a group to be successful at contract speculation. There's no need to approach planning board members tactfully, no need to present and re-present plans to prospective and committed limited partners, no need to take anyone out to dinner or to send "business" Christmas presents. This is an investment vehicle in which you can work alone.

Work alone, however, does not mean work without regard to the community or communities in which you're investing. It goes without saying that you must know what's going on in local politics and who's planning to build (or tear down) what. But you must also know people. The first hint of a particularly good deal might well come from a friend or business associate who knows a builder in need of some ready cash and also knows that you deal in contracts. Or a buyer for your contract might just be referred to you by someone with whom you've previously done business. Even in this real estate vehicle, success can depend on your networks.

In fact in cities with low apartment vacancy rates and tight, fast co-op markets, social contact may be the *only* way to get in on preconversion subscription agreements. Most tenants in a building about to undergo the conversion process suspect that "something is going on" long before the intent to convert is actually announced. These tenants may alert investor friends who do not live in the building so that the investors can move into the vacant apartments themselves or make contact with other current tenants who do not wish to buy but are willing to sell their subscription agreements.

SELF-CONFIDENCE AND NEGOTIATING SKILL

Contract speculation is *not* recommended as a vehicle for the beginning investor: the risks are too great and the need for real estate insight too crucial. To enter this booth in the real estate marketplace, play, and come out a winner, you must have experience, lots of it, for experience is the predominant factor in building the self-confidence necessary to gamble serenely for thousands and tens of thousands of dollars at a throw.

To win in the big games, you will also need superior, well-honed negotiating skills. If you don't have extensive negotiating experience but are determined to try contract speculation, start by contracting to buy a single condo unit or a single house in a development. You will then be treated exactly like a home buyer.

Once you've been through the process once or twice, however, you may decide to enter the game as a professional speculator. As such, you'll be contracting to buy several units or houses, each scheduled to close at a different time. The developer will know that you're a speculator (no masquerades of innocence allowed) and you will, of course, be open about your motivation: you want, and intend, to make money. Your message to the developer is a clear and simple one: *I have X amount of dollars available for your use, how much investment property will that buy me and under what terms?*

There's no space here for emotional pegs, no *look at the fabulous skylights* sales pitch. You and the developer talk money and time, trading, giving, taking, until each party is satisfied that the deal is a good one. This kind of negotiation is usually best done face to face, at a table if possible. There's no need for real estate agents running between separated parties with newly retyped or heavily deleted and initialed contracts. The contracts are usually written *after* handshakes all around.

.   .   .

HOW TO SELL YOUR CONTRACT

Of course you'll tell everyone you know that you have a contract available for assignment that will allow a buyer to save $20,000, or whatever the figure is, on a brand-new house in Happy Acres Estates. But if no friend-of-a-friend calls, newspaper ads usually work well. Keep the text simple, starting with the town and then the name of the development. Here's a sample:

> **Gainsville:** Happy Acres Estates. You can buy a brand-new 4 bedroom colonial at $20,000 less than the builder's current price. Call 555-1234. No brokers please.

The "no brokers please" is important because you want the reader of the ad to know that you're not a real estate agent.

When you get calls on your ad, give the callers the house or lot number (or unit number if you are selling a condo or co-op) and suggest that they drive by and call you back if they are interested. You *want* them to stop in at the on-site sales office where they will get a sales pitch, floor plans, perhaps a tour, and a price list.

If they call back, arrange a meeting. You have a very interested party. The rest is presentation, yours. You will need to explain how contract assignment works, stressing the fact that they as the new buyers will take over all the obligations and priviliges of your contract. These include home buyer's insurance if it's available from the builder and any extras that have been written into the contract, such as upgraded floor covering or lighting. You may have to negotiate on the price, so leave yourself some space.

If you sense both interest and anxiety (a common conflict in buyers unfamiliar with the assignment process), suggest that you all get together with an attorney of their choosing and go over the papers. You can bring your attorney along if you like, but it isn't usually necessary.

TOOLS OF THE TRADE

KNOWLEDGE

At the risk of sounding like a broken record, I *must* repeat: *knowledge of the real estate marketplace is absolutely essential to successful contract speculation.* This is not a vehicle you can ride to wealth after attending three one-hour lectures or listening to a few mail-order tapes. You should have previous investing experience and you should start small. Contract to buy *one* condo unit in what you think is a *sure thing* development, wait out the construction time, and then sell your contract. That trial run will teach you more than this book or any seminar leader can give you; it will teach you if you have the personality for speculation. If you discover that you're not quite the gambler you thought you were, there *are* other investment vehicles available that will not bring on migraines or insomnia. Read among the other chapters until you come upon one that seems right for you.

WAITING TIME

You may think that signing a contract for a unit to be completed in nine months will mean a waiting time of six to seven months before selling your contract. It's almost never the case. Construction projects that are completed on time are so rare that they often make the newspapers! Consider the waiting time indicated in the contract as a target date at best. You may not sell your contract for several months after that date. Or, if prices are skyrocketing, you may be able to sell for a good profit sooner than the date in the contract, even though the building itself is nowhere near completion.

WORKING TIME

None. Unless, of course, you count worry time, inspection time, and keeping-up-with-what's-going-on-in-town time.

START-UP CASH

Absolutely essential. You must have cash down payment money in order to deal with a developer in multiunit contracts. Even in a single-unit contract speculation, you must have the customary and usual earnest money deposit, in cash. And in either case, *the money should not be borrowed money.*

CASH FLOW

None. There is no income until you sell your contract. There are also no expenses except your lawyer's fee.

•   •   •

TAXES

Your profits are taxed at your ordinary income rate. There are no depreciation benefits in this vehicle, but if you *lose* money in a deal, I strongly recommend that you consult with a tax accountant, especially if you have other real estate investments. Many tax questions regarding passive loss and gain and, in fact, exactly what *is* passive investment are determined by individual circumstances.

THE BOTTOM LINE

Is there money to be made in contract speculation? Absolutely. *How much?* It depends.

Not very much of a guideline, is it? But it's the best I can do. Just consider again these relevant factors:

- the national economy
- the local economy
- interest rates
- the quality of construction
- events within the local area
- the accuracy of your estimate for future value
- luck.

SOME SUCCESSFUL INVESTORS

EXPERIENCED SPECULATORS

The Highlands is one of the largest multizoned residential developments now under construction in the United States. On 440 acres, housing will be built for approximately 4,000 people. Among the types of real estate that are or will be for sale are luxury houses priced over half a million dollars, prestigious two-story town house condominiums, modest and low income high-rise condominiums, and a small shopping center.

About one fourth of the town house condominiums (all of what was designated as section one) had been completed and occupied when Irene and Bud Pindar decided to invest their $40,000 in preconstruction contracts. Their plan was to take two units in section two, one in section three, and one in section four all at $100,000 each with 10 percent down on each. Without hesitation, the real estate agent told them the plan was impossible. Humongous Corporation was only selling units in section two at this time. The price was firm: $100,000 each no matter how many you might buy.

Bud asked to speak directly with an officer of the corporation. Instead, he got the broker who ran the real estate agency. The couple explained their plan again. The broker shook his head, said it was impossible, talked for forty-five minutes about buying all four units in section two, and then finally agreed to arrange a meeting between them and a representative of the corporation. Mr. Julian Silvershine, the representative, advised the Pindars to buy four units in section two. The Pindars refused, saying that buying all four units in one section represented too much risk and not enough opportunity. They were walking out the door when Mr. Silvershine called them back. Perhaps something could be worked out after all.

After much negotiation, the deal was set up as follows:

- One unit in section two with a scheduled completion date in nine months for $100,000; $10,000 down payment.
- Two units in section three, one with a scheduled completion date in fourteen months for $115,000 and one with a scheduled completion date in eighteen months for $120,000. Each of these section three units would require a down payment of $15,000.
- All deposit monies were to be released immediately to the builder.
- All three contracts were to be drawn individually and separately and all three were to be assignable.

It took three years before they were completely out of the deal, but the Pindars did well.

- Apartment one in section two was completed eleven months after the contract was signed. By that time, its neighboring units were priced at $119,000. The Pindars sold their contract for $20,000, doubling their $10,000 investment. (The new buyers bought a $119,000 apartment for $110,000.)
- Apartment two in section three was completed twenty-one months

after the Pindar contract was signed. Comparable selling price at that time was $145,000. The Pindars sold their contract for $32,000, more than doubling their $15,000 investment. (The new buyers bought the apartment for $132,000, saving $13,000.)

- Apartment three in section three was completed three years after the Pindar contract was signed. By that time, condo units were selling for $179,000. The Pindars sold this contract for $53,000, more than triple their investment. (The new buyer paid $158,000 for a $179,000 apartment, saving $21,000.)

Gross income: $105,000. Investment: $40,000. Net income: $65,000. Expenses: negligible. Work required: negligible.

LUCKY TENANTS

Lane Swenson is a literary agent in New York City who works out of his home. There was plenty of space in his three-room apartment for a desk and file cabinets until his two sons were born. Unhappy then with the crowding and the crying, he rented another apartment in the same building to be used as his office.

Six months later, a red herring (the term New Yorkers use for a conversion notice) arrived at his door. Lane did *not* want to move and he did not want to buy, so he organized and led the tenants' opposition group. The building was converted despite the objections of the tenants, but their efforts resulted in an insider's price offer almost 60 percent below market value. Lane bought the two apartments for $40,000 each. Within fourteen months he had sold them both and moved uptown, a wealthier man.

The selling prices? $109,000 and $114,500. That's a before-tax profit of $143,500, $74,500 of which would not be taxed but carried forward with the purchase of his three-bedroom home/office condominium at $167,000.

• • •

Andrea Tomkins got started with a lucky break. She graduated from college in 1980 and then changed jobs in 1981, just about the time mortgage rates reached 19 percent. Everywhere she looked during her relocation housing hunt, she saw FOR SALE signs. Sometimes, however, the signs read FOR SALE OR RENT. Interested, she toyed with the idea of actually having a whole house to herself.

An aggressive real estate agent worked out a deal for her: a three-year lease with an option to buy at the listed price of $75,000.

Three years later, the house that couldn't attract a single offer at $75,000 was surrounded by houses that were selling for $125,000 and more. Andrea's real estate agent urged her to exercise her option and buy. "You could turn around and sell it for $125,000 in a day!" he pleaded.

"Bring me a buyer," challenged Andrea. She had carefully read the lease that the real estate agent had filled in and the seller had signed without the assistance or review of a lawyer. It allowed her to sublet and/or to assign the option.

The house did not sell in a day. It took three weeks before the agent found people willing to pay Andrea $50,000 to buy the option that would allow them to buy the house for $75,000. Andrea pocketed $50,000 and bought herself one of the nicest condos in town. The original seller of the house got $75,000 for his property *minus* the 6 percent real estate commission.

"That's terrible!" you say.

Yes, it is. But it's also a very good example of *why* a seller should always avoid giving a tenant an option-to-buy in the lease. And why any tenant who's offered one should always take it.

MOVING ON

Well, there's Las Vegas, Atlantic City, Monte Carlo . . . No, seriously, if you're successful in contract speculation in your hometown area and you like doing it, you might investigate the vacation-home marketplace. This market is more volatile than conventional housing, but if you choose a location that becomes a trendy hot spot, the profit potential is very great indeed.

But let's push the *if*s a little farther. Let's assume that you're wealthy and have considerable cash to invest but you don't have much time to devote to your investments. Let's also assume that your several ventures into contract speculation have been successful and that in the process you have come to know several developers and a good real estate lawyer rather well. Perhaps, then, it's time to consider a joint venture.

How does that work? The principle is quite simple. *You* put up the working capital, a builder does the work. The profit is split 50-50 or according to whatever arrangement is mutually agreeable. If you're interested, have a talk with the local developers you know and then visit with your attorney.

• CHAPTER 13 •

Hammer and Nails Conversions

Charlotte McGinty is thirty-seven, recently divorced, and a college professor. She has flexible hours, a modest income, and about $75,000 in cash from the sale of the house she had owned with her husband. She wants security, minimal housing costs, and appreciation potential. Investment vehicle of choice: the conversion of a rambling old house near the campus into three apartment units.

Bill and Marjorie Hardy are about to retire. They have paid off the mortgage on the ten-room house where they raised their five children and have about $250,000 in equity, plenty of cash to buy a nice little condo in Florida. But they have no intention of leaving the community where they have lived for over thirty years. And, in fact, they'd like to stay right in their own home. Source of income and investment vehicle of choice: conversion of their one-family house into a two-family house.

John Wassermann has dabbled in handyman specials for five years now and made a good deal of money at it. His building skills are well honed and he has established a working relationship with suppliers, subcontractors, and crafts people. He'd like to move from handyman specials into something bigger and more profitable. Investment vehicle of choice: Hammer and nails conversion.

•   •   •

Drive through almost any mid-sized or larger U.S. city and you'll see an array of houses built before 1930. Some of these are three-story town houses or brownstones built wall to wall against the properties next door. Others are rambling Victorians of fourteen or fifteen rooms. And still others are relatively modest boxlike structures, sometimes with incongruous additions.

"So?" you say. "This is the American cityscape. What does it have to do with investment real estate?"

Look again. Focus on doorways. Isn't it strange that many of these houses seem to have two or more front doors? Check out the windows. Funny how the curtains and the furnishings you can glimpse from the outside are inconsistent, no family resemblance at all. If there are driveways, look at the parking spaces. Two, three, four cars to a building!

You are now looking into the character of "home" in late twentieth-century urban America, and it's a far cry from the typical household of the early twentieth century, when most of these buildings were designed. Husband, wife, several kids, a dog, and perhaps a servant are no longer the typical inhabitants of urban housing. Today, single-person households have increased in number faster than anyone predicted and account for a major housing demand. Two- and three-person households are right behind. Where are the middle-class families with three and four children? Those that still exist can be found in the housing developments of the suburbs and exurbs.

The American life-style has changed, but available American housing has not. Oh, there's the condo to be sure. But we can't just toss away all those fine buildings of an earlier time of growth and prosperity. So what are we doing with the brownstone, and the Victorian, and the ten-room cottage? We're converting them. Sometimes legally, sometimes illegally, although the illegal part is becoming about as protested as opening a store on Sunday in most parts of the country. We're converting them with hammer and nails into buildings that hold two, three, or more independent households. And the people doing the conversions are *making money*.

Whether you're a single, self-employed person looking for a self-supporting place to live, a retired couple looking to tap the family homestead for a little extra spending money, or a real estate professional carefully figuring his profit margin, hammer and nails conversion is an appealing investment vehicle, *if you know how to get it done.*

CHECKPOINTS FOR THE INVESTOR

IMAGINATION AND CREATIVITY

If you look at a building and see only what's there, this is *not* the right vehicle for you. No, you don't need a degree in architecture to participate in it, but you do need the imagination to enjoy sitting at your kitchen table and making sketches of what could be or might be. An architect will almost surely be called in to redo those sketches for structural soundness and better traffic flow, not to mention amenities, but the original idea, the vision, must be yours. You should also feel excitement and anticipation at the thought of creating something new, beautiful, and practical.

Making money is definitely a motive in conversion, but it is rarely the only motive (there really *are* easier ways to make money.) This is an opportunity vehicle. For some beginners it may be a one-time opportunity to create housing that answers contemporary needs within structures that might almost be called historic. For others, it can be an opportunity to create housing from structures never intended as housing: warehouses, churches, department stores, movie theaters, or even parking garages or barns.

LEGAL CONSTRAINTS

The subdivision of interior housing space probably breaks the on-the-books laws of more communities more often than any other real estate venture. Some owners simply don't know that zoning laws and building codes exist and proceed happily with a money-making idea without consulting anyone in the town government. Others are aware of the laws but look around and say, "Just about everyone else in the neighborhood has done it, so why not me?"

It's a fact that many, many municipalities across the country are simply disregarding the changing character of certain neighborhoods from single-family residences to buildings housing two or more separate households. In these cities, you'll often see advertisements in the real estate sections of local newspapers that are headlined LEGAL TWO-FAMILY. On the books, the neighborhood remains zoned for single-family residences, but the book in which the law is written hasn't been opened in decades.

INVESTOR DEMAND PROFILE

	1	2	3	4	5	6	7	8	9	10
1. Positive Action and Reaction										
2. Willingness to Take Risks										
3. Decision-making Ability										
4. Commitment—the Will to Follow Through										
5. Logical and Rational Evaluation of Options										
6. Ability to Deal with Numbers and Finances										
7. Ability to Deal with Legal Constraints										
8. Organization and Management Skills										
9. Foresight										
10. Imagination and Creativity										
11. Self-confidence										
12. Patience and Tact										
13. Self-control										
14. Social Contact										
15. Negotiating Skill										

CONSIDERING ZONING ORDINANCES

Every town, every neighborhood, every house is unique. Which means *you* must make the decision. Suggestions, however, are pretty universal. Here are a few to get you started.

- Check to see what zoning laws *are* on the books. Don't accept hearsay; your friends and neighbors might just be wrong. Zoning laws are open to the public and available at the town hall.
- Talk with your neighbors or prospective neighbors. Who has done what in the neighborhood? How many houses have been converted? When? Have there been any problems? Ask people if they would object to your plans.
- Read back issues of the local newspapers if you're not right on top of the topic. Is housing conversion an issue in the community?
- Check on the building codes. You should know what the law requires before you start your project. It's less expensive to structure compliance into your restructuring than to take down newly erected walls in order to comply once a complaint has been filed.

Should you buy an old house in such an area with plans to live in part of it and convert the remaining space to apartments? Should you go to the board of adjustment with your plans? Or just go ahead with them quietly? What are the risks and consequences?

Well, if you start conversion work without approval and someone complains, the town could stop you with your nails only half into your boards, as it were. If you do apply to the board of adjustment, there is always the chance of refusal, and even when that's slim, there will certainly be a long wait. Three to six months awaiting approval is not at all unusual, and that's just the beginning. Then you will wait, and wait again, for the buildings inspector at each designated stage of your work.

Applying for the zoning variance and building permit is certainly the safest way to proceed. It completely eliminates the possibility of loss due to a *cease and desist* order. If you are a gambler, however, and you look about the neighborhood and see that 50 percent or more of the buildings are already converted, you might decide to go ahead without the required approvals. Why? Most such gamblers would tell you that it's hard for the town to say *no* to you when in fact nothing has been done about all the other people who have done it.

Know the local scene. Making a judgment call on interior restructuring is entirely dependent upon local circumstances. Some towns with housing problems are actually *encouraging* the conversions despite the fact that laws to the contrary are still on the books. But if you use that fact to do a restructuring in Anytown and Anytown is *not* one of those towns, you could lose a great deal of money. Hammer and nails conversion of single-family houses to two-or-more-family houses is an area of endeavor where it's better to be a follower than a leader.

If your conversion goals are larger and more complex than one family to two or three, you will almost certainly have to go before the planning board of your community. Let's say that you want to convert an old high school into an apartment building. Now that's an undertaking that is hard not to notice. People will talk. People will wonder how much money you're making. And someone will complain. If you haven't obtained the proper permissions, your project will be a political hot potato. Talk about delays . . . Your grandchildren may be old enough to act as your attorneys before the project comes out of the courts.

Among the best places to look for investment property for interior restructuring are the so-called T zones of a city. Not all cities designate these neighborhoods as T (transition) zones, but they exist almost everywhere. These are areas that were once residential but are gradually becoming commercial. A few neighborhood stores have moved in (with proper zoning board approval) and a few offices (doctors, lawyers, Realtors, a hairdresser, perhaps a daycare center.) If you can find a rambling house in such a neighborhood with parking space available on the lot, you might well consider developing a mixed commercial/residential property. Here you would lease the street-level space for offices and keep upper floors for residences. The return on your investment dollar is usually excellent. You should plan to make an appointment with your tax counselor before buying, however, since you'll be dealing with two different depreciation schedules when you file your federal income tax return.

One final word of caution: *watch out for parking problems.* In some cities where restructuring of interior space has become so prevalent that the planning boards have essentially thrown up their hands and abandoned efforts to stop it, focus has shifted to the question of where to park the cars. Ordinances are on the books in many of these areas requiring off-street parking for one, or even two, vehicles for each new unit being created. If you come upon such a law, be sure the lot upon which your prospective property stands is large enough to provide adequate parking space.

POSITIVE ACTION AND COMMITMENT

You may have the imagination and creativity of Leonardo da Vinci, but unless you're willing to tear yourself away from the Sunday football game and *do* something with your plans and dreams, your financial well-being will not change for the better.

And once you *do* begin work on your hammer and nails conversion, be prepared for setbacks. There are approval setbacks, weather-related setbacks, materials availability setbacks, subcontractor setbacks, and just plain mistakes. If you are living in the house while restructuring it, these can be devastating. There's nothing quite like a six-by-four-foot hole in the bedroom floor to trouble your night's sleep, even with the kitchen chairs surrounding it so you won't fall through.

Beyond being a doer, there is the question of commitment. You'll need a lot. First of all, you have *got* to get the job finished. Reward (financial) is dependent upon completion rather than good intentions. So when you're sick and tired of the sawdust and sweat and you want to run away, take a half day off, but go back to the project. And when your plumber doesn't show up, call him and set up a new date, or get a new plumber.

Once your single-family-to-apartments project is complete, you become the owner of a multifamily house. Whether you plan to live in it and rent out part, sell it immediately for a profit, or hold it while renting all the units for a positive cash flow investment, you must be aware of the positives and negatives of multifamily house ownership in order to achieve optimum profit. I'd suggest that you go back to Chapter 5 and read the Checkpoints for the Investor and Tools of the Trade sections. You should be absolutely sure that you want to take on this investment vehicle *before* you buy a piece of property that you intend to convert to multifamily housing.

If your conversion is a large-scale one creating seven or more units, its completion will make you the owner of a small apartment building.

And, of course, I'd suggest then that you read Chapter 9 on small apartment buildings, whether you intend to aim at an economically sound venture into landlordship or to sell as soon as possible.

RISK TAKING AND FORESIGHT

You can minimize your financial and time-commitment risks by paying careful attention to:

- zoning practices in the immediate neighborhood
- the prognosis for demographic and economic growth in the local area
- the timeless and universal criteria of good real estate investment: *location, structure, and cash flow*
- a logical and rational evaluation of the possibilities for restructuring interior space and the probable return on the money you'll invest in that restructuring.

LOGICAL AND RATIONAL EVALUATION OF OPTIONS

Your first question should be: *Is this a good place to buy?* Second, you should ask: *Is this a good place to do a hammer and nails conversion?* And third: *Can the building be converted given its physical characteristics and the prevalent zoning practices of the town?*

The answers to the first two questions should come from the real estate savvy that you've developed. For the answer to the third, however, you may well need some professional help. I highly recommend that you consult an architect about your plans. A good one will save you more than his or her fee in mistakes avoided and right choices made. Most will also be able to recommend subcontractors in your area they know are reliable. Some architects (for a fee) will even oversee the construction work.

Do I also recommend using a lawyer to get through the zoning maze? Not always. Much depends on the size of your project and the prevalent attitudes toward zoning law compliance in your area. But if you are the least bit unsure of yourself or worried, get one . . . a *good* one.

If your project is large enough or the zoning laws strictly enforced enough, you might do well to bring in legal help. Remember, however, you *can* have a clause written into your contract to purchase that makes the sale of the property contingent upon zoning board approval of your conversion plans. The seller may hold out for more money because of

SOME QUESTIONS TO THINK ABOUT WHEN YOU EVALUATE A BUILDING FOR POSSIBLE HAMMER & NAILS CONVERSION TO RENTAL UNITS

- Does your subdivision of interior space *work*? What will the traffic pattern be in each apartment?
- Will heat be provided by separate heating plants with separate meters (tenant pays) or by one heating plant (landlord pays)? If separate heating plants are to be used, will walls have to be removed to put in heating mechanisms? If one plant, will it be adequate?
- Can water and waste pipes be brought to the appropriate rooms? Economically? Or at great expense?
- Where will the space for stairwells to upper-story apartments come from?
- What about windows? Windowless rooms are unpleasant at the least, illegal in some parts of the country.
- Will each unit have a rear door? Or a fire escape?
- Will you need some soundproofing? Will someone's bedroom wall back up to someone else's washing machine?
- Where will necessary storage space come from? You'll need to consider closets in your redesigning of space. Will there be basement storage space for each tenant?
- Is electrical wiring adequate? (Probably not.) Calculate the cost of new wiring in your figures.
- Can you conceive of someone wanting to live in one of the units you are creating? In other words, will they be appealing?

the risks and delays involved in such a contingency, but if you get it, you will have fail-safe protection for your investment plans.

NUMBERS AND FINANCES

How much will the conversion cost? Where will I get the money? How much of a return will I get on my investment? These are the key before-you-buy questions.

HOW MUCH WILL THE CONVERSION COST? If you use an architect, he or she will give you fairly accurate estimates of costs for both materials and labor. Be sure to tell the architect, however, exactly what work you plan to do yourself.

If you do not use an architect, you should do some calculating, some research and planning, and some legwork. Make a chart for each room involved in your restructuring project. Under the room heading, list the projects that must be completed in that room and the materials that will be needed for those projects. Don't forget hallways, stairwells, extra doorways, fire escapes (if necessary), and the addition of utilities, appliances, and storage space in the basement. Bear in mind that you must not only list the materials you need, but also the quantities and the approximate costs. You can't, for example, just list *wallpaper*, you must list how much wallpaper and at what price.

You can get estimates for materials costs by going to the appropriate retail stores and comparing prices. You can get estimates for labor costs by calling subcontractors and asking them to bid on the job. Unless you are using an architect who has a selected list of subcontractors, get estimates from at least three different subcontractors for each type of labor required, that is, three plumbers, three electricians, three heating men, etc. Comparing estimates is your primary safeguard against overpricing. Asking about in the community for references is another tried-and-true method of protecting yourself from scam operators who promise the best job you'll ever see and deliver nothing.

WHERE WILL I GET THE MONEY? If you have cash to invest, the question changes to *do I have enough?* If you must borrow for the project, you should weigh the cost of the loan against the income it will bring. If you find a slight negative cash flow, however, don't throw in the towel. Estimate what will happen to that cash flow if you raise the rents in a year or so. It should turn positive, and after five or six years, if you choose to live in the house that you convert, you may even be living cost free.

Home improvement loans and, more frequently, equity credit lines can be used to convert properties in which you already live. They can be obtained from banks, credit unions, and specialty mortgage lending firms. Be sure to compare interest rates and other loan terms before choosing your lender. If you are buying for investment only, consider financing both the purchase and the conversion under one loan. Take your plans to the bank along with an estimate from a professional appraiser as to the value of the property once your conversion is complete. Many lenders, particularly smaller community banks, will work out financing based upon the projected value. A word of caution, however: don't overmortgage thinking that you could take out a large enough loan on this house to give you the cash down payment for another one. The income you project from the newly created units should come close to carrying the costs of the property. Long-term negative cash flow has become a losing concept under the new tax laws. It can leave your bank account registering empty while you see no tax savings come April 15.

HOW MUCH OF A RETURN WILL I GET ON MY INVESTMENT? You'll have to do some walking about in the marketplace to answer this question. Go out and look at apartments advertised for rent in your local papers. When you find some that are similar in space, amenities, and neighborhood to the ones you plan to create, make a note of the rental asking price and then watch the newspapers to see how soon the ad disappears. If it remains in the paper for weeks, the rent is too high.

Once you have estimated rental figures for your apartments, you'll know your probable income. Now deduct your estimated expenses and you'll have your net cash income. Subtract taxes and you will have a ball park idea of the return on your investment dollar. Remember, however, that this figure will change each year. In a good investment, it should increase in most years.

If you're a seasoned investor, you can do this calculating yourself, and your estimates will be fairly accurate. If this is your first run, however, get the help of an accountant.

ORGANIZATION, MANAGEMENT SKILLS, AND DECISION MAKING

Planning space and improvements, choosing and ordering materials at the best possible price, scheduling (and sometimes rescheduling) work to be done, and keeping track of the money (outgoing and incoming) are all important factors in successful hammer and nails conversion. Once the conversion is complete, the usual landlord management and organizational skills take over.

If you are supervising a conversion yourself and doing some of the work too, be certain that you obtain evidence of contractors' insurance from each subcontractor that you hire. If your subcontractor does not carry insurance, you could be held liable for expenses and damages if an accident befalls a workman on your property. Hire only subcontractors who willingly provide you with verification of their insurance.

You should also take steps to assure yourself that a mechanic's lien will not be filed against your property. Every company that furnishes building materials and every subcontractor hired to work on the construction of a building has the right to be paid for his materials and/or work. If he is not paid, or if he thinks he is not paid a sufficient amount, he can impose a lien on the property. In some states such liens can be foreclosed in much the same way as a mortgage.

To avoid the messy legal entanglements of a mechanic's lien, ask each subcontractor to sign a lien waiver once he is paid in full. A lien waiver is a signed statement voluntarily giving up the right to file a mechanic's or a materialman's lien during the statutory period allowed in a given state. Your lawyer can supply you with a few sentences that you can machine copy for as many forms as you will need. Keep the signed waivers with your records of bills paid.

SELF-CONFIDENCE

Do I need to tell you that self-confidence is important to successful hammer and nails conversion? All the creativity and imagination in the world, and even all the will to act is but sound and fury unless you have the self-confidence to believe that you can change ideas into solid reality.

PATIENCE, TACT, AND SELF-CONTROL

Whether you do the work yourself, hire subcontractors, or both, you'll need a bountiful supply of patience, tact, and self-control. I absolutely guarantee that things will go wrong during your conversion process. And that schedules will be delayed. And that hidden problems will quite literally jump out of the woodwork, especially if you're working with an older house. A blocked fireplace, termites, clogged plumbing, insufficient supporting beams . . . Space limitations and good sense keep me from going on with an extensive list of every possible problem.

I do have a special word of caution for you, however, about obsessive behavior. Some people throw themselves into a conversion project so completely that they forget that the world is still turning. Wife, children, social obligations, even their "real jobs" all can wait and "I've got to *get it done*" becomes a driving force. This is the stuff divorces are made of. Or the stuff that drives many a person into therapy. Try to put the conversion into perspective as an investment, a moonlighting job. Find time to laugh and have fun, and, as the saying goes, to smell the flowers.

If you do, you'll find that self-control is no longer something to work at. Temperamental explosions at workmen, planning board members, prospective tenants, or neighborhood children, not to mention your spouse, will be few and far between. And your blood pressure will be lower, too.

SOCIAL CONTACT

Knowing the right people in town could help you through a variance application but it's unlikely to assist you in finding good property. This is a job you must do alone. Once you do find a property, however, and are ready to start your conversion, the people you know in the business, will become important indeed. Materials suppliers whom you trust can help you to estimate your needs accurately. Subcontractors with whom you have established a good relationship are more likely to show up on the appointed day.

NEGOTIATING SKILL

Negotiating plays a bigger role in hammer and nails conversion than you might suspect. It's not just the price of the property that is open to discussion, it's also the *cost* of the conversion. If you're good at negotiating, you can come to an agreement (one different from the published price) with subcontractors, materials suppliers, and even your friendly banker. And you can save thousands of dollars.

TOOLS OF THE TRADE

WAITING TIME

Waiting time in hammer and nails conversion is dependent upon a whole array of variables. Let's list the most common, keeping in mind that others might just crop up in your particular job:

- the amount of work to be done in the interior restructuring
- your decision on zoning law adherence
- if you apply for a variance, the number and complexity of petitions before the planning board or board of adjustment
- the number of buildings inspectors available in proportion to the demand for inspections; the delays in obtaining a Certificate of Occupancy (CO).
- the availability of subcontractors: the hotter the housing market in your area, the more difficult it is to get subcontractors to come out for what they probably consider a small job even though it's very big to you.
- the availability of materials: strikes at the plant, bad weather, paperwork mixups, any number of factors beyond your control could cause delays. Try to have alternative sources of materials lined up whenever you can.
- your decision to rent the property as a positive cash flow investment for a period of time, or to sell immediately for a profit.

WORKING TIME

Working time will depend upon *who* does the work and *how much* work there is to do. If you subcontract everything, then your working time is minimal: the time you spend on the phone, the time you spend choosing materials, the time you spend negotiating, the time you spend visiting the site to inspect the work you have contracted for, and the time you spend writing checks and keeping records.

If your project is small enough that you can choose to do most of the work yourself (especially if you're already living in the building), try to come to terms with the fact that the working time will be longer than you expect. At first you'll roar along, but then there will be the day you come home from the office late and tired (no work), or the days you have the flu (no work for those days and perhaps a week more), or the days you just have to get away to save your sanity.

Hammer and nails conversion, however, is not for the dilettante. You don't dabble in this investment vehicle, because the longer it takes the more it costs, both in money spent and in money not earned from rents. And there's no way to calculate the cost in terms of stress on the people involved in the conversion, especially if they're living in the property being converted.

So you're between a rock and a hard place. It's going to take longer than you planned but the longer it takes the more it costs. I'm telling you to take time off and I'm telling you to work hard. What to do? If you are converting your own home, try to make a realistic evaluation of your skills and the time you have for the project. You can often save money by spending some on a good subcontractor, or two, or three.

$ If you are converting a large building into apartments, spend your time supervising or hire a general contractor. You might even be able to work out a joint venture deal with a reputable contractor, a local lender, and yourself. You supply the building that you have already bought, a lender supplies the money for the interior restructuring, and the contractor takes on the responsibility of getting the job done. You split the profits according to a mutually agreeable arrangement made *before* work begins.

START-UP CASH AND CASH FLOW

There's no rule of thumb here. Some converters invest little or no cash, using home equity loans or cost-plus-improvements financing from local lenders. Others mortgage the building and use cash for the conversion.

Your choice of financing options should be based upon your goals and your projected cash flow. Remember that a negative cash flow for a year or two is not necessarily bad financial practice, but don't choose financing that has no chance of bringing in positive cash flow in the easily forseeable future.

TAXES

If you live in the house that you convert and you designate it as your primary residence, the mortgage interest and property taxes for the portion you live in are deductible on federal income tax returns. Depreciation, interest, taxes, and expenses for the portion you rent can be deducted against the rental income from the property. If you use an equity line to finance your conversion, the interest allocated to your residence is deductible up to the original cost of the property, plus improvements. Since conversion could well be considered an improvement, allocating and figuring taxes can become something of a juggling game.

Your local IRS office has tax booklets available that will give you guidelines and information needed to file your return. If this is your first time through filing a return that includes rental property, however, I suggest that you also consult with a tax adviser.

If your conversion is strictly investment, losses generated by the property (paper or otherwise) will not be deductible against income from other nonpassive sources. If your adjusted gross income is less than $100,000, however, you may deduct up to $25,000 in passive real estate losses. Between $100,000 and $150,000 adjusted gross income, this deductible amount decreases until it becomes zero deductible at $150,000. And these special loss provisions are available only to those who "actively manage" their properties. (Hiring a management company does not disqualify you from active management. Using a limited partnership as your investment vehicle does.) Here again the IRS has printed matter available for the asking. Get the booklets and study them *before* you make your investment decisions.

The Bottom Line

Most conversions are profitable. Even though you may not be creating more living space, you are dividing the space into more units. Given the same building in the same location, three units of 900 square feet each will bring in considerably more income than one unit of 2,700 square feet. The single unit (an eighty-year-old Victorian, for example) might bring in a rental income of $800 a month. The three apartments created by conversion could easily bring in $450 each, a total of $1,350 a month. The converted house therefore brings in $550 a month more.

In figuring your bottom line, you must consider how long it will take for the extra rental income to pay off the expenses of conversion. Only after that is the conversion truly profitable.

Unless, of course, you sell immediately after doing the conversion. Then you must estimate the market value of a big eighty-year-old Victorian against the three-unit investment property you've created. The investment property price will almost invariably be higher, but how *much* higher depends upon your local marketplace. The difference should cover your conversion expenses and leave a profit worthy of your time and work.

·   ·   ·

Knowledge and Skills

Of course construction knowledge and building skills help in achieving a successful hammer and nails conversion, but I want to caution you not to rely completely on your own skills. Call in subcontractors when you need them and, perhaps even more important, use a professional home inspection service before you buy or decide to do an internal restructuring. A qualified outside opinion can save you thousands in expensive errors. Do *you* know if the current cross beams will support a bathtub? One that's full of water? With a person in it?

SOME SUCCESSFUL INVESTORS

Live-in Landlords

Charlotte McGinty bought the 2,700 square foot Victorian that I mentioned under "The Bottom Line." The price was an amazingly low $89,000. Despite her $75,000 in ready cash, she mortgaged to a maximum 80 percent loan-to-value ratio and used her cash for the renovation and conversion work.

Since she subcontracted virtually everything, the total expenditure approached $50,000. She was allowed to take 10 percent of those costs as a tax *credit,* however, since the building was constructed and placed in service before 1936.

Charlotte lives in one of the three apartments she created and rents the other two. The $900-a-month income she receives falls just short (by $80) of covering her monthly mortgage and property tax payments. Of course there are still maintenance and insurance costs, but essentially she has achieved her goal of secure, comfortable, and inexpensive housing.

Visionary Craftsmen

John Wassermann is the handyman-special investor mentioned in the lead profile of this chapter. The hammer and nails conversion investment he embarked upon surprised even himself. He bought a $3-million estate with the assistance of a wishing-to-remain-anonymous joint venture speculator.

With board of adjustment approval, he created from the twenty-three-room, eleven-bathroom main house nine congregate housing rental units for senior citizens. Each unit has a sitting room, bedroom, and bath (some of the large bedrooms in the original house were divided into sitting room and bedroom). The tenants share the huge living room with its magnificent stone fireplace, the dining room, the kitchen, and the porch and patio. The two maids apartments are occupied by the superintendent and the groundskeeper.

From the fourteen-stall stable, the five-bay garage, and the building containing the caretaker's, chauffeur's, and stableman's quarters he created twelve condominium apartments, deeding three acres of land to the condominium community for parking and green space.

Were John Wassermann and his invisible partner making money from these conversions? Not exactly. The income from the sale of the condominium units just about wiped out John's construction and conversion costs for both the congregate housing for seniors and the condominiums. The income from the rental units in the main house, however, comes nowhere near covering the carrying costs of the mortgage on the original $3,000,000 purchase.

"So why did he do it?" you ask.

For the land. Besides the 3 acres for the condominium community, the 1.5 acres for the seniors' housing, and the 7.4 acres he dedicated to the town for walking trails, John Wassermann was deeded 47 acres of gently rolling landscape in the estate purchase package. While he was working on the hammer and nails and the condominium conversions, he was also doing the paperwork for a subdivision of the land. His civic responsibility (or so it was viewed) in creating rental housing for seniors and condominiums for moderate-income families prompted the town's planning board to look favorably on his plans for the development of the remainder of his land. They approved just about what he asked for.

There will be thirty-six one-acre-plus lots along Wassermann Lane. Upon them thirty-six houses priced in the $400,000 range will be built. Even the construction financing is already arranged. It seems everyone, including John Wassermann himself, believes that he is ready to become a professional builder.

VACATIONERS

Claudia and Michael Vallejo owned a fifty-year-old eleven-room summer place on the ocean. By renting at $1,800 a week during July, they were able to pay all expenses and spend August at the beach with their four children.

Finding tenants at $1,800 a week wasn't always easy, however, and the Vallejos discovered more often than not that two and sometimes three families were sharing the costs and the house. It seemed that the summer place was always crowded during its rental period, and badly used.

After one particularly odious cleanup, Michael had an idea. Why not convert this huge house into three units: two one-bedroom apartments for rental and one three-bedroom apartment for themselves? If it worked, the family could spend the entire summer at the beach. Claudia would be there to oversee the tenants, there would be little inclination for overcrowding the house, and there might still be enough income to cover mortgage payments, taxes, insurance, and upkeep.

Some detective work revealed that four other large beach houses in the community had been converted to apartments units and no one had objected. Going rate for a bedroom, living room, kitchenette, and bath on the ocean ranged from $600 to $850 a week. Not quite $1,800, it's true, *but* there would be *two* rental units and both could be rented for the *entire* summer. Such a plan would actually bring in more income while providing the Vallejo family with more vacation time.

It cost the Vallejos $27,000 to do the conversion, but they'll tell you they don't regret a penny. The house pays for itself, even with the extra payment for the home improvement loan. And everyone enjoys the long summer.

MOVING ON

If you do a conversion, make money, and enjoy the work, you might well move on to others, perhaps bigger and more creative. And you might eventually decide to leave your current occupation and do renovation, refurbishing, and interior restructuring full time.

But there's another kind of conversion that isn't exactly an investment. It's more like a venture, maybe an adventure. You've probably guessed that I'm referring to condominium conversion.

If you buy a rambling old house, refurbish it and convert the interior into four beautiful living units, why not sell those units individually as condominiums? It's happening all over the country, and generally the profits from the sale of four condominium units far exceed those from the sale of the refurbished building with four newly created rental units. Before you start on this venture, however, be sure you talk with an attorney very familiar with real estate procedures in your area. Condominium conversion laws differ from state to state and you must conform to yours.

· C H A P T E R   14 ·

Commercial
Property

*Sarah Robinson is a dentist. She is looking for a permanent location
for her office at minimal cost to herself. Investment vehicle of choice:
a building with capacity for three to four offices, or a mixed commer-
cial/residential building.*

*Joe Fiske has a top middle-management job at a huge corporation.
His skills at time/efficiency management are among the best in the
business, but he feels that he has no upward potential in the corporation and he would like to be his own boss. His real estate experience
consists of the subdivision of a parcel of land which he sold to a builder,
one conversion of a single-family house into a three-family house, and
the three homes he has lived in. He has $300,000 equity in his present
home with a very small mortgage payment, and he has $400,000 in
available cash. Investment vehicle of choice: commercial property.*

·   ·   ·

It wasn't by chance that I placed this investment vehicle last in the
order of chapters. It was quite simply a matter of numbers. Commercial property, you see, is suitable only for a small percentage of
investors.

Oh, don't get me wrong, there's money to be made in this part of the marketplace, big money. But there are big-money risks too, and the demands upon time, experience, and commitment are tremendous. Look at the investment demand profile. A demand level of *10* in *nine* of the fifteen character traits! To choose this investment vehicle you must have either a personal need for commercial space or a well-considered desire to move into commercial property speculation as a career. And in either case, you had best have a good financial reserve that will carry you through at least a year or two.

CHECKPOINTS FOR THE INVESTOR

RATIONAL AND LOGICAL EVALUATION OF OPTIONS

If you are a self-employed professional looking to buy a building that will provide you with office space for yourself and rentable space that will bring down the cost of housing your own business, your primary points of consideration are those of virtually every investor: location and structure.

In considering location, evaluate accessibility, demographics, and parking. In considering structure, read Chapter 13, Hammer and Nails Conversions, and then ask yourself if the building is suitable for commercial or mixed commercial/residential use. Be aware of zoning restrictions as you consider both location and structure and be aware that some businesses require special utility services (a hairdresser would need extra plumbing and electricity, for example). Can you get zoning board approval for the use you wish to make of the building? Are you willing to put in the extra services a special tenant might require or will you restrict your tenants to those that require no special alterations?

§   Bear in mind during your search for property that location and structure, not the price, are the most important evaluation criteria. *Do not buy simply because a building carries a bargain price tag.* If that bargain is in a second-rate location, the odds are that the income from the rental units that you create will be second rate, too, if you can get the space rented! And the importance of location doesn't stop there. Income from the business that *you* are running within the building could also fall short of its potential.

After location, the quality of the structure and its suitability to your

INVESTOR DEMAND PROFILE

	1	2	3	4	5	6	7	8	9	10
1. Positive Action and Reaction										
2. Willingness to Take Risks										
3. Decision-making Ability										
4. Commitment--the Will to Follow Through										
5. Logical and Rational Evaluation of Options										
6. Ability to Deal with Numbers and Finances										
7. Ability to Deal with Legal Constraints										
8. Organization and Management Skills										
9. Foresight										
10. Imagination and Creativity										
11. Self-confidence										
12. Patience and Tact										
13. Self-control										
14. Social Contact										
15. Negotiating Skill										

needs and plans are so important that I urge you to spend the necessary money to have a professional engineer inspect the premises before you buy. (You can make your contract to purchase subject to this inspection.) If you make an error in evaluating structure, it can be almost as costly as an error in choosing location. Unanticipated repair or restructuring problems can throw you into a ruinously negative cash flow, not for a month or two but for years to come. Then your efforts to find least-cost housing for your business will, in fact, have purchased you high-cost housing (much higher than rent for comparable space). And your investment will be a difficult one to liquidate.

If you wish to become an investor/speculator in commercial property, your evaluation of options is far more extensive. Before any other decision is made, you must choose the type or types of property in which you intend to invest. This is not an easy pick-a-card, any-card game, for not every type of investment property will be profitable in every area. Again I must fall back upon the most essential rule of the real estate game: *Know your local marketplace.*

Ask yourself which of the following commercial ventures is likely to succeed in your area, and for which can you find, restructure, or build property that is so eminently suitable that tenants or buyers will make your venture a genuinely profitable one.

INDUSTRIAL BUILDINGS: As a beginning commercial property investor, you are unlikely to have the funds, knowledge, or business connections to come upon, recognize, and develop the perfect site for American Nissan. But you might be able to develop factory or factory-and-office space that could be subdivided to house several fledgling companies, including American Sake, which might someday become as popular as Old Grandad. If you take on such a venture, some of your fledgling tenants will survive and prosper (and may just rent more space from you or hire you to develop a new plant location for them) and some will surely fail. Which means that turnover and change in this type of venture is a high probability, one with which you must deal on a continual basis. To help carry over vacancy periods, some developers of such "incubator" buildings convert vacant space into short-term warehousing facilities.

Before you jump aboard this particular investment vehicle, be sure you do your homework. You should have rather clear cut information indicating that such facilities are in demand within a twenty-five-mile radius of your selected site. Incubator industrial buildings usually do best when located on the outskirts of major metropolitan areas where growth is very strong, markets for the products readily available, and transportation facilities excellent. Work with the Census Bureau, the local Chamber of Commerce, and/or private research groups to get facts on demographics, vacancy rates in the area, new business ventures, business failures, and proposed future development.

OFFICE BUILDINGS: You don't have to duplicate Trump Tower to get started in office building development, but you do have to know a lot about business and services in the local area. You must establish first that office space is in demand and that new construction now under way or in the proposal stages will not create an over-built situation that will cause a high vacancy rate. Once you establish high demand and low supply, location is the key to success. A long-deserted, rambling estate from the 1890s can be restructured into a splendid office park and bring in rents that will buy you that condo on St. Croix you've been dreaming of, if its location is good. If it's on a back country road that everyone misses, however, it may just stand empty, or nearly empty, *permanently*. Not even lowered rents will bring out new commercial tenants. There will be no vacation condo, not even a shack in the mountains, coming from this venture. In fact you could even end up abandoning it as a tax loss. Or you might spend more money to convert it to an apartment building, which will fill up if the rents are low enough, but *how long* will it take you to recoup your investment? The goal, you must remember, is *positive* cash flow.

RETAIL SPACE: This venture carries the same considerations as the development of office space with the added restriction that most successful retail space must have street-level access. (With the exception, of course, of two- or three-story indoor shopping malls, which I don't usually recommend as a beginning investment vehicle.)

What I do recommend is mixed commercial/residential property. Consider buildings that will house a pharmacy, barbershop, stationery store, or other relatively small, one-level business or businesses on the street level and three, four, or more residential apartments above the street level. The rents from the residential space may just keep you going during a vacancy in the retail space.

OUTLET CENTERS AND WAREHOUSES: Inexpensive is the key word here. If you can find the land and buildings cheap enough to rent them cheaply and still make a profit, *and* if you have a large enough population from which to draw both tenants and customers, you *may* be able to convert buildings once considered unusable into profitable multiuse centers. Parking and road access are important factors to consider, and don't forget zoning.

MOTELS, HOTELS, RESTAURANTS, RECREATION FACILITIES, AND NURSING HOMES: These are personal-use facilities and the success of such ventures is very much dependent on the demographic profile of your area. There exist printed guidelines and rules of thumb that might say something like "there should be one restaurant for each five thousand people," but these are worth little or nothing without a good socioeconomic profile. For example, restaurants range from Burger King to Le Petit Auberge, and a community that might support six Burger Kings might not support *one* expensive French restaurant. Or consider a roller skating rink. The statistics might say one rink per 45,000 people. Would one succeed in an area of 75,000 people known for its

retirement appeal? If you are considering the development of personal-use facilities as your investment vehicle, you must add socioeconomic data to location and structure as your primary considerations.

To say that this little summary has scratched the surface of commercial investment possibilities would be an exaggeration. The field is very big and very complicated. If you really want it, be prepared to research, research, and then research a bit more.

LEGAL CONSTRAINTS

A few weeks ago, I spent two days in the office of an attorney who deals primarily with commercial real estate clients. When I made the appointment, I thought I knew quite a lot about real estate law and commercial real estate dealing. Those two days were a humbling experience for me.

As I expected, the attorney was involved in several petitions to the zoning board, several contracts, and a closing that went on for three and a half hours. What I didn't expect was the complexity of the commercial leasing *negotiations* and the attorney's direct involvement in them. Attorneys can and do spend hours debating the wording of a single phrase.

ABOUT LEASES

This is a primer, an introduction not meant to stand in for the advice of an attorney. But knowing even these few terms will help you to understand some of what your attorney is talking about.

FLAT RENTAL LEASE: This lease names a periodic rental payment (usually monthly) that is fixed for the entire term of the lease.

GRADED LEASE OR GRADUATED LEASE: The tenant agrees to a fixed rental amount at the inception of the lease but there are provisions for graduated increases or decreases at specified points during the term.

NET LEASE: The tenant pays rent and all operating expenses for the portion of the property which he or she occupies.

NET NET LEASE: The tenant pays rent and all operating expenses, and all insurance premiums on the space he or she occupies.

NET NET NET (TRIPLE NET) LEASE: The tenant pays rent, all operating expenses, insurance premiums, and property taxes on the space he or she occupies.

GROUND LEASE: A ground lease covers the use of land alone, usually land without improvements. Often the tenant constructs his or her own building. Most ground leases are long term; ninety-nine years is common. A valid ground lease can sometimes be used as the down payment for construction financing, allowing an investor/speculator to put up the building with 100 percent financing.

Commercial real estate contracts that run to ten or even twenty pages are quite common. Expect your legal fees to be high in this investment vehicle and *don't* try to save money by hiring your friend Sam's cousin who's primarily a divorce lawyer but will take care of your contract and closing as a favor. Speculating in commercial property must be based upon a thorough knowledge of *both* real estate law and business law. Choose as your attorney the most experienced person you can find. And if you should waver from this advice because you are put off by the amount of that attorney's fee, just make a little comparison between law and medicine. Would you hire your child's pediatrician, the best in the area, to do the double bypass heart surgery your aging father needs?

NUMBERS AND FINANCES

Do you recall the chapter on small apartment buildings which I began with a sign that read NEOPHYTES BEWARE? One of the factors that inspired that sign was the importance of numbers in a successful apartment building venture. Expenses, taxes, the servicing of debts, and income for the apartment building must be carefully balanced. If that balancing were likened to a seesaw in the playground of the real estate marketplace, the balancing of the numbers and finances in a modestly sized commercial venture would be something like a forty-foot Ferris wheel. Yes, there's that much of a difference.

First of all, the numbers are usually much larger. But more important, they are so very sensitive and subject to change, their weight shifting according to the gross profits of tenants whose leases are tied to income, or upon vacancies, or new competition in the area, or local and national economic swings. And financing? That is often a complex arrangement in which the lender shares in the profits of the venture. Your accountant should be a specialist and every bit as good as your attorney.

SELF-CONFIDENCE

It does look a little odd, doesn't it? A rating of 5 in self-confidence in this the most demanding of investment vehicles. Well, rest assured, it's not a printer's error. Too much self-confidence in an arena that demands the talents of people trained in many different professional disciplines can be the fatal flaw of the would-be commercial real estate entrepreneur.

This is *not* a do-it-yourself marketplace. Don't overestimate your abilities and your knowledge.

ORGANIZATION AND MANAGEMENT SKILLS

Just as you will need to depend upon the knowledge and skills of lawyers, accountants, bankers, and perhaps commercial real estate agents to acquire your property in a potentially successful manner, you will also need to delegate the work of building, renovating, renting, and managing it.

"Of course!" you exclaim. "That goes without saying, considering the picture you've painted so far. But why have you stopped short of giving this personality trait a ten? Isn't it just as important as numbers, rational evaluation, risk taking, and the others?"

Yes. And no. Except in the smallest commercial ventures (a building to house your business and one or two others, for example, or the investment in your first mixed commercial/residential property), commercial property speculation and development will require the management and organization skills of more than one person. In fact, a personal weakness in this area can be compensated for by hiring a particularly skilled manager and organizer who might rate only 3s or 4s in most of the other personality traits we've been discussing. Again: commercial real estate speculation is not a do-it-yourself venture. *Know* your strengths and weaknesses and act according to your knowledge.

RISK TAKING

What American hasn't walked or driven down a city street where at least half of the stores were vacant and boarded up? "Tough times" or "bad area" are our common responses. But how many of us have ever looked up from the storefronts to examine the upper stories of the buildings in these neighborhoods? Those who do usually see curtains at the windows and sometimes even a few geraniums on the fire escapes. Business may be bad, but there are still people *living* here. And *that* is the difference in risk between residential and commercial real estate investment.

Inhabitable residential space can almost always be rented if the price is low enough. The cash flow then may still be negative, but the owner/investor does not carry all the expenses of the property while waiting for a turn in the economic climate. Tenants contribute.

In contrast, commercial space does not rent easily and quickly and lowering the rent often has no effect whatsoever on the likelihood of finding a tenant. A poor choice of commercial investment property therefore may result in *no income* rather than diminished income. And that situation can become the Waterloo of even the most experienced investor. The risks in this investment vehicle run neck and neck with the rewards.

. . .

COMMITMENT, DECISION MAKING, AND POSITIVE ACTION AND REACTION

If you have worked your way through the real estate marketplace to the commercial property booth, you must certainly possess these three essential qualities of the serious investor, for absence of any *one* usually guarantees failure.

Without commitment, projects would stand unfinished, and incomplete work almost always sells for a loss (or goes into bankruptcy). Without commitment, projects would also be poorly managed, which diminishes both value and return.

Without the ability to make decisions, every sticky question would be tossed from one involved party to another, considered and reconsidered, worried over, complained about, found fault with, and proposed against without proposing a viable alternative. And while everyone waits for *someone* to say, "This is the way we'll do it," time ticks away, taking money with it.

Without positive action and reaction, apathy and despair could reign undisturbed. To be your own boss in a business that hinges upon *doing* things, you must be a self starter. To handle the many things that go wrong in every real estate venture, you must be willing to react with an attitude based upon the affirmation, "Here's what we can do" rather than a resigned, "What can you do?"

FORESIGHT

Some investors, speculators, and developers pour hundreds of thousands of dollars, sometimes millions, into projects because they feel gut reactions that say, "This area is gonna go!" And sometimes they're right. When they are, they may just earn millions in return for their time and intuition. But intuition is a shaky foundation upon which to build a fortune. Foresight in commercial property ventures derives from knowledge, research, study, and calculations. Intuition is but the catalyst that transforms concrete into gold.

IMAGINATION AND CREATIVITY

Just as hammer and nails conversion of residential property requires an eye for architectural potential, commercial real estate ventures require an eye for business potential. You have to be the kind of person who can forget time, and food, and music, and sex while you're immersed in the bunch of sketches, plans, dreams, and calculations spread upon the table before you.

In commercial ventures, however, you must pay even closer attention to rational and logical evaluation of all the possible pros and cons, to legal constraints, and to the balancing of the numbers, for there is far less room for error in this investment vehicle than in any residential venture.

PATIENCE, TACT, AND SELF-CONTROL

Commercial real estate development is a profession, almost never an avocation. By the time you enter this part of the marketplace, you should be experienced in the use of patience, tact, and self-control in the business arena. There are times to be patient and times to step forward and act; times to be tactful and times to be blunt and demanding; and times to be self-controlled and times to express your anger and exasperation. If you wish to be successful in your commercial ventures, you should be able to tell the difference.

SOCIAL CONTACT

Being a commercial real estate investor/speculator is a lonely business. You will find few people in the social circles of even major cities who can understand your dreams and your problems. Oh, certainly you'll find some camaraderie among professional groups, but remember that these professional friends are also your competitors. Be careful what you talk about with them (good property and good ideas are hard to come by but easily stolen).

Your business as a commercial investor/speculator will also involve some necessary business socializing: obligatory luncheons with planning board members, materials dealers, buyers, sellers, real estate agents, and prospective tenants, not to mention your attorney and your accountant or your property manager and your foreman. So why have I given social contact so low a rating in the investment demand profile? Because most of these "social luncheons" will really be negotiating sessions. Those that aren't will probably be occasions during which you formulate plans or give directions. In truth, there is precious little socializing in the work day of a commercial property investor/ speculator.

NEGOTIATING

If your previous negotiating sessions have brought about sleepless nights and/or acid indigestion, you might want to consider some other investment vehicle as your means to wealth, for the commercial property investor/speculator seems to spend more time negotiating than anything else. Think about the possibilities:

* negotiating for the purchase of property,
* negotiating for zoning changes or variances,
* negotiating the cost of materials,
* negotiating the cost of labor,
* negotiating the terms of leases,
* negotiating the sale of property.

Bear in mind also that each of these activities is many times more complex than anything you've encountered in the residential marketplace.

TOOLS OF THE TRADE

WAITING TIME

Most commercial property is purchased with long-term investment in mind. It is important, therefore, that the cash flow be positive and the potential for appreciation be, at the least, good. Remember also that commercial property is an illiquid investment, you *cannot* count on a quick sale, even at a reduced price. A year on the market is not a particularly long listing term and some properties can take as long as five years to sell.

WORKING TIME

Working time depends on the role or roles you choose to play. If you do "everything" yourself, you could well work an eighty-hour week. If you gather competent people about you and learn to delegate

SOME NEGOTIATED BITS AND PIECES

Think of these items as a handful of confetti thrown to wish you well. And remember there are much, much bigger things ahead.

RENT ESCALATION: Many commercial leases provide for rent escalation during their term. How much and when are the points of negotiation. Theoretically, this escalation provides coverage against increased operating expenses to the owner of the property. Sometimes, however, rent increases can exceed expenses, especially when rent escalation is tied to an index unrelated to the business of the tenant (the Consumer Price Index, for example). Some rent escalation clauses are tied to utility costs and/or local taxes. Generally, you will find no government rent controls on commercial leases.

LANDLORD FIX-UP: Will you, the landlord, agree to remodel to suit the tenant or will the tenant be responsible for remodeling and redecorating? If the landlord remodels, the lease should define exactly what is to be done, naming as many product names and quality standards as possible. If the tenant remodels, the lease should specify what remains in the building when the lease is terminated.

NONDISTURBANCE CLAUSE: This clause guarantees the tenant possession of the premises for the entire term of the lease, even if the ownership of the building changes. Consider it carefully if you hope to sell in the forseeable future.

THE RIGHT TO SUBLEASE: If the tenant is allowed to sublease all or part of the space he leases from the landlord, he collects the rent (any rent he desires to set) and then pays the landlord the rent specified in the lease. The right to sublet protects the tenant who comes upon hard times, but it can bring an undesirable business into a building. The landlord can protect his interests by requiring his approval before a sublet can be arranged.

THE RIGHT TO ASSIGN THE LEASE: In an assignment, the tenant finds another tenant to take his or her place and abide by all the terms of the lease. The landlord should protect his or her interest by requiring approval of the assignment.

RENEWAL OPTION: Many if not most businesses plan to remain in the same location for long periods of time. The renewal option is a means of protecting the right to occupy a space. It may or may not specify the rent during the option period.

ARBITRATION OF DISPUTES: Some disagreement is almost inevitable. It's a good idea to name an arbitrator when there is no dispute, that is, when the lease is signed. Be sure you name an impartial person.

both tasks and authority, you might get several afternoons a week on the golf course and certainly four or five evenings at home with your family. In other words, working time is something *you* control. And the amount of time you put in will not necessarily be in proportion to the amount of money you make. Effective time management is an important factor in successful commercial ventures.

START-UP CASH

Nowhere in the marketplace is financing more complex. Banks, life insurance companies, syndicates, REITs, private individuals, the federal government, and other groups are all in the business of financing business ventures. Some write long-term mortgages, some short-term construction loans, some require large cash reserves by the developer, others mortgage the total cost but take a share of the profits in the deal.

If you've been in the real estate investment business for a number of years previous to your venture into commercial property, you probably have financial sources where you have already established a good credit record. They are the best place to start in your search for capital. If you have no established sources, be sure to use a commercial specialist as your real estate broker since he or she will be able to direct you to a number and variety of lenders.

In some situations, usually after you are well established in commercial development, a major corporation may not only hire you to find a site for their new building, but also to find financing for the construction work. Once the work is complete, you take out a mortgage and lease the building back to the corporation, at a profitable cash flow, of course.

CASH FLOW

Positive. *Positive. POSITIVE!* One goes into commercial real estate investment and development to *make money.* Tax writeoffs are a thing of the past. Check the numbers again and again to be certain your project will produce a positive cash flow when it is fully leased. (And it's a good idea to have it fully leased or at least to have an anchor tenant—one who occupies a majority of the space on a long-term lease—before you start construction or renovation.)

Taxes

It would take a separate (and very heavy) book to discuss tax laws as they apply to commercial real estate, and before the ink was dry on its pages, there would be changes in those laws. So I will not try to summarize commercial real estate tax law in two pages. But even if I could or if I were willing to write the all-time tax tome, I would still end my work with this same sentence: *It is imperative that you use a good tax accountant if you choose commercial real estate as your investment vehicle.*

The Bottom Line

Some of the nicest millionaires I know made their money through commercial development. This is probably the most lucrative vehicle in the real estate marketplace, but it is also the most risky and the most demanding.

Knowledge and Skills

I won't put you off with another hammer blow to the knowledge-and-skills message I've been repeating in this chapter. Instead, let me just list some points of information with which the prospective commercial investor/speculator should be very familiar:

- the value of land locally
- the cost of building materials
- the cost of specialized labor
- land use regulations and zoning laws
- the time delay to be expected in zoning board appeals
- the availability of subcontractors in the area
- environmental protection regulations
- types of financing
- sources of financing
- leases
- business law
- real estate taxation (local, state, and federal)
- local demographics
- market potential regarding a specific type of investment
- the local building codes

- building inspection procedures (and expected delays)
- accounting principles
- outlook for the local economy
- negotiating skills.

SOME SUCCESSFUL INVESTORS

SELF-EMPLOYED BUSINESS PEOPLE

Sarah Robinson, the dentist in this chapter's lead profile, bought the big gray house on the corner of Maple and Elm streets. It had two turrets, a front porch that wrapped around two sides, a yard big enough to park twenty cars, and enough space between it and its neighbor properties to allow for separate entrance and exit driveways.

Why had no one seen the possibilities? she wondered. Fourteen rooms and only one block from Main Street . . .

Sarah wondered if she could be making a mistake. Perhaps there was some fault she was not seeing. Something obvious that everyone else knew. But her research, the professional inspections, even the projected numbers fit together. She decided the problem was in the listing. The house had been on the market for eleven months as a *residential* property. There had even been two price reductions, first from $240,000 to $209,000 and then to $189,000.

Sarah had three estimates for renovation and conversion work that ranged from $60,000 to $82,000. The work, when complete, would create three multiroom medical or legal offices. The going rental rates for such space were approximately $800 to $1,000 a month. If she could get the house for $175,000, the rents from two units would more than carry her $135,000 mortgage *and* the property taxes. The $60,000 or so improvement loan would cost her a little over $800 a month, an amount equal to what she would otherwise have to pay in rent for her office space. And better yet, the two income-producing units would almost certainly bring in more revenue over the years, while the cost of her unit would remain fixed. And of course, the building would appreciate, especially after its conversion to office units in an area where more and more professionals were moving in.

.   .   .

MID-LIFE CAREER CHANGERS

Joe Fiske was offered a "management incentive." If he left the company during its current staff reduction, he would be paid a year's salary over two years. It was the nudge he needed to bid farewell to the ten-hour days and the office politics he hated.

With most of his available cash, he bought a parcel of land half a mile down the road from the site of a proposed eight hundred-unit condominium development and abutting the site of the new post office under construction. He planned to build a small shopping center with facades and interior details modeled after Williamsburg, Virginia.

While busy with work for the planning board, Joe was also hunting for financing and for an anchor tenant to occupy the largest of the rental spaces he would build. In the same week, he found both. A Publix Market would take a long-term lease and a local bank and a private investor with some venture capital would provide construction money.

The details of this story could fill a book on their own. The setbacks, the dreams, the delays; the day the backhoe broke the town's sewer line; choosing from among the prospective tenants; the newspaper stories; the guy who wanted to put in the gay bar; the how-to-do-everything bookstore lady . . . The project took three years of Joe's life, sometimes seven days a week, and often more than the ten hours a day he had been spending in his old job at the corporation. But when it was done, he could point to something and say, "I built that." No committees, no corporate policies, no anonymity. And when it was done, Joe Fiske was $2½ million richer.

MOVING ON

As I suggested earlier, a good place to start in the commercial marketplace is the mixed commercial/residential building. There you will be introduced to the principles of commercial investment/speculation without becoming completely dependent upon the commercial lease for cash flow. Building management is also relatively simple and consumes little time. If you see potential growth in your area or the need for a specific type of building, you might consider moving on to commercial renovation work. I've seen an old movie theater converted quite successfully into a branch office of a bank, complete with drive-through tellers. Or perhaps a closed department store or supermarket might be converted to a nursing home. Or a house to a restaurant. The possibilities seem endless given enough imagination and the supply/demand data to back it up.

Once you do a renovation or restructuring or two and have a good feel for the work, you might move into a small strip shopping center with perhaps a brand-new A & P as your anchor tenant. And after that . . . perhaps you know of a cannery in San Francisco or an unused seaport in New York City.

If you can renovate and/or build commercial real estate, well, the sky's the limit, and you no longer need this book.

Negotiating in the Real Estate Marketplace

Win/Win is very fashionable nowadays. Look around a bit and you'll certainly come across an array of books, magazine articles, corporate and private seminars, and even television programs that promise to teach you win/win negotiating techniques, win/win management techniques, win/win honeymoon and marriage techniques, and even win/ win child-rearing techniques. The prevailing cultural attitude (or at least the attitude prevailing in the media) seems to assume that every educated person should (and would choose to) come away from a confrontation wearing a corners-of-the-mouth-turned-up smile that says quite clearly, "We both won."

If you believe this pop-psychology pablum, your potential earnings in the real estate marketplace will be limited. Have you ever seen team players jumping into the air, clapping their hands, hugging each other because the contest was declared a draw? Yet that's the purported goal of win/win negotiating—a tie, no real winner declared. Win/win is *not* the goal of successful real estate professionals (despite what their books and seminars may say). In fact, no one should enter the marketplace without the expressed intention of winning. To do less is to settle for mediocrity and mediocre rewards.

The secret of successful real estate negotiating is in creating a strategy for winning. In other words, *how* you play the game is of utmost importance. If you play all-or-nothing, if you play for a shutout in each negotiating game, you will win occasionally but you will probably tire of the real estate marketplace long before you become rich there. For a sustained winning record, you should learn to play with, as well as against, your opponent, leaving space for his or her pride and self-satisfaction, allowing him or her to move the ball and even to score an occasional goal.

Remember one word in dealing with others—Reciprocity.

That was the message in a Chinese fortune cookie I opened at dinner almost six months ago. I have kept it pinned to the bulletin board above my desk ever since. Its advice is a master key in a marketplace where you must often be willing to give up some things in order to get others. In the end, the successful negotiator *wins* by getting those goals that he or she thinks *most important*. Winning what is most important may be the equivalent of winning by a score of 21 to 18. But that's a good deal better than a score of 6 to 6.

"In the end" is another key phrase in the formulation of negotiating strategy. Rarely does one achieve goals in the first moves of a negotiating game. Negotiating is a process. The beginner must recognize it as such and learn to use time and strategy in the process. Impatience will usually cause failure or, at least, diminished success. So will the desire to drive forward without due regard to the movements and strategies of your opponent.

What else contributes to working the process successfully? Sensitivity, intuition, planning, research, role playing, tact, and respect for the goals, intelligence, and skills of your opponent.

BUYER NEGOTIATING

The most widely held misconception about negotiating in the real estate marketplace is that it begins when a prospective buyer makes an offer. In fact, the first offer is closer to the midpoint of the game for both the buyer *and* the seller. For the buyer, the process really starts just after he or she first *sees* a property that is appealing.

. . .

Determining Market Value

Most such properties will have a price tag attached and that tag begins your game. Your first move is to test the asking price against what you think is the value of the property. Remember, there's no fair pricing code in the real estate marketplace. A seller can quite literally ask whatever he or she pleases for a piece of property. Overpriced properties usually hang around a long time on the market. Underpriced properties often get snapped up before they hit the shared listing system of the real estate agents in the area. And those in between? Well, they get negotiated until someone wins.

There are several ways to estimate real estate value, none of which works every time or for every type of property, so you must become familiar with them all and use them together or singly as they apply to the particular transaction in which you are involved.

THE COMPARISON METHOD: Also called the *market data* method, this is the method most often used in the single-family and multifamily home marketplace, the condominium marketplace, and the vacation home marketplace. It is also used in evaluating small apartment buildings and mixed commercial/residential properties when enough facts are available.

To do a market data analysis, you will need the help of a real estate agent. Ask to see the *comparables file*, sometimes referred to as "comps." This is a compilation of listing sheets for properties in the area that have sold during the past year or so. Each listing will contain a complete profile of the property plus information on the original asking price, the actual selling price, and the length of time on the market. This information will be the key factor in your evaluation.

From the file, choose several properties that are similar to the property you want to buy. Pay particular attention to location, size, age, and amenities. Then compare the actual selling prices of those comparable properties to the asking price of "your" property. Allow for amenities, better location, lot size, or whatever else might make one property more valuable than another, and allow also for any change in the mood of the marketplace between the current time and the time your comparable was sold. (The comparables may have sold in a slow market or a slow season and you might be buying in a superheated market. Market value on the property you want to buy would then be higher than the comps. Or reverse the scenario, and the market value for "your" property might be lower than the comps!)

Come up with what you think is the market value of the property you want to buy, but *do not* mention this number to your agent. (If you do, you'll probably end up paying that amount.) Ask the agent his or her opinion as to market value and ask how that number was arrived at. This information will help you to corroborate *your* estimate. Do not, however, commit yourself verbally to agreeing or disagreeing with the agent's estimate. In negotiating, like poker, you must hold your cards close to your chest.

REPLACEMENT COST ESTIMATE: There are three steps in the appraisal method that uses replacement cost as its basis.

1. A value must be assigned to the land. This is especially difficult in cities where there is virtually no vacant land for sale. Tax assessments might help in establishing relative value, but they cannot be relied on for accurate market value. Unless you are something of an expert in your local real estate marketplace, it is probably advisable to consult with real estate agents or an appraiser to determine this figure.

2. An estimate must be made for the cost of comparable new construction. You can get a figure for the usual cost per square foot of home construction in your area from your local chapter of the National Association of Home Builders. National headquarters are at 15th and M Streets N.W., Washington, D.C. 20005. Phone: (202) 822-0200. A call will get you the address and phone number of your local affiliate.

If the property you're considering is something larger than a home—an apartment building or commercial property, for example—it's advisable to seek out a general contractor who does that type of building and ask if he can give you a dollars-per-square-foot estimate of new construction costs.

3. From the cost of new construction, you must then subtract depreciation because of age and wear and tear.

Replacement cost estimating is valuable as an appraisal technique in establishing the upper limit of market value. It tends to be most accurate when evaluating a relatively new building, but even then it should *not* be the only appraisal method used in your evaluation. Combine it with market data or income evaluation, or both.

INCOME EVALUATION: This appraisal technique is used in evaluating income-producing properties, from apartment buildings, to small industrial plants, to huge shopping centers. It can also be used effectively, however, in evaluating multifamily houses that the buyer does not intend to occupy.

The first step in this evaluation process is to obtain accurate gross income figures based on rent roll and other income such as concessions. An estimate for vacancies must be factored in to obtain an estimate of gross revenues. Operating expenses are then subtracted from the gross revenue figures to obtain a net operating income figure. This number is then capitalized at a given percentage which yields the estimate of current market value.

For example, $50,000 a year net operating income capitalized at 8 percent yields a property value of $625,000: $50,000 divided by 0.08.

The trick in this appraisal technique is finding the *correct* capitalization percentage. Real estate generally runs from 6 to 20 percent (the higher the figure the higher the risk in the property). But there are many variables that might influence a capitalization percentage estimate—the local economic picture, state and federal tax laws, the expected life span of the building, potential for a change of usage, just to name a few. It's almost always advisable to get professional advice in establishing the capitalization rate. An accountant specializing in local real estate could help, and so could a good commercial real estate agent.

HIGHEST AND BEST USE: This is an appraisal factor rather than an appraisal technique. It is most often applied to land purchases or to buildings that are to be converted, renovated, or restructured. Evaluating at highest and best use assumes that a future use will make the property more valuable for resale or productive of greater income than it currently is.

Comparison is made between the value of other properties used at the same level as the property you are considering and the value of properties used at the level to which you aspire. If the numbers look good, you might be willing to pay a premium price for a property *because* you believe the future holds a still greater reward for your efforts. But remember to give due consideration to the cost of conversion and the time it is likely to take. Some offers and estimates of value are made contingent upon municipal approval of the change in use.

Once you have estimated the market value of a property, you're ready for the next step in the negotiating game, but you are *not* yet ready to make an offer. Yes, you have a price guideline, but price is not the only factor in a real estate transaction. If it is your *most important factor*, closing date and financing terms can help you to win your best possible price. If financing, renovation, rezoning, or some other factor is most important, price can be one of your most powerful trading chips. Now that you have a fairly accurate idea of market value, it's time to take an inventory of your goals and your trading pieces.

Setting Up for Action

First of all, you really should save all those scratch pages you used in arriving at your market value estimate. You may need them later to help the seller see the market realistically (the way *you* see it, that is). After you've gathered them neatly in a file folder, buy a spiral-bound notebook, the kind kids take to school. This will be your negotiating diary. Such a diary is one of the real estate negotiator's most effective tools, yet most beginners are completely unaware of its value.

Use only the right-hand side sheets in your diary. It's important to keep the back sides of these sheets (the left-hand side as the book lies open before you) clear for notes or comments that you might add later. Number each right-hand page consecutively as you use it and beneath the number enter the date. If you think this sounds like busywork, think again! Those seemingly insignificant dates can become crucial later if negotiations heat up to a point where you must know on what date who said what to whom, or upon what date you determined such-and-such and has-your-opinion-changed-since.

On the first page of your diary, write the address and asking price of the property you want to buy. If available, write the name and address of the seller, and the phone number if you can get it. Staple the real estate agent's card to the page also, so his or her phone numbers will be readily accessible whenever you want them. This is now your easy reference page.

.   .   .

YOUR PRICING PAGE: Page two will be your pricing page. Copy this format:

Asking price   _____

Estimated market value   _____

Ideal price   _____

[This is the price at which you would like to "steal" the property.]

Top-dollar price   _____

[This is the price you might agree to pay if financing, extras or some other special terms sweeten the deal. It is often slightly above your market value figure.]

First offer   _____

[This figure is usually slightly under your ideal price, but you may want to leave it blank as you fill in this page, since factors to be considered on several of the following pages will influence it.]

On this pricing page, you now have a record of the range of your price negotiations as you see it on the date listed. Stop here a moment to do some evaluating. Where, for example, in the range of these numbers does the asking price fall? If it's far above your top-dollar figure, you may have to negotiate long and hard before you come out a winner. Or you may negotiate long and hard and finally have to realize that you will not be able to buy this particular property at a price that's potentially profitable to you. Acknowledge the fact that some sellers hold out for prices that are unrealistic. You may, however, be able to make the deal after four or six months more on the market!

If the asking price of the property is at or near market value or below market value nearer to your ideal price, don't rush out immediately to make an offer at full asking price. Look again at your evaluation. Have you made an error? Is there some factor you don't know about that makes the property less valuable than it seems? Ask questions of the real estate agents and, perhaps more important, of neighbors or business-people in the town.

Part of the function of this pricing page, and in fact of the entire negotiating diary, is to keep your negotiations on a rational basis. Emotion in investment real estate is rather like arsenic, the speed at which a winning deal dies is directly related to the amount used. It's important that you not get caught up by a desire to own a particular property so strong that it blocks out the realistic market evaluation you have made. If a property can't be purchased at a winning price and terms, go on to another.

LISTING YOUR GOALS: Once you've completed the pricing page, you'll want to prepare your goals list. Consider:

* price;
* your optimum closing date;
* any extras you would like included in the purchase price;
* your optimum financing arrangements;
* any contingencies to the purchase.

Get your priorities straight by listing these goals in order of importance, or by assigning each a number on a scale of one to five that indicates its importance to you.

Use this goals page as a check against any contract you may consider signing. In the heat of negotiations, it's quite common to forget an item that you considered an important goal at the outset.

YOUR TRADING CHIPS: On the next page of your diary, you should list your trading chips. This is really a rehash of your goals list with a different perspective. It is, in effect, a test of how important those goals really are to you, for you are now evaluating how much trading space you have in each one.

* *Money.* This is what most people think negotiation is about. How many trading dollars do you have between your ideal price and the market value price? And from there to your top dollar price? The span will determine how large your increments can be as you add dollars to each new offer. If you have a lot of space here, money may turn out to be your primary negotiating chip. If there is little space in the money category, you may have to negotiate with other items.
* *Time.* Closing date is another common trading chip. How flexible can you be? The more flexible, the more time trading chips you will have. If, however, a quick closing is one of your goals, or a very long period before closing, and for some reason you cannot afford to change this date, closing date may not be a trading piece at all. Instead, it

will become a primary goal and you will negotiate with money and/ or other items.

• *Financing.* If there's any kind of seller-assistance available, how money is to be paid out will become a major trading chip. Sometimes a payment schedule or interest rate that is important to the seller can be traded for many thousands of dollars off the asking price.

• *Condition of the building.* Condition is a point the buyer *always* brings up as a reason behind the low offer. Everyone nods and agrees and then doesn't take the point too seriously. But consider it seriously for a moment. How much would it be worth to you if the *seller* were to repair certain items *before* closing? Sometimes repair work done in advance can save so much time that it becomes worth more than its actual cost. Especially if you were planning to do the work yourself and you add in your effort (sweat equity).

• *Contingencies.* Inspections, leases that may or may not survive the closing, zoning changes, the lifting of certain environmental restrictions, parking restrictions, and building permits are all items with which you can negotiate. Dropping the need for one of these from a contract may be a factor in lowering the price significantly. Be careful, however, that the contingency you drop is not essential to the value of the building. For example, a property might be worth $350,000 if it can be converted to mixed commercial/residential use, but only $200,000 as a four-family house. In this case, price would definitely be related to a contingency in the contract that the zoning variance be allowed.

• *Extras.* What can you bargain over? Almost anything that is not actually *attached* to the land or building. Carpeting, draperies, yard equipment, dishwashers, washing machines, dryers, other home appliances, furniture, office equipment, commercial fixtures, shelving, building equipment, the condition of the furnace or heating system, air conditioning units, new hot water heaters, even fill if you happen to be dealing in land. A top-dollar price which includes many extras for which you would otherwise have had to pay out-of-pocket cash at new merchandise prices can still be a winning deal.

YOUR FIRST SELLER PROFILE: Your market evaluation is done, and, with your goals prioritized and your trading chips evaluated, you have created a good image of your negotiating position. The next step is to make an offer, right?

Wrong. You have only half an image of the negotiating game when you have a complete picture of your own side. Most negotiators learn the other half as they play, discovering their opponent's goals and trading chips by making bids and getting responses. In some cases such blind negotiating may be the only way to get that essential information, but not always. The master negotiator therefore takes some time before making the first offer to evaluate the seller. You should do likewise.

Turn to the next page in your negotiating diary and title it with the seller's name and property address. Here you will draw your first tentative image of your opponent's goals, strengths, and weaknesses. You may redraw this image several times as negotiating proceeds, but each time you will be honing your strategy for maximum effectiveness.

To draw your seller image, you'll have to ask questions of and talk with real estate agents, the neighbors, tenants, property managers, business associates, materials suppliers, subcontractors, local officials, and anyone who has business contact with the seller or the building. Try to find out the following:

- *Why is the property being sold?* This is a key factor in evaluating how low your initial offer can be. You are looking to discover the degree of pressure-to-sell upon the seller. If this is a property which he or she can no longer manage or if the financing on the property has been structured for tax shelter and it is therefore losing money under the new tax laws, you probably have a strong negotiating position. If the seller has left the area and is losing money because of poor property management, you certainly have a strong position. If, on the other hand, the seller is doing well on the property and is just fishing for a top-dollar sale, you might not be able to win this game.

   Probably the strongest buyer position is a seller who has bought another property and must sell "yours" to meet financial commitments or who wants to buy another property but must sell "yours" first. If you come upon that situation, start your negotiating with a low price and a distant closing date. Raise the price only slightly as you move the closing date closer. Closing date for that seller is probably more valuable than cash.

- *Who is the seller?* How much experience in the real estate marketplace does he or she have? How great is the need for cash? *Is* there a need for cash?

- *How long has the seller owned the property?* Often, the longer the seller has owned the property, the more space there is for negotiating price and terms.

- *What did the seller pay for the property?* You can find out this figure wherever town records are kept. In instances where the seller has owned the property for a short period only, this number may be crucial. Factor in commissions, and you may well have the seller's rock bottom figure without asking.
- *How long has the property been on the market?* Sometimes even grossly overpriced properties can be negotiated down to below-market-value prices if they have been long on the market. Listen carefully to hear that the seller is "sick and tired" of the place. That can mean a bargain no matter what the asking price. Bid very low.

THE MOOD OF THE MARKETPLACE: "Okay," you say, "I know all I can find out about the seller and I'm willing to continue to reevaluate him or her. Now I should make the first offer, right?"

Almost. You need one more evaluation page in your diary. Title this one "the local marketplace" and consider these questions:

- *What's the mood of the local real estate marketplace?* Are properties selling quickly and near asking price? In that case, your seller will have a stronger negotiating position than you will. Are properties standing long on the market and then selling at prices well below asking price? In this case, *you* will have the stronger position. The first situation is called a *seller's market*, the second a *buyer's market*, for obvious reasons.
- *What's happening demographically?* Is the population growing? Is the median age growing older or younger? Are businesses moving in or out? Answers to these questions will give you an indication of what kinds of real estate will do well in future years. The trick, of course, is to buy such a property before the seller is aware of the positive demographic trends.
- *What's happening on the local political scene?* Is there a tax increase looming? Many sellers are motivated to "unload" their properties when threatened by tax increases without ever calculating if small rent increases will cover the changes.
- *Does the local area support appreciation in the kind of real estate being sold?* An answer of *no* to this question may indicate a fabulous deal for you. Make your contract contingent on a change of usage, with municipal approval, and you'll see dollar signs in your dreams.

Most neophyte buyers jump into negotiations without sufficient planning. They also respond to each new step in the negotiating process without using past steps as an evaluation tool. It's a bit like stabbing in the dark at a moving target that can stab back. And it requires about as much luck to make a killing.

Don't use the stabbing technique in your real estate negotiating. I strongly favor the process of keeping a negotiating diary because it slows the impulse to jump in without preparation and to respond too quickly. The very act of writing provides an incentive to think and evaluate. And the fact that your evaluation is a *written* one provides checkpoints in time against which you can judge your negotiating progress. If you keep a negotiating diary, you'll make fewer mistakes in a game where mistakes can often mean failure. You'll also be using a technique favored by the most successful real estate entrepreneurs as well as business executives and lawyers.

THE FIRST OFFER

Everyone wants how-to-do-it advice when it comes time for the first offer. "How much below the asking price should I offer?" is the question I hear most frequently. It is a question which I cannot answer. There is no valid rule of thumb. There is no percentage below asking price guaranteed to get the results you want because there are no controls on asking price! And because there are so many other variables that affect each individual deal.

You're on your own now. You have the tools and the knowledge; you must make the decisions. One word of caution, however. *Do not reveal the information in your negotiating diary to anyone.* This is a situation something like the rights the police read to apprehended criminals on the television screen: *anything you say can and will be used against you. . . .* If you tell your real estate agent your top-dollar figure, you might just as well agree to pay that figure at the outset because that is exactly where your negotiations are most likely to end up.

When you decide upon your first-offer price, take a new page in your negotiating diary, date it, and enter all the pertinent facts of your offer on that page. Keep this first offer simple. A price and a closing date, perhaps but not necessarily the contingencies you'll need to make the property profitable. As the seller responds you can add extras and requests for financing or special terms to your offers as you increase your offering price. This technique works well in the spirit of reciprocity. *I'll give you this much more money, but I also want . . .*

THE SELLER'S FIRST RESPONSE

The first response of the seller often sets the tone for the entire negotiating process on that particular property. Let's look at a few possibilities and some appropriate reactions.

The seller responds to your first offer by lowering his or her asking price by $1,000. You're still $20,000 apart. This seller is probably indicating that he or she wants to continue negotiations, but your price is too low by far. Consider market value. Can you make another offer still below your market value estimate? Ask for something additional with the new offer, but save your trump cards (closing date and/or financing) for later in the negotiating process.

The seller responds by lowering his asking price $10,000 and asking for a closing in forty-five days. This seller probably wants very much to sell. Raise your offer somewhat with a sixty-day period until closing. You can come down to forty-five days if it suits you in your next offer, which may or may not include a still higher price.

The seller says "no," just "no," to your offer. No counteroffer at all. This seller thinks your offer is far too low and does not want to start negotiations with the midpoint so far below his or her expectations. Or this seller is not particularly motivated to sell. But don't be put off. Make another offer at a somewhat higher price, if the property merits it.

The seller comes down $5,000 and says "That's my final offer, not a penny less." Don't take anything as final until you test it. Make another offer just under market value and spend some time with the agent going over your market value analysis calculations so that the information can be carried back with your second offer.

The seller surprises you by responding with a price $4,000 above your first offer. That counteroffer, however, is tied to a six-month delay to closing. You calculate that the counteroffer is already under market value. If you can, raise your price by $2,000 and accept the six-months' closing, especially if you're in an appreciating market. Here you're setting a price in today's market that will probably be low in the market six months from now. This has got to be a winning deal, but if you want to try for even more, ask that your escrow money be held in an interest-bearing account and that the interest be credited to you.

Now don't think for a moment that these five examples cover anything more than five glimpses into the negotiating world. Their relationship to the potential for negotiating situations is rather like the snippets you see in the previews for a three-and-a-half-hour movie. Negotiating possibilities are as vast and varied as the kinds of people who participate in them.

ROLE PLAYING

Write the details of your seller's counteroffers in your negotiating diary and date each one, just as you write the details of your subsequent offers. As the negotiations go on, however, do some role playing. Try to imagine yourself as the seller. What goals are most important? How would you feel about the offer the buyer just made? How would you respond? What would be your arguments that *your* suggested sale price was a fair one? How could a buyer make his offer sweeter to you?

The ability to put yourself in the shoes of the seller can be a major tool in your negotiating. If you are good at this kind of exercise, you'll be able to answer objections before they're voiced. One very successful professional investor whom I know works this technique so thoroughly that you can watch him moving his hands and changing his facial expressions as he silently plays through negotiating scenes in his mind. Don't laugh. His bank account is one you'd wish were yours.

FACE-TO-FACE NEGOTIATING

In most situations, it's better to use a real estate agent as an intermediary. If you must negotiate directly with the seller, however, use the same protective techniques used by professional investors and commercial developers. They arrive at face-to-face negotiating sessions either as a group of buyers or with two or more advisers (lawyers, accountants, professional engineers, environmental experts, etc.) to sit at their sides.

When an offer is made that seems plausible but imperfect, they withdraw to *discuss and consider* it. Often they ask for a day or two before the answer.

You too should always have someone with whom you "must" confer before accepting an offer or making a counteroffer in a face-to-face negotiating session. You don't necessarily *have* to use that someone if everything is going your way. But that's a rare piece of luck. Your someone will get you out of a tough situation and allow you to use time lapse to your advantage before making a counteroffer. Your someone will also be especially valuable if negotiations get heated and you want them to cool a bit.

FEELINGS

Anger, pride, love, prejudice, greed, fear of failure, and an array of minor emotions all make their appearance at the negotiating table from time to time. Be aware of your emotional responses and keep them apart from your rational evaluation of the property in question and the progress of the negotiations.

Even lawyers don't wreak as much havoc with real estate deals as emotional responses do. If you see your opponent responding emotionally, move away for a time (consideration time in another room, or sleep-on-it time) and approach from another direction as you restart negotiations.

RESOLUTION

Once you've made a deal and signed the contract, don't rehash the negotiations in your mind. "Maybe we should have—" can get you nothing but headaches. Go forward with your deal. If you have negotiated carefully and rationally, you *can* make it a profitable one!

Unless you have considerable experience in the real estate marketplace and can rely quite comfortably on your own legal judgments, however, I strongly recommend that you include in your contract a *legal review clause*. It should read something like this:

> Buyer may choose to have an attorney review this contract. If the attorney disapproves the contract for any reason, notice must be given to the seller within three working days. The contract will then be considered terminated and all deposit monies returned.

If you include a clause of this type in your contract, you are not required to take advantage of the right to legal review, but it's available. If you or your lawyer come up with a major stumbling block to a successful purchase during those three days, you do have a way out of your contract, or the option of allowing your lawyer to insert protective wording or change certain clauses.

SELLER NEGOTIATING

Most sellers have been buyers at least once in their lives and therefore have some experience in the negotiating game. The principles, rules, and strategies of seller negotiating are pretty much the same as those of buyer negotiating. Only the goals and vantage point are different.

SETTING THE PRICE

Sellers, like buyers, should do a market evaluation before they set the asking price on their properties. Be aware, however, that market value is *not* a good asking price. Everyone wants to negotiate in a real estate purchase. Even if you set your price at market value and print FIRM after it, you will get offers well below that asking price. Many buyers refuse to pay full price just *because* it's full price, even if they agree that the price seems "more than fair." When you become a seller, therefore, leave yourself space to come down from your listed price.

"How much space?" you quite logically ask.

It depends.

As I have said many times, real estate is a *local* game subject to the events and moods of the local marketplace. How much negotiating space you should leave in your asking price depends upon what's happening in and around town.

In a seller's market, I like to list high, at least at the outset. Who knows, you might just find someone willing to pay above your market value estimate. If nothing happens in response to your high asking price, you can always stimulate activity by lowering that price. In a buyer's market, however, you should not list more than 10 percent above market value. If properties are moving slowly, an overpriced property will go nowhere. Ten percent keeps you in the selling ball park but still allows you space to negotiate with the buyer.

THE NEGOTIATING DIARY

You, as a seller, should also keep a diary. It will differ slightly from your buyer's diary, however, in that it may contain the histories of several prospective deals before a buyer with an acceptable offer appears on the scene.

Each offer should be dated with the name, address, and phone number of the prospective buyer noted. The business card of the real estate agent who presented the offer should be stapled or taped to the page and the pertinent facts of the offer should be listed.

On the page following each offer notation, write out the details of your counteroffer *before you make it*. Note also what your actual goals are as you write out each point of your counteroffer. You will have to judge both the marketplace and your buyer as you decide how much to give at each step.

To do this, of course, you should have both a goals and a trading chips page similar to those described for the buyer's diary, and you should refer to these pages as you plan each step of your strategy.

If a deal cannot be made with one prospective buyer, try to evaluate why. Reconsider your goals. Are they realistic? Evaluate the prospective buyer. Why did he back away from the deal? Use this information in forming your strategy for the next offer.

Be sure to keep all your negotiating records in *one* negotiating diary and in chronological order. As you evaluate and reevaluate progress and points of contention, ask yourself: *what are the least costly changes I can make that will enhance the possibility of an agreement?* These changes may be physical (repairs to some part of a building) or they may be conceptual (Is my market evaluation correct? Am I holding out irrationally on some point?)

With the first offer of each prospective buyer, also take time to do a buyer profile. Try to get as much personal information as possible. What does the buyer do for a living? What is his or her annual income? How much down payment is being proposed? Will the buyer qualify at a conventional lender for the financing needed? And most important, why does this buyer want to buy this property? The answers to these questions are usually available from a real estate agent who has done his or her homework and properly qualified the customer.

•   •   •

TRADING CHIPS

You, as seller, have essentially the same types of chips as the buyer: price, closing date, condition, contingencies, and seller financing. How you use them will determine the character of your deal.

A word about seller financing, however. Although it is often a strong incentive to wrapping up a sale, most professionals avoid using it unless market conditions make other arrangements impossible. Why? Because it ties up cash that could be used to make other investments. Oh, you'll be getting interest on your money, but that interest is rarely equal to the return you might make by investing cash elsewhere in the real estate marketplace.

YOUR ADVISERS

As is true for the buyer, it's a good strategy to have someone with whom you "must" confer before saying *yes* or *no* to a particular proposal. Referring to your lawyer, accountant, or even your husband or wife can buy you strategic thinking time or necessary cooling down time.

THE MEETING OF THE MINDS

When the giving and taking, the trading of one chip for another is done, have a clean contract drawn. Do not accept one that is scratched out, scribbled over, initialed, and reinitialed. And consider if perhaps *you*, as seller, might not also want a legal review clause.

Once the legal review period is over, you can then begin to think of new investments for the money you've just made. Or perhaps . . . Well, it's about that sailing yacht you've always wanted . . .

Index

money, time value of, 23–24
moneymarket funds, 24, 37
mortgages, 22, 45
  for co-ops and condos, 138–39
  for down payments, 45
  interest on, 7, 69, 120, 121
  for land, 79, 96
  nonrecourse, 195
  purchase money, 45, 96
  second, 45, 75, 117–19, 199
  for vacation homes, 117–19
  VA-guaranteed, 45
multifamily houses, 8–9, 13, 36–54
  appraisal methods for, 281–82, 283
  cash flow and, 46
  commitment to, 40
  conversion to, *see* hammer and nails conversions
  creativity and, 41
  decision making and, 41–42
  evaluation of, 42
  expected return on, 47
  finances for, 37–39
  foresight and, 39–40
  how to buy, 49–50
  legal considerations and, 40–41
  location of, 49–50
  maintenance of, 47–48
  management skills and, 41
  negotiation and, 43
  resale value of, 37, 39–40
  risk in, 39–40
  social contacts and, 42–43
  start-up cash for, 45–46
  tact and, 42
  taxes on, 46–47
  as vacation homes, 103
  waiting time for, 44
  working time for, 45

National Apartment Association, 171
National Association of Home Builders, 282
National Association of Realtors, 119

negotiation, 18, 279–96
  as buyer, 280–94
  for commercial property, 271, 272, 273
  contract speculation and, 233
  diary for, 284–90, 295
  emotional responses in, 293
  face-to-face, 292–93
  first offers in, 285, 290–91
  goals in, 286
  for hammer and nails conversions, 253
  for handyman specials, 63
  for land, 81–83
  marketplace mood and, 289–90
  market value appraisal in, 281–84, 294
  for multifamily houses, 43
  reciprocity in, 280
  resolution of, 293–94
  role playing in, 292
  as seller, 294–96
  seller profile and, 287–89, 292
  seller's first response in, 291–292
  trading chips in, 286–87, 296
  for vacation homes, 116–17
  win/win, 279
net leases, 267
noise pollution, 71
nondisturbance clauses, 273
nonrecourse loans, 195, 212

office buildings, 265
options:
  on land, 82, 88–89, 98–99
  renewal, 273
options to buy, 72, 224–25, 239; *see also* contract speculation
oral lease, 40–41
ordinary income, 6
outlet centers, 266

paper castles, 142, 143, 149–50
parking, 49, 247–48
passive income, 6–7
patience, 17